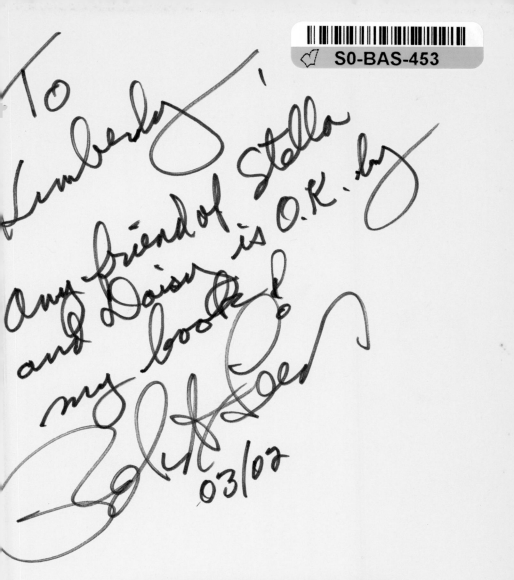

To
Kimberley,

Any friend of Stella
and Daisy is O.K. by
my book!

Elliott Cohen
03/02

**REVIEW COPY
NOT FOR RESALE**

S0-BAS-453

Love
Is
A
4
Legged
Word

DOG

Nick Kenny

A faithful dog will play with you,
And laugh with you,   or cry.
He'll gladly starve to stay with you,
Nor ever reason why.

And when you're feeling out of sorts,
Somehow he'll understand.
He'll watch you with his shining eyes,
And try to lick your hand.

His blind, implicit faith in you
Is matched by his great love,
The kind of faith that we should have
In Our Master, up above!

When everything is said and done,
I guess it isn't odd,
For when you spell "dog" backwards,
You will get the name of God.

Love Is A 4 Legged Word

By **Robert X. Leeds**

EPIC PUBLISHING COMPANY
NEVADA

Copyright © 2001 by Robert X. Leeds
All rights reserved under the Pan-American
and International Copyright Conventions.
Printed in the United States of America
Published by Epic Publishing Company

This book may not be reproduced in whole or in part in any form or by any
means, electronic or mechanical, including photocopying, recording, or by any
information storage and retrieval system now known or hereafter invented,
without written permission from the publisher.

ISBN 0-9674025-2-2
Library Of Congress Catalog Card Number 94-12045

Cover design by
Evan Hill Design, Inc.

First Edition

This book may be ordered from all major bookstores.
In the event you are unable to obtain additional copies
from your local bookstore, copies may be ordered
directly from the publisher:
Published by Epic Publishing Company
8814 Big Bluff Avenue
Las Vegas NV 89148-1418
702/871-7263

DEDICATION

"Dreams are highways of the heart.
You make a wish and your journey starts."

To my wife Peggy, my traveling companion.

To Leslie, Marc, Gail, Michael, Myong Ok,
Damian, Marcus, and Heather.

"When the cause is just, just men will rise to the cause."

A special expression of gratitude is due my son, Marc,
who rose to the cause. Peggy and I were
never alone in our quest.

And to all those women and men of the pet care industry
who share in a noble mission for the welfare of
our companion animals.

CONTENTS

CONTENTS

ACKNOWLEDGEMENTS

I do not accept that any achievement is without the effort of many unseen and unheralded collaborators. Certainly ours was not. Though there were many who made our struggle easier, I would be remiss if I didn't pay special tribute to the following Doctors of Veterinary Medicine.

Robert W. Abell, Warren Anderson, J. W. Barnes, Alvin M. Becker, Leland Carmichael, Fred S. David, Lynn Doner, David I Epstein, Robert F. Going, William Grant, Roger A. Halvorsen, Ralph O. Holstein, Debbie J. Hasse, Jan Mahr, A. Thomas Maiolo, Douglas McGregor, Imre Pagi, Roy V. H. Pollock, Robert G. Schirmer, Lewis Seidenberg, Erwin Small, Ralph S. Wilhelm, Thompson T. Wright, and Phillip Zand.

I also wish to express our appreciation to the entire staff of the following veterinary clinics and hospitals:

A-Northwest Emergency Veterinary Center, Abell Animal Hospital, Barnes Bone Animal Hospital, Bayshore Animal Hospital, Berwyn Veterinary Association, Blum Animal Hospital, Bone Animal Hospital, Care Animal Hospital of Arlington Heights, Countryside Animal Clinic, Forest Lakes Animal Clinic, McCormick Animal Hospital, Misner-Holley Animal Hospital, Niles Animal Hospital, Rand Road Animal Hospital, Riser Animal Hospital, Rohlwing Road Animal Hospital, Terry Animal Hospital, Wauconda Animal Clinic, Wheaton Animal Hospital, and Wilhelm Veterinary Clinic.

I would also express my appreciation to the Oil Dri Corporation, Quaker Oats Company, Ralston Purina Company, Simonson Mills Company, and the Suburban Surgical Company,

Inc. for their assistance in the development and success of our facilities, procedures, and programs.

I also need to acknowledge a debt of gratitude to all the men and women who, as employees, have shared and been a part of this grand experience. In particular, six young ladies deserve being cited: Carol Samp, Tracy Dornik, and Julie Wamback came to us as fledgling groomers many years ago and still, while managing the chores of a full family, continue to work grooming their "old timers." Dawn Brtek and Irene Schall were also among our early hires and still continue to work full time caring for "their" animals. They manage this despite the veritable zoos in their own homes. Lastly, but far from least, is Kim Young. Kim started with us as a novice animal attendant when we opened our pet motel in Sarasota, Florida. When we moved back to Chicago, she also moved and today manages the entire pet motel. When you work in an animal facility you wear many hats; janitor, animal attendant, driver, receptionist, bookkeeper, bather, groomer, and the list goes on and on. Kim did, and still does, all these things and manages to smile. How fortunate the animals would be if we could clone her.

Seven people deserve singular recognition for having made possible the happy ending to this chronicle: Ralph Brown of Schwyler, Rosche & Zwirner, Robert O. Case of McBride, Baker & Coles, David R. Bromwell, D.V.M., Director, Illinois Department of Agriculture; Jim Corbin, Professor of Animal Science, University of Illinois, and Jane Jordan Browne of Multimedia Development Corporation.

Introduction

It was a bright, warm Monday in July when the telephone rang at our newly opened pet motel. My wife Peggy answered the telephone and a serious voice on the other end of the line said, "I'd like to reserve a room for a camel. Do you have one?"

Peggy paused for a moment, but she was prepared for these unusual jokes.

"Boy, are you lucky. We just had a cancellation in the camel suites," Peggy replied.

The reply seemed to catch the caller off base and there was a short pause.

"Are you sure you can take care of a camel?"

"Absolutely," Peggy replied cheerfully. "We can board anything that walks, creeps, crawls, swims, flies, slithers, or hops, as long as it's not vicious or poisonous."

"Well, there is one thing," the caller cautioned. "Bernice is pregnant."

"Not a problem," Peggy assured him. "We also have a maternity ward and veterinarians are on call twenty-four hours a day. Your camel will be safe with us."

"Well, Bernice is very special to us and we want to be sure she gets good care. I understand you have wall-to-wall carpeting with brass beds, Sealy mattresses, and Snoopy sheets. Will she also have these amenities?"

It was Peggy's turn to pause. Then she explained to the

caller that such accommodations were only available in the Imperial and Regency Suites for dogs. A camel would have to settle for something less–a bed of straw in the stable or barn.

After several more minutes of sparring, the caller introduced himself as Wally Phillips, a well-known Chicago radio talk-show host. A recording of the conversations was played for his audience for the next week.

For Peggy and me, the call was not at all unusual. We built and operated a million-dollar motel for animals just outside of Chicago, in Prairie View, Illinois, and the amenities she had just described were but a few that we offered to our animal guests. For twenty-six years we catered to that unique and specially privileged member of the American household–the family pet.

To deny that we were directed to this vocation by some unseen hand of fate would be to ignore the substance of providence. What sane reasoning would support forsaking a secure and comfortable middle-age existence to embark on such a dubious quest as bringing reform to the pet-boarding industry?

It was not logic that directed us to this mid-life interest. Instead, like thousands of pet owners, our concern was inflamed by the tragic and needless loss of our own pet in a boarding kennel. Unlike many pet owners, however, we did not choose to forget the incident, nor did we want to forgive the prevailing system that encouraged it. We wanted a change in the way pets are cared for.

Our entry into the pet-boarding industry was not without incident, and it is true that there were times when exasperation or exhaustion tempted us to flee.

Yet, whenever these doubts arose, we had only to hear the joyful yapping of a departing four-legged guest, or the shrill chatter of voices issuing from the variety of brightly plumed birds in the aviary, to reassure us. The quest was worthwhile, the goal worth striving for.

The heartfelt pleasures derived from working with animals and with the handful of other kennel owners who shared our concerns more than mitigated the occasional adversity. In the end, our labors forged an example that would not tarnish before the acid recriminations of those intent on perpetuating an unprincipled industry.

Some detractors may still claim that American Pet Motels was nothing more than a glorified kennel, but it is a fact that we boarded more than ten thousand dogs, cats, birds, and miscellaneous animals each year, and we did it without any of the problems our peers predicted.

While America's largest kennels boasted when they grossed $100,000 a year, we soon were taking in that amount in a single month. But, it was not the quantity of pets served or the amount of dollars received in which we took our greatest pride. Our outstanding achievement was the virtual elimination of any illnesses, injuries, or deaths to the pets while in our care. From the beginning, we said it could be done. It had been our sole objective and remains our most prized accomplishment. We conceived a radically different concept for the public care of people's pets, and we brought that concept into being with an unbelievable degree of success.

I admit our entry into the pet-boarding business was an act of arrogant brashness. Neither Peggy nor I had any training or experience in the pet-boarding industry. To compound the ridiculous, we wanted to build a $250,000 pet motel that would not only board dogs and cats but any type of animal that a person would call a pet.

In revealing our plans to our closest friends and the family veterinarian, we refuted every conceivable argument with the same impenetrable self-assuredness. This was due to something deep inside us, something that refused to let us accept that collies couldn't be boarded because "they would just pine away," or that it was natural that some pets always died from loneliness, or "grievance disease," as our own veterinarian called it.

Nor could we accept that it was normal for someone's pet to run away from a shelter or to become injured or maimed while being boarded there. Perhaps what disturbed us most was the passive attitude of veterinarians and kennel operators toward the conditions that were actually responsible for those tragic occasions.

With very few exceptions, those in the industry maintained that conditions could not be changed. Instinctively, we were just as sure that a facility could be built and operated that would eliminate all the evils associated with kenneling an animal. It was our dream to build and operate such a facility. To dispel any doubts about our intentions, we would also introduce two changes that were unheard of in the pet-boarding industry. Our boarding contract would specifically accept liability for every pet boarded with us. The second policy was a written guarantee that everyone's pet would go home in as good, or better, condition than when it came in to us or we would reimburse the owner up to two hundred and fifty dollars to return the pet to its normal condition. To those in the business, it was insanity. To us, it was a challenge. We knew it could be done. We knew we could do it.

Prologue Chapter 1

"And God created the heavens and the Earth and on the Evening of the sixth day brought forth all the animals that would dwell thereon; and it was good . . . and God saw that it was good. Then, He said, "I shall create mankind and give it dominion o'er all the Earth and the animals that dwell thereon that he shall reign with understanding and with compassion. But, God was very tired, so He appointed a committee . . . Alas!"

RXL

1

IN THE BEGINNING

As I sat across from my boss's desk one bleak December day in 1970 and told him what I planned to do, I can only imagine what he must have been thinking.

I had had a few odd pets in my lifetime, but I was an engineer, not a zookeeper. I had started at General Motors seventeen years before as a clerk and now occupied the position of Director of Industrial Engineering and had two secretaries, a private office and perks and privileges most employees would have been eternally grateful for.

In addition to a very generous salary, I was receiving an annual bonus and shares of stock in the company. I was able to select five company cars each year, changing them as soon as the odometer reached three thousand miles. This was a luxury that afforded me the opportunity to drive the first Corvette Stingray that Chevrolet produced.

For the first time in a lifetime of insecurity and frequent periods of unemployment, Peggy and I enjoyed a sense of security.

My manager reviewed all the advantages of working for General Motors for me. At forty-three years of age, there was still opportunity to garner an even larger share of the good life.

After all, he reasoned, I hadn't started with the company until I was twenty-six. Over the past years, I had not only proven my ability as an industrial engineer, but I had worked equally hard during my "free" time, acquiring first a bachelor's degree and then a master's degree from Wayne State University. Because I had dropped out of high school to enlist during World War II, I began my college studies without even an eleventh-grade education. I not only graduated with an MBA, but I graduated with honors and was awarded the Sigma Iota Epsilon scholarship key.

But it was General Motors that made it possible. Among the perks was a College Tuition Program that permitted any employee to further his or her education while the company paid the tuition.

In addition, I had been chosen to serve as a consultant with the corporation's manufacturing staff and on several occasions was sent to the General Motors' Institute for advanced courses in engineering, financial, and managerial techniques. The company had invested in my education, but we had both benefited.

"Are you really going to give all of this up to run a dog kennel?" my manager asked incredulously.

"Not a dog kennel," I corrected him politely. "A motel. A pet motel."

He kept his eyes focused on mine as he re-folded my letter of resignation and placed it back in its original envelope. He held his arm out with the envelope only inches from me.

"Why don't you take it back and think about it for a few days." Almost confidentially, he said, "I won't mention it to anybody. Think it over." His head was nodding up and down almost as if he was giving his consent.

"No," I replied, smiling. My stomach was churning inside and there was a strong temptation to take the letter back, but inside I knew I mustn't weaken. I pushed my chair back out of reach and shook my head. This newly awakened concern for animal welfare and the forces that had compelled me to make a commitment were stronger than any logical persuasions. I didn't dare procrastinate. This had to be it.

I struggled to stand up, almost falling over the chair, as I tried to move out of reach of the envelope. I had given my official notice. I was saying good-bye to all my unearned shares in the stock bonus program, my pension program, and the alluring benefits one struggles a lifetime to achieve, and I was turning it all in for a dream.

When I drove my freshly washed car out of the company garage that night in December 1970, my feeling was one of exhilaration. It had to be the kind of feeling a fellow with a past due mortgage feels when he learns he's won the lottery.

If I had even the remotest suspicion of certain future events, I might have gone right back to that office and pleaded for the return of that envelope. For some, it is a fine line that separates a dream from an obsession. For me, there was no line at all.

During almost all of my childhood, my family had always had some kind of mutt as a household pet. I never really conceived of a family as being complete without a dog or cat to share the daily experience of family life.

When Peggy and I acquired our first home, our next order of business was acquiring a dog. It just seemed a natural order of priorities. However, after eleven years of marriage, three children and several dogs, I thought it would be nice to diversify. So, on our twelfth wedding anniversary, I presented Peggy with a six-month-old coatimundi, a racoonlike carnivore that lives in South America.

I don't know how many readers have ever seen a coatimundi, but Amigo looked like a cross between a raccoon, an anteater, and a teddy bear. In the jungle a long, muscular snout is useful to probe insect mounds. In a contemporary setting the long, muscular snout is useful for getting into trouble. Despite his beady eyes and his ungainly long nose, which he used as a lever and crowbar when he wanted to get into something, to me he always seemed to possess an innate quality of beauty–a quality not always apparent to strangers and certainly not apparent to Peggy.

Unfortunately, because I had to travel clear across Detroit to pick Amigo up, I arrived at our anniversary party almost two hours late and after all the guests had arrived.

A coatimundi, even as young as six months, is not an easy thing to conceal and very impractical to gift-wrap. When I walked from the foyer into the living room and confronted the stares of family and friends, I could think of nothing more appropriate to say to my awaiting wife than, "Honey . . . this is for you."

I could hardly wait for her to unveil her gift and I sensed everyone else's eagerness to behold this wondrous surprise gift.

After only a brief moment of deathly silence Peggy burst out in sobs. At first I couldn't imagine that my being two hours late had affected her so. I have since come to acknowledge that perhaps a sentimental occasion, such as a wedding anniversary, might better be celebrated by a gift of a less animate nature.

In some respects, Amigo was much like a trained dog. He was allowed to romp around the house or yard and rarely entertained the idea of roaming beyond our lot line. Before long it became routine for Peggy and Amigo to meet me when I arrived home from work. I would pull into the driveway and there the two of them would be waiting to embrace me. If Peggy had moved faster, she might have gotten to me first but she was no match for my little furry friend. However, there was another factor involved in Amigo's boundless enthusiasm. He loved cigars!

Amigo had a voracious appetite and in addition to the dog food and fruit that comprised his regular diet, he delighted in searching through the lawn for the little tidbits of insects or plants that his palate might savor. But this variety, while satisfying the bulk of his appetite, did not diminish his addiction to tobacco, and I always carried cigars in my coat pocket.

As soon as I left my car, Amigo would bound into my arms and as I instinctively grabbed him, his long snout would home in on the location of my cigars and he would leave my arms with two or three cigars dangling from his mouth as he sought some sanctuary where he could chew them up undisturbed.

The other quality that tested Peggy's patience was Amigo's penchant for climbing. Curtains held no attraction for him but drapes! Drapes were jungle material. On more than one occasion we would walk into the den and find Amigo hanging from her beautiful gold brocade drapes. A stern reprimand usually would dislodge Amigo, but a stern reprimand directed to me by Peggy did little to prevent Amigo from doing the same thing the next time we were absent from the scene. My assurance that it was a normal and harmless habit did little to assuage Peggy's growing ire.

Perhaps because of his age, Amigo had seemingly boundless energy. This, plus his affinity for fun and games, eventually forced me to agree to confine Amigo when we retired for the night.

Amigo had brought about this incarceration by tactlessly choosing that hour of the night when we had just fallen asleep to start playing leapfrog across our bed.

As if that was not bad enough, more than once Peggy was awakened from a deep sleep by the sensation that some foreign creature was hovering just over her head. Sure enough, when her screams died down and I managed to find the light switch, there would be Amigo hanging from the headboard with his long snout only a few inches from Peggy's own nose. Why he enjoyed studying her face in that upside down posture as she slept was an amusing topic of conversation for everyone except Peggy.

Nighttime confinement was an amicable alternative to some of Peggy's other suggestions.

The first two or three attempts to keep Amigo confined failed to produce an escape-proof enclosure. My final product was almost a masterpiece of engineering. It was a heavy, reinforced wood cage about three feet in height, length, and depth. Because of its size, it was necessary to keep it in the basement. In anticipation of his wily deftness for getting in and out of impossible places, I secured the door with a heavy padlock. Since the cage weighed almost seventy-five pounds, there appeared no reason to construct a bottom for it, as I knew he could not dig through the concrete floor.

But there was a reason, and it arrived in the form of my monthly shipment of Madura Palma cigars from Florida. On this particularly hot and humid June evening, the entire house boasted the aroma of fine, tender Madura leaf but only two of us really appreciated the promise it held.

That evening, I placed the new shipment of cigars inside my handsome walnut humidor, locked Amigo in his cage, and we retired for the night.

Early the next morning, I was jolted awake by the unrestrained screams coming from the family room. I ran toward the screams expecting to see some unspeakable horror. I recognized none. But, perhaps horror lies in the eyes of the beholder, for all I saw was darling little Amigo sitting up in one corner of our good leather couch, staring innocently up at us.

A closer inspection found his fingers and mouth stuffed with the remains of one-hundred fine leaf Madura Palma cigars, some fresh, some regurgitated. From one end of the room to the other, our prized sculptured orange carpet bore the remains of the rest of the cigars. Not only the carpeting, but the walls and drapes were liberally soiled with soggy, chewed tobacco. To make matters worse, the abundance of tobacco was more than poor Amigo's system could tolerate and the carpeting and sofa bore more than just tobacco remains.

Apparently, with the proper motivation, Amigo's powerful nose had sufficient strength to lift his cage up from the floor and permit his escape. Freed of our restraint, he went directly to the family room and to my cigar humidor.

Like any normal man, I cannot remain indifferent to a woman's tears. With great reluctance, I agreed that maybe Amigo would be happier in a home where there would be fewer temptations. That afternoon, I telephoned a want ad into the local newspaper. "Adorable pet coatimundi for sale or trade." After all, Peggy didn't say how I should get rid of him.

If I had had twenty coatimundis, I still would not have been able to meet the demand and if the number of callers surprised me, I was amazed at the variety of animals I was offered in exchange. I had no idea so many exotic pets existed outside the Detroit zoo.

My attachment for Amigo extended far beyond any monetary value, so my main concern was to find a new owner with a nature sympathetic to his peculiar behavior.

My final choice appeared to provide me the best of both worlds. Not only did the woman know all about the raising of coatimundis, but also one of her rare exotic cats was pregnant, and our agreement gave me my choice of the litter. What a deal!

The litter finally arrived in late fall and a few months later I received a call to pick up my cat.

For some inexplicable reason, I had neglected to tell Peggy about the terms of this arrangement, so I found myself once again bringing home an unexpected pet to an unsuspecting wife. It was a particularly cold and windy day when I arrived with a wicker basket full of shredded rags and a tiny bundle of striped fur. I tried to shield the basket with my coat and hold the storm door with one foot while I pushed open the front door. I was counting on at least getting into the foyer before being discovered by Peggy or the children. Unfortunately, as the door finally swung open, I was confronted by Peggy's curious glare.

"What's in the basket?" she asked in a suspicious tone.

"Nothing special," I assured her, a bit sheepishly.

"There's got to be something in it," she said with conviction.

I set the basket on the tile floor and attempted to put my arms around her and give her a big greeting kiss. Her lips avoided mine and she tilted her head to one side, her eyes glued to the motionless mound of rags in the wicker basket.

"What's in the basket?" she demanded more firmly.

"Well . . . I paused, trying to think of some way to phrase a plausible explanation. "I brought you something." In that brief moment I also was thinking, "Oh my God. What have I done now?"

She had stopped smiling and was standing there suspiciously eyeing the motionless basket.

"It's really something *special.*"

Still, she didn't move, remaining in my embrace with her head tilted down toward the basket. Finally, she pushed herself out of my arms and clutched her hands tightly together. I recalled a similar reaction the first time she saw Amigo.

"It's a kitten," I explained reassuringly, hoping to head off any violent reaction. "I knew you'd like it the moment I saw it." This was stretching the truth more than a little. Peggy was not at all inclined towards cats. In fact, on a number of occasions she actually expressed a natural antipathy toward felines. The attitude had been fostered during her childhood in Finland, where her mother insisted that cats were bad luck. The mere sight of a cat prompted members of her family and many of her friends to make a motion of spitting, which was thought to ward off bad luck.

She moved toward the basket and knelt, watching for some kind of movement. Cautiously, her fingers began peeling back the layers of towels and rags, finally revealing a tiny ball of tricolor tufts of fur. The animal was no larger than her hand and it lay there almost motionless, with only a barely perceptible stomach movement when it breathed. Its markings bore the spotted pattern most people would associate with a leopard. On the back of each ear was a white circle amidst the dark fur. There was something very obviously different about this cat.

"What kind of cat did you say this was?" Peggy asked. Her voice had mellowed and had lost its harsh, critical quality.

"It's an ocelot," I answered. "Sort of a cat that lives in South America. They're quite common as house pets there," I added trying to reassure her.

Although the woman who had bartered him to me in exchange for Amigo had told me this, I hadn't the slightest idea if it was true or not.

"They only get to be about twenty or twenty-five pounds— just a little more then an ordinary house cat."

Noticing that her interest was now totally absorbed in the tiny bundle of fur, I continued on with a recitation of the virtues of owning an ocelot. The previous owner had told me some of the things. Most I merely made up to embellish the prospects of ownership.

At last Peggy spoke up. "When did it eat last?" She was holding the tiny kitten level with her eyes and seemed to be studying its face. "I'll bet this thing is starving to death! Kittens this small have to be fed frequently. I don't think it's ever been weaned."

I shrugged my shoulders. I hadn't really taken into account these considerations. Nor could I imagine how she could be so certain of impending disaster unless it was some instinct peculiar to women. However, I could only interpret her immediate concern as a favorable omen, so I agreed and suggested that we feed the kitten immediately.

"Feed it? Feed it what?" she asked sarcastically. "Did you bring home any Esbilac or baby formula? You can't give a little thing like this a roast beef sandwich!" Having made her point, she continued on in a more moderated tone. "I don't think this little guy is more than five or six weeks old. He sure doesn't look good. I wonder it it's even been fed today?"

Then she abruptly placed the tiny figure back into the basket and covered it. "Put the basket next to the kitchen register and let's get to the store before it closes."

Once we were in the car, the serious questions started. "Who?" "How much?" "Where?" "When?" "Why?" And, in response to any of my replies, "Don't give me that! Tell me the truth!"

Still, despite all the questions and doubts, I felt a strong sense of relief that her voice lacked that certain bitter quality she was capable of expressing when she was really angry. I kept my eyes riveted on the road ahead, but inwardly I was grinning like the Cheshire cat. I was sure she was going to accept the ocelot.

After several trips around the racks of baby foods and

baby supplies, our shopping basket contained an ample collection of cereals, baby and junior foods, plus a variety of baby bottles and nipples. During the early years of our marriage, shopping was frequently an exercise in controversy. Peggy would pick an item from a shelf and then I would search the shelves for a similar, but lower priced product. Then she would replace my choice with her original selection and an argument would ensue. It is a marital ritual I still see practiced whenever young couples do their grocery shopping together. It only ends when the wife learns not to include the husband in her weekly shopping excursions. On this occasion, I made no effort to audit her choice of products. If she had filled the cart with imported caviar, I wouldn't have said one word. Instead, I stood to one side, searching the store with my eyes for any signs of neighbors. I could just imagine the rumors this scene of purchasing baby products could provoke. When she was satisfied that she had everything she needed, Peggy advised me that we were now going to find a store that offered a book on how to raise ocelots.

Since I had not even known such an animal existed, I seriously doubted that we were going to find the book she described, even in a pet shop.

However, I didn't want to do anything that might prejudice Peggy's growing interest, so I agreed to chauffeur her from one pet shop to another until she came to the same conclusion. Fortunately, her intuition withstood the trial, and by the sixth or seventh pet shop, some forty miles from our home, her perseverance was rewarded. She pulled a thin, glossy jacketed booklet from a wire rack and read the title aloud. *"How to Raise Ocelots,"* by Catherine Cisin. "Here it is!" she exclaimed, as if she had always known for sure it existed.

On the cover was a picture of a beautiful, sleek jungle cat. Once inside the car, Peggy opened the book and began to read the text aloud. She would pause and repeat what she felt were critical passages and then would pause again as if to allow the information to sink in. By the time we arrived back home, I think she felt she had mastered the situation and knew exactly what had to be done.

Having raised three children, Peggy prepared the bottle of baby formula as she had so many times in the past, even to the testing of the temperature by forcing a few drops from the bottle onto her wrist.

Next, she picked the small bundle of fur from its nest of torn rags and placed it on a towel on her lap. It lay there motionless. Although we could see a very slight movement of its stomach with each breath, it failed to open its eyes or show any other sign of activity. Peggy pried the tiny mouth open and moved the nipple back and forth, trying to get the kitten to accept it. There was no response.

"It's too weak to eat," she said, slowly turning the bottle in an attempt to evoke a response. "Get me an eye dropper!"

I removed our only eyedropper from an old bottle of baby medicine and carefully rinsed it out several times in hot water. Peggy poured some formula into an open cup and, after checking the eyedropper to confirm I had cleansed it properly, filled it with formula.

She carefully tilted the kitten's head backward and drop-by-drop let the formula trickle into its throat. It was a slow and tedious procedure, but Peggy was convinced the animal was on the verge of death and only an ample infusion of nourishment would save it.

While our three children looked on with obvious delight, our poor mixed Labrador retriever, Plato, didn't appear to share in the spirit of the occasion. Instead, he sniffed the new arrival and then lay down in a corner of the kitchen to watch the proceedings from afar. Perhaps, by some uncanny canine sense, Plato realized that this intruder would soon take over his place as top dog, so to speak, in the Leeds' household.

I woke up the first two or three times Peggy got up that night to feed the kitten, but I finally managed to fall into a deep sleep that was interrupted only by the alarm clock. Peggy was not in bed. I've often wondered if it isn't some genetic trait that makes it possible for women to absorb the demands of motherhood. Regardless of the lack of sleep and the physical and mental exhaustion, they're up at all hours of the night and day and meet the exigencies of babyhood.

That morning Peggy greeted me with a smile. "The formula is going down much better," she said. "You can see its tongue move now." The broad smile never left her face as she related the entire night's events in detail.

I knew then that despite our first misadventure, Peggy was going to accept the ocelot. Neither of us mentioned the potential difficulties of raising such a wild animal in a home with three small children and a dog, but Catherine Cisin's book revealed it had been done and was being done.

By the third day, the cat was able to nurse from a bottle, and we all shared a sense of relief and accomplishment when it took its first wobbly steps, fell over, and then got back up and tried again. I watched Peggy's face as she urged the small bundle of fur to walk to her and when it reached her at last, we all gave a cry of joy.

The cat had managed to do more than just take a few steps. He had managed to walk into our hearts, and from that moment on became another of America's millions of pampered pets.

He was now a permanent member of the Leeds household. He was our "cat's meow."

Prologue Chapter 2

TRILBY

Herbert H. Taylor

Trilby was my companion
  She shared my joys and tears,
Tried and true and faithful
  For ever so many years.

She was tender and kind and gentle
  And followed wherever I led,
And I loved–as a man loves his sweetheart
  Every hair in that little dog's head.

Her instinct was more than human,
  Her affection almost divine;
And she trembled with joy when I petted
  This little Scotch Collie of mine.

Her beautiful hair was glossy
  And black as a raven's crown,
And over her eyes–that looked so wise–
  Were two little spots of brown.

And when one day she left me
  With a sad farewell in her eyes,
I knew what it is men suffer
  When the nearest and dearest dies.

And I crept downstairs in the morning
Just at the break of day,
And called her my little sweetheart
And kissed her–and went away.

And I thought of the Christian teaching
That God has the power to save
The sinner whose sins are blackest,
But a dog's life ends in the grave.

But I knew as she lay before me
There in the early dawn,
That that which I loved was missing,
That which loved me was gone.

For a labor of love was ended
In a look which the brown eyes cast,
And a great big soul went–somewhere–
When a little dog breathed her last.

2

A LESSON LEARNED

I should have suspected this euphoria would be short-lived, for once this period of crisis passed, Peggy's innate sense of pragmatism came to the fore. The animal was, after all, an unknown quantity. Order and cleanliness were obsessions with my wife. In order for the animal to stay with us, it would have to conduct itself in accordance with the rules of the mistress of the house.

In fifteen years of married life, even I hadn't been able to satisfy her criteria for neatness and order, and I argued that such demands on a creature of the jungle were much too severe. Each day the discussion arose and we each argued their side of the arrangement. After weeks of arguing, I decided the only fair way was to compromise. I gave in. You just can't plead a case to a deaf jury. I actually conceded because it was only right that certain conditions were the sacred right of the homemaker. I also recognized that the provision of certain domestic luxuries, not the least of which was her weekly batch of homemade bread, could best be assured by my concession to what was probably a reasonable demand. What really jeopardized my chances of prevailing was when we took our differences to a jury of our friends. Every single woman sided with Peggy while my good friends and childhood buddies just sat there and grinned. I should have asked for a change of venue but it was too late. In the end, the children and I agreed that if the animal did not conform to her rules or if the rest of us failed to monitor his behavior and to clean up after him, Socrates would have to go.

It was this understanding that led us to name the cat Socrates. His future was dependent upon his own behavior.

Over the next five years, Socrates grew from a half-pound weakling into a lovable fifty-five-pound bundle of muscular energy. His diet of baby formula soon gave way to chicken necks, supplemented with whatever fish or meat the nearby supermarkets wished to dispose of at a reduced price. I might add that there were also occasions when we failed to put some food item in a secure place, only to find it missing when we went to look for it. Even Peggy could not blame Socrates for taking advantage of the situation, but the children and I were not spared a warning and a lecture.

One occasion occurred while we were all watching television one evening. Preparing for our Sunday meal, Peggy had set a huge roasting chicken in the middle of the kitchen table to season it. Called into the family room to view something on television, she placed the large roasting pan in the center of the table, where it appeared secure from this twelve-inch baby carnivore. Logic would have you believe that a one-pound cat isn't going to jump forty-two inches to a tabletop and run off with a chicken four times his own weight. (Experience will teach you something else.)

Suddenly, there was a loud, thump from the direction of the kitchen. Peggy and I were on our feet in a second, running to investigate the noise. There, moving slowly across the kitchen floor was our next day's dinner. Only partially visible from behind the chicken were two familiar upright furry ears. Our little doll baby had his teeth embedded in the chicken and, with all the strength he could muster, was dragging the chicken backwards toward the deserted hallway. That afternoon I ate a toasted tuna fish sandwich while my houseguest dined on fresh chicken.

Yet, of all the foods we brought into the house, none provoked him as much as the ordinary banana. His fondness of bananas equaled or surpassed Amigo's penchant for tobacco. Learning this early on, we made it a point to always store bananas on top of the refrigerator. Unfortunately for him, there was no way a little tyke like him could leap the six-foot distance that separated them. Unfortunately for us, we failed to realize that he was growing, and his ability to defy the law of gravity grew at an unexpected progression. With the disappearance of a bunch of bananas one day and the tell tale residue of banana skins, we were ready to accept that Socrates had matured to the point where he could scale tall buildings in a single leap, and he earned the affectionate nickname of Super Cat.

I have had the pleasure of being in the company of numerous people who have lived with exotic animals, from the large gorillas, leopards, and tigers to small raccoons, skunks and monkeys, and I have learned that even within a specific species, animals, like people, have different personalities. There are those I would trust. There are those I would not.

Socrates was an animal I would trust.

As he matured, he seemed to recognize the differences in each family member and treated each of us differently. His behavior was very different, depending on who was present. Never during his life with us was he ever confined in a cage. We even replaced a basement pane of glass with a rubber flap that led to an outdoor fenced enclosure. Being a nocturnal animal, he appreciated the ability to get up during the night and go outside to romp.

If he was ill or otherwise not feeling well, such as the time we had him de-clawed and neutered, he persisted on staying in our youngest daughter's bed. Being only six years old, Gail delighted in treating Socrates like a doll and would sit for hours petting him as another child might play with a doll. Generally, Socrates would seek out some secluded spot to sleep in. But during the entire time of his recovery from surgery, he slept with Gail. When he felt well enough, he returned to the seclusion of his hidden retreats.

Marc, who was eight years old, was Socrates' access to

the outside world. Each day, as soon as Marc arrived home from school, Socrates would begin hounding him until Marc attached his harness and leash and led him out into the woods, where he would eliminate and then climb up and down the numerous trees and stalk some imaginary prey.

The process was somewhat different when winter came and the ground lay buried in snow. Then it was a veritable ordeal to get Socrates to go outside. Marc would have to catch him and carry him out to a nearby tree, where a struggle would ensue to disengage the cat from his hold. If Socrates was really disinclined to be set down in the cold snow, he would lock his powerful front legs around Marc's neck and hang on for dear life. On more than one occasion, Marc would finally lie down in the snow and that would result in the cat relinquishing his grip. The cat would always relieve itself immediately and then leap back into Marc's arms to be returned to the warmth of our home.

Our oldest daughter, Leslie, was a teenager, and Socrates soon learned that his pleasures with her depended upon her changing moods. Usually he was content just to lie in her lap awaiting the arrival of the master of the house.

In addition to being a source of love and affection, Peggy seemed to represent for Socrates a pantry door. From her came all the vital nutritional requisites necessary to sustain life. At a certain time every day, Socrates would find his way to the kitchen and check his feeding dish. If Peggy was preoccupied with some other task and had forgotten to fill his bowl, or if he felt hungry even though it wasn't time for his meal, Socrates would walk behind her, gently nipping at her heels. Never would he bite down hard enough to damage the skin, but always firmly enough to let her know that he expected food.

There finally came a time when Socrates' request for food was inopportune for Peggy, so she shooed him away by waving her hands at him and ordering him to go away. Socrates stood a few feet from her and studied her face. As soon as she turned around, he returned and again began nibbling at her heels. This time Peggy yelled at the cat and sent him sprawling across the floor with a sweeping motion of her foot. Again the cat sat up in surprise. Then, as Peggy turned her back to him, Socrates turned around, raised his tail up straight, and shot a stream of urine with unerring accuracy onto the foot that had just vanquished him.

The first time this happened, we treated it as a fluke. When it occurred a second time, it was Peggy's behavior that changed. From that time forward, whenever the cat nibbled at her ankle, her immediate response was to give him food. The cat seemed content with the resolution.

For me he reserved the dubious honor of sparring partner. Barely would I enter the house when he would begin his game of stalking me. He loved to sit on his haunches and provoke me by striking out with one of his forelegs until I would accept the challenge and wrestle with him. After acquiring a number of painful scratches, I finally invested in a pair of heavy leather welder's gloves into which he could sink his teeth without injuring my hands.

His favorite game was to wrap his four legs around my arm and hang upside down while he snarled and chewed on the rough leather fingers. From time to time, I would forget to put the gloves away, and the next morning I would retrieve little more than a finger or two.

One of his greatest delights was to wait until I had relaxed in my favorite armchair to read my newspaper. Socrates would slink unnoticed into a position at my feet and then suddenly spring up right through the paper. After a few traumatic experiences, I learned to sense his approach and to prepare for his sudden intrusion. But try as I might, even though I anticipated his leap, it was still a shock when he came bursting through the paper.

Our mixed lab, Plato, found no comfort in Socrates' presence. While the two might enjoy the same space without an altercation, Socrates could not resist the urge to stalk the dog and then pounce on him when he least expected it. Worse, Socrates would grab the loose skin on the back of the dog's neck in his teeth and the poor dog would go galloping through the house until someone came to his rescue. Whether the cat was reacting on a primitive instinct or not, we could not take the chance. The only safe arrangement was to never leave the two together unattended by an adult.

Except for close friends, most of our neighbors were totally unaware of Socrates' existence. Although we were not deliberately secretive, we did not parade him around or seek attention. After a while however, his residency became so matter of fact that we hardly considered him in our daily routines and this led to some amusing situations.

One of the things Socrates liked to do was to ride with us in the car. He would always climb up on the shelf between the rear seat and the rear window and watch the traffic behind us. One day we were driving along when a state police car approached from behind with his lights flashing. I was surprised when it pulled abreast of our car and signaled us to pull over. I assured Peggy that, to my knowledge, I had done nothing to warrant a ticket and the two policemen confirmed that immediately. Apparently they had spotted the cat in the rear window a few miles back and had been following us trying to ascertain whether it was a doll or real. When it became obvious the ocelot was real, it became pretty obvious they wanted to hold it or at least pet it. Socrates must have had a great respect for law officers because he let them hold him and even gave one of them a big slurp across his face.

Somebody else must have heard about this incident, because a short time later the advertising agency for Chrysler Corporation called and asked if they could use Socrates for a photo shoot of their new Chrysler. The advertisement came out beautifully. It showed an old woman with gray hair and a knit scarf around her neck seated in the rear seat of the new Chrysler. Socrates was perched on the rear window ledge looking into the camera and the caption read, "Quiet As A Kitten." Not having been able to attend, I inquired how the photography session went. The agent smiled and assured me that it was great until that picture was taken and the cat responded by grabbing the model by the nape of the neck, scaring the hell out of her.

21

Another incident involved our water softening service. Seeking various ways with to amuse himself, Socrates discovered that he could use the open joists of the basement ceiling. There was no apparent problem or threat in letting him climb and jump from one joist to another so we did nothing to discourage it. Quite often, when he tired of being upstairs, Socrates would go down to the basement, climb up onto a joist, and just lie there.

The first few months after subscribing, whenever the service man came to the house to recharge the tanks, Peggy made sure the cat was locked in one of the bedrooms. On this occasion Peggy was busy baking, so she asked our daughter, Leslie, to secure the cat. As a typical teenager, instead of locking the cat in a bedroom, she simplified everything by just asking the serviceman if he was afraid of cats. She neglected to mention that this particular "cat" was an ocelot and weighed fifty-five pounds. When the serviceman answered "No," Leslie simply directed the man to the basement and left.

About a half-hour later, Peggy remembered that the serviceman was still down in the basement. Going downstairs her gaze fell upon a man standing immobilized with Socrates perched on a joist just above him, reaching down and licking the man's bald head.

When the man became aware of Peggy's presence, he rolled his eyes toward her and asked, "Ma'am, does this animal bite?"

Peggy assured him the cat was quite friendly and that he was free to move about without being terrorized. Instead of being irritated, the man found the situation hilarious. On future calls, he would always insist that Peggy leave the cat loose so they could visit while he replenished the softener supplies. While we never could prove it, we became highly suspicious that Socrates had found more than a playmate. He had found another source of nourishment. We were quite certain the fellow was smuggling fresh meat to Socrates each time he visited. You never saw Socrates scramble to greet anyone like he did when the water softener man called. After several months, the serviceman was transferred to another route but traded a customer with the man who was replacing him so he could still service our account. This same service man continued to take care of our water softener (and Socrates) until we moved to another city. Socrates made the nicest friends.

Our move to Birmingham, Michigan, meant a change of schools for each of the children, and this meant becoming known and meeting new friends. For our youngest daughter, Gail, there was an obvious solution. She wanted to take Socrates to school for "Show And Tell."

I will never understand what led Peggy to capitulate, but one sunny morning she, Gail, and Socrates took off for the local grade school and "Show And Tell."

The event was spectacular. I guess every teacher and his or her class was present for the event. They had a table at the head of the room, and Socrates was placed in the middle of the table. He actually seemed to enjoy it as each child passed in a single column for the opportunity to pet him. Regrettably, the spectacular event turned into a more spectacular spectacle when the school's nurse moved in for a closer look. Socrates had only recently recovered from having his claws surgically removed, and apparently, the white gown of the nurse reminded him of the veterinarian who had given him considerable pain. With one loud shriek, Socrates leaped from the table while spraying everything and everyone with a bodily discharge. While the children clamored for more, "Show and Tell" was brought to an abrupt halt and Peggy and Socrates were politely urged to use the nearest exit to return home.

In July 1965, the family decided to take a three-week vacation and drive out West. This precipitated the dilemma of arranging for someone to care for the dog and an ocelot. The local kennels were willing to board our dog, but Socrates was something else. Even the veterinarian who serviced our regular needs declined to have him as a regular guest.

We called several kennels before we found one that said

their facilities and experience were adequate to hold an ocelot. The owner not only had an attractive ad in the Yellow Pages but also claimed to be experienced in caring for all types of exotic pets. The price was steep, but since he was the only one we could find who had experience with exotic pets (and since no one else was willing to board Socrates at any price), we confirmed the arrangement.

Our plans called for us to leave directly after work on Saturday, so to save time we arranged to take Socrates to the kennel on Friday evening. When we arrived, a sense of foreboding came over me. The facilities bore no resemblance to the beautiful buildings depicted in the Yellow Pages.

The kennels were comprised of several old wooden farm structures whose interiors had been partitioned off into pens. There was no evidence of air conditioning, but the windows were open to permit an occasional breeze to pass through. Several young children were running around and yelling for the dogs to be quiet, but except for the man who met us, no other attendants were to be found.

This was the first time I realized how important it was to visit a pet boarding facility before leaving a pet there. Not even guessing the worst, like most pet owners I figured I had no alternative but to go ahead with the arrangement.

The kennel operator apparently sensed my disappointment and hastily sought to assure me that he had special areas within his house for special guests like Socrates.

As he had promised, the inside of the house did contain several enclosures adequate to contain Socrates with a degree of safety. There was a perceptible odor of urine emanating from the wooden partitions and floors, but except for a hot water tank and some water lines in these areas, there appeared ample room for Socrates to sleep and play. My apprehensions were lessened when the operator inquired about Socrates' diet requirements, and I was further relieved when I saw how the man handled and played with the cat.

While I still harbored some latent fears, since we were due to leave the following day, I convinced myself that there was no apparent alternative. With more hope than conviction, I reassured Peggy and the children that everything would be all right until we returned.

The following morning, I arrived at work to find a message asking me to call the kennel immediately.

I placed the call and recognized the owner's voice when he answered the phone.

"Mr. Leeds, I'm afraid I've got some bad news."

"How bad?" I asked, aware of the multitude of things Socrates might have done.

"I'm afraid your cat is dead."

Neither of us spoke. While I could anticipate some problems, I was totally unprepared for this. I felt a large lump forming in my throat as I struggled to hold back the tears.

Finally, the man from the kennel broke the silence. "He must have climbed up on the water heater during the night and weaved in and out between the pipes. Apparently, he jumped off and the leash snagged on the pipes. We found him in the morning, hanging."

When I was able to gain a measure of composure, I asked the man how he could even think of boarding a cat with its collar and leash on. It was a stupid thing to do. His excuse was that one of the young boys put the cat in his room and apparently was afraid to take the collar off.

Suddenly I realized how stupid it all was. You don't have hot water tanks or any other obstruction inside an animal's enclosure. You don't board a pet you love in a kennel that compromises its care by using immature children in place of qualified attendants. You don't board your pet in a makeshift facility that appears to be falling apart and that reeks of urine and feces.

Certainly the kennel was guilty of gross neglect. But inside I knew that I was equally guilty for having boarded Socrates without first checking out the facility.

Only a person who has lost a pet can understand the depth of grief one feels when his cherished pet dies. It is much worse when you feel responsible.

For all of us, the loss was tragic and profound. But it would also affect our lives in a way never imagined at the time. Whether preordained or not, it was Socrates' needless death that eventually caused me to resign my position with General Motors and catapulted Peggy and me into a venture that promised to revolutionize the entire pet-care industry and change our own lives forever.

Prologue Chapter 3

ON BUYING A DOG

Edgar Klauber

"I wish to buy a dog," she said,
"A dog you're sure is quite well bred,
In fact, I'd like some guarantee,
He's favored with a pedigree."
"My charming friend," the pet man said,
"I have a dog that's so well bred,
If he could talk, I'll guarantee,
He'd never speak to you or me."

PET BOARDING
IN AMERICA

One of the first questions I asked myself after Socrates' death was why there wasn't a single modern kennel in the entire Detroit area–a kennel designed and built to provide some measure of the security and comfort that a household pet enjoyed at home? Was it because there were not enough animals boarded to warrant the investment in modern, efficient facilities? Maybe the employment of children or other family members was the only way a kennel could survive in the absence of a viable market. I doubted this was true. I couldn't believe there weren't thousands of pet owners like me who would gladly pay a little more for the satisfaction of knowing their pets were well taken care of.

With the memory of Socrates fresh in my mind, I decided to take a look at the pet-boarding business.

For the past several years, a part of my responsibilities with GM had been the preparation of feasibility studies for new plants and products. I was well schooled to conduct an analysis of the pet-care industry.

My first task was to determine whether or not there was such a thing as a pet-boarding industry. To garner the necessary data, I designed and mailed out an innocuous four-page questionnaire to the eighty-one dog kennels serving the Detroit area. An analysis of the results would provide me with much of the information I required.

My market studies showed there was certainly a demand for boarding facilities. In 1965, Detroiters spent $1.67 million at boarding kennels. I was more impressed when I realized that close to that amount was also spent with veterinarians who were boarding dogs and cats in their hospital cages. This latter market was one I had entirely overlooked while doing my initial research. The results of my study more than vindicated my impression that boarding animals was an industry, but like a ship without a rudder. There were no more doubts in my mind. It was an industry that begged to be developed in a positive direction.

Visiting kennels became a preoccupation during my free time. These personal visits did even more to affirm my resolve to transform the industry than the unfortunate death of my own pet, which had spawned this obsession.

My visits revealed an industry almost totally lacking in pride or cohesiveness. Except for a handful of dedicated kennel operators, the majority of those in the industry were unprofessional and unscrupulous. Nonetheless, perhaps because of the lack of alternatives, pet owners patronized these businesses and by so doing, encouraged their undeserved success.

Not a single kennel I visited was willing to accept any liability for the pets it boarded. To the contrary, if any kind of written boarding agreement was offered to the pet owner, it always contained the specific clause, "If your pet runs away, disappears, becomes ill, is injured or dies while boarding, we are not responsible." In fact, many of these boarding contracts go on to state that if your pet bites someone or causes any damage to the kennel or to anyone
else's property, you, the pet owner, are responsible for the damages. I shook my head and thought, "What a hell of a way to run a business."

The conditions I found inside those kennels that permitted me access supported the logic of a boarding agreement that denied liability for anything and everything. The exterior appearance of a kennel is often indicative of what you might expect to find on the inside, but this is not always the case. I recall one very attractive facility, just outside the city of Des Moines, Iowa, which displayed a huge sign advertising heated and air-conditioned kennels. Inside, I found the kennel freezing and the water in the water bowls frozen hard as a rock. The temperature inside that kennel had to be the same as it was outside: zero!

There was a kerosene space heater at one end of the kennel, but it was either inoperative or it had run out of kerosene sometime during the night. The owner tried to persuade me that he always kept the kennels at a "comfortable" temperature and had even installed an alarm in the house that would ring if the temperature in the kennel fell below sixty degrees. I found absolutely no alarm system of any kind.

The conversion of garages, barns, and other outbuildings into kennels frequently resulted in the use of portable kerosene heaters that presented more of a health threat than they did a solution to the cold. Each year newspapers carried the stories of kennels burning to the ground with tragic loss of animal life due to defective heating systems. Most of these fires did not have to happen.

One of the most successful kennels in the Detroit area was located on a major highway in northwest Detroit. The owner never flinched when she told me that every month one or two dogs managed to escape and run out onto the highway and get killed. It never occurred to her that installing a six-foot chain-link fence around her property could eliminate the problem.

My son Marc was fourteen years old when he went to work for this lady during a summer vacation. The woman's two young children were the only other employees. Each day, Marc would return home and relate pathetic stories of what transpired at this supposedly outstanding kennel.

Like most kennels I investigated, this one advertised heated and air-conditioned facilities. But as was so often the case, the equipment was seldom used because of the expense involved.

On one particular summer day, Marc returned home visibly upset. That morning, one of the owner's children had forgotten to open the windows in the garage, which was filled with cages of dogs, stacked one on top of the other, from the floor to the ceiling. The outside temperature went up in the nineties but inside the garage the additional heat generated by all those dogs added another fifteen or twenty degrees. By the time this was discovered, several dogs had already died and a number of others were suffering from heat exhaustion and were near death. Marc was able to see bodies on the kennel floor before he was chased away by the owner. It was typical of the problems that arise when unsupervised children are used in a kennel instead of mature trained employees.

As happens all too often in such cases, the kennel owner got her own veterinarian to address a note to each pet owner stating that the cause of death was due to heart failure.

On Long Island, New York, a personable young lady who operated a grooming parlor advertised that she would board your dog in a family environment in her home. However, instead of taking the dogs home, she had her fourteen-year-old mentally retarded son take the dogs to the basement of her grooming parlor, where they were placed in cages under his care.

While her grooming parlor was bright and attractive, the portion of the basement where she kept almost 50 dogs lacked even the least amenity. She was aware that her son never fed or checked the animals on weekends or holidays, but she gave no consideration to the condition of the animals unless one died or the stench became so bad that she had to force her son to clean the cages. On one occasion when the odor became unbearable, she went down into the basement and found one corner of the basement filled to the ceiling with dog feces and urine-soaked newspapers.

One of her groomers related the story to me only after he quit because he was ordered to bathe and brush out a dog that had been dead for several days. The grooming was ordered because the owner didn't want to return the body of the dog in such a filthy condition. This grooming shop owner is the same woman who would always tell an owner that his or her dog "just keeled over from a heart attack" while being played with in her home. Although owners paid for the services, few of the pets were given their vitamins, medications, or special diets, even though the owners provided them.

Such reports helped shape my own future employment criteria. For one thing, I resolved never to employ young, irresponsible children as animal attendants. Another promise was that, although I would employ the services of veterinarians, any relationship would be maintained at arm's length. I would never ask a veterinarian to lie for me and I would never work with one who was willing to do so.

The conditions and problems I discovered were not entirely unknown to the pet-owning public. Still, for some reason, few good people seemed inclined to enter the pet-boarding business with the intention of conducting it on a professional level. Even to this day, despite the tremendous growth in pet ownership, the industry has remained fairly static, with as many kennels going out of business each year as there are new kennels being built. The result is that during the summers and holidays, pet owners are forced to accept undesirable accommodations for their pets because nothing better is available. It remains the ideal trade for the unscrupulous entrepreneur.

Abuses were not only rampant among breeders and unskilled kennel operators, but, surprisingly, were common almost to the same degree among veterinarians who sought extra income by providing boarding services in addition to their skilled medical services. It was particularly disturbing to find educated and trained professionals guilty of all the bad practices existing in the boarding industry.

One lady told me about her experience, which added another dimension to unprincipled kennel management by veterinarians. This lady received the dog back with one of its eyes gouged out and with more than twenty stitches in its body. I would surmise that the dog was boarded in a cage or pen with one or more other unrelated dogs, a trade practice called "double dipping." When the owner received her dog the veterinarian advised her that, having absorbed the expense of once treating the dog, he would not be responsible for the cost of any further treatment should any problems arise from these injuries. However, the veterinarian did explain his rational for his decision: "If I had to absorb the cost, I would be too tempted to use the cheapest drugs and treatment–and that would be against my ethics!"

It is a common practice for veterinary hospitals to board perfectly healthy cats in cages next to cats with feline leukemia, a contagious form of cancer spread by a virus. Although there are a number of conditions that would have to be met in order for the healthy cat to contract leukemia, it is a senseless risk. Diseases and ectoparasitic conditions such as hemobartonella, coccidiosis, infectious peritonitis, conjunctivitis, toxoplasmosis, sarcoptic mange, parvovirus, and coronavirus can be spread to a healthy animal when it is boarded in the proximity of animals carrying these disorders. In many cases, the disease may be present for many years before any symptoms are apparent and by then, other household pets may have become infected. After several years, the pet owner rarely traces the cause back to a boarding or hospital confinement. In some cases, the results are terminal and the pet's life is cut short. Vaccines are available today to prevent many of these known diseases but there are still diseases out there for which no treatment or cure is available. It is not a good practice to board healthy animals with sick animals under any circumstance!

In the past, almost every veterinary association was on record opposing the boarding of healthy animals in veterinary clinics and hospitals. Still, it was done regardless of the known hazards. Today, due to the increase in the number of veterinarians and the increased emphasis on profitability, veterinary associations have

33

been pressured by their members to rescind this restriction from their bylaws.

Conscious of this problem, many new veterinary clinics (and some of the older ones) have been built with a kennel separated from the clinic. These are the kinds of kennels and veterinarians a pet owner should be considering.

Without a doubt, kennels account for the majority of boarding problems, but not every problem can be laid at the door of the kennel.

There are, however, two unethical practices that cause many needless injuries and deaths of boarded pets: double dipping (also referred to as "community boarding") and splitting of runs.

As previously mentioned, double dipping is the practice of placing several pets from different owners in the same cage or pen. This practice leads to occasional fights and subsequent injury or even death to one or more of the animals.

An equally abhorrent practice is the splitting of runs, a deception common in kennels that advertise "indoor-outdoor" runs. Perhaps because they have already experienced the problems of "community boarding," these kennel owners simply lock the door between the inside run and the outside run and place one animal on each side.

The problems arise when the temperature outside goes into the nineties or drops below freezing. In most kennels, the outside runs offer no protection for those dogs put there.

Because of the Christmas holiday, another one of the major boarding kennels north of Chicago filled its outside runs with dogs when it ran out of space. That year, Chicago experienced the worst blizzard in its history with the wind-chill factor dropping to eighty-one degrees below zero. On Christmas morning, the employees were horrified to find many of the dogs locked outside frozen to death. In this case the operator was punished. She could not cover up the product of her greed and was forced to close the kennel and sell the property.

In Texas and other southern states, there is the opposite

problem during periods of oppressively hot temperatures. I have been in one kennel in Las Vegas during one hundred degree heat where I saw several large dogs tied to stakes in the sandy yard area. There were no trees or other protection from the scorching sun. The owner must have seen my surprise, so he sought to assuage my concern by assuring me that he only kept large dogs staked outside. The dogs locked in the outside areas and those locked in the inside of non-air-conditioned kennels are easily subject to strokes and death from heat prostration. Unfortunately, the profitability of these procedures, for those who do not accept liability for the pets, encourages the practice. A kennel with only twenty or thirty runs can board several times that number of animals by resorting to substandard confinements.

Being an outspoken critic of the industry, I was challenged one time at a meeting of the American Boarding Kennels Association. In this instance we were discussing the meaning of ethics. The kennel owner was trying to convince me that the vast majority of kennel owners were the embodiment of good character and ethical behavior. I was unmoved.

I told him about the experience of a friend who had boarded his twelve-pound Yorkshire terrier. He had driven many miles to a nice looking rural kennel where he was assured that his dog would have its own private indoor-outdoor run. My friend arrived back from his vacation two days early and like pet owners everywhere, he headed straight for the kennel to get his dog. The lobby was jammed with people bringing their pets in for the upcoming weekend.

When he asked for his dog, he could see the color drain out of the owners' faces. My friend followed one of them to an adjoining office where the man began searching among several cat-carrying cases sitting on the floor.

Finding the correct one, he opened the front panel and the dog's head poked cautiously out. Suddenly, the dog bolted past both men and ran to the lobby exit door where, literally screaming, he tried to claw his way out of the building.

Apparently, for the better part of two weeks the dog had

been cramped into a small cat-carrying case that was so small he couldn't even stand up in it. There is no way to be certain, but it is likely the dog had been forced to eat, sleep, and eliminate, within the confines of that small container.

These kennel owners were no different then hundreds of other kennel owners. The standing joke of this industry is that "Dogs never tell."

It is a common practice to assure dog owners that their dog will have a private, spacious indoor-outdoor dog run, but as soon as the owner is out of sight the dog is put into another run together with other dogs, or it is shoved into some kind of crate unfit for a living animal. The "spacious indoor-outdoor run" is then rented to the next unsuspecting pet owner.

The kennel operator I was telling the story to was shaking his head from side to side.

"That was unethical," he agreed. "They should have at least built a wall so people couldn't see into their office."

I continued my research into every aspect of pet boarding for almost five years after the death of Socrates. The investigations and studies were organized and completed with the same thoroughness I would have used had I been studying the merits of a major project for General Motors.

I used every available free moment to visit kennels and animal research facilities throughout the country. Ralston Purina, Quaker Oats, A. J. Carlson Research Institute at the University of Chicago, and dozens of other institutions were all kind enough to permit me to inspect and study their facilities and to discuss the problems of commercial pet boarding.

I initiated acquaintanceships with as many veterinarians and kennel operators as I could, soliciting information. More often than not, I detected a slight tinge of resentment if I revealed my intentions to some of these people. Over and over again, I was assured that the investment of substantial monies in a pet-boarding facility was folly. "The successful mass boarding of all types of animals is impossible." "Too many viruses going around." "Too many bacterial infections." "Too many unsolvable problems."

"It has been tried before and always failed."

My dream was already someone else's nightmare.

I was thoroughly tutored in the industry's faults, and despite assurances that nothing could be done about them, I was still convinced that remedies were available. Good pet care was possible, and I was going to prove it was economically feasible.

One of my friends offered to comfort me with the assurance that no failure is so great that it cannot be exceeded by blind faith and unreasoned effort!

Prologue Chapter 4

PAW MARKS

W. J. Hickmott, Jr.

On the floor I see the marks of muddy footprints.
My favorite chair is graced with long grey hair.
The windowpane has smudgy little nose marks.
But you know — I love to see those dear marks there.

There's a bone behind the davenport, I fancy.
A rubber doll lies lonesome on the floor.
A little leather harness on the table,
A dog leash on the handle of the door.

I know they're out of place and look untidy,
But yet, I think I like them on the whole.
They make a house a home –a place that's happy,
A little puppy's paw marks on your soul.

THE PERFECT
PET CARE FACILITY

There were no school courses or textbooks available on how to build or operate a kennel. Even the state's Department of Agriculture, which had jurisdiction over pet-boarding facilities, could not offer a single printed document to guide a newcomer to the industry. There was no trade association, nor were there any trade magazines from which a person might learn. It was no wonder problems were common and had persisted over the years.

The director of the Carlson Research Facility did offer me a government pamphlet that included recommendations of the Committee on the Guide for Laboratory Animal Facilities and Care of the Institute of Laboratory Animal Resources, National Academy of Sciences-National Research Council. In addition, we contacted the Government Printing Office and obtained copies of all Congressional acts that pertained to animal welfare.

Although this information related to animal research facilities and to the interstate transportation of animals, at least it offered data on ventilation and sanitation that were not available elsewhere. While some of these requirements might be thought of as being too severe for a commercial boarding facility, we felt their incorporation would only add to the safety and welfare of our guests. The recommendations of the National Academy of Sciences became a part of our specifications.

After interviewing several architects, we made our selection and contracted for the development of a formal set of plans and specifications for a four hundred room pet motel that would serve as a model to anyone in the business, as well as anyone wanting to enter the profession.

To begin with, we concentrated on the problem of stress. From all of the information we garnered, there was one common area of agreement. Stress was responsible for more illnesses and deaths among boarded pets than any other single factor. With young animals, it led to enteritis and subsequent dehydration. With older animals, it contributed to kidney failure.

To remedy this problem, a separate area was designed for each type of pet. Only dogs were to be kept in the kennels. Cats were to be housed in four-foot-high "apartments," in two separate catteries. Not only would they not be able to see the dogs, but also they wouldn't even be able to hear them when they barked.

There are many homes where a dog and cat live together in complete harmony, but this is a learned condition and not natural. As a rule, when a dog comes into the proximity of a strange cat, the natural tendency is for the two animals to display a strong animosity toward each other. The result is an abnormal degree of stress in both animals.

I have been in many kennels and veterinary hospitals where the cats are enclosed in portable cages or crates and stacked on top of the dog runs in the kennels. The dogs bark continuously at the cats, and the cats scream back their own peculiar hiss of defiance. When the pet owner calls for his pet, he gets back a neurotic animal that will take months to straighten out, if ever.

Since the problem of such stress was a major consideration for all species, not just dogs and cats, our design had to ensure that no animals with a natural hostility toward each other would ever be boarded in the same area. Besides kennels and catteries, separate facilities would include an aquarium, aviary, serpentarium, stable, and a small-animal room, our "Bunny club."

Each area was designed to hold a specific number of animals without overcrowding and designed so a specific number of attendants could adequately service that area.

Special ventilation systems would provide up to twenty complete fresh air changes an hour while maintaining comfortable temperatures during the most extreme weather conditions Chicago could suffer.

Published studies indicate dogs and cats relax when serenaded by soothing music (and are agitated when exposed to hard rock music). This prompted us to incorporate a special communications system that would carry soft music to every pet area, both inside and outside the buildings. A master control in the manager's house would allow him to monitor each animal area with the push of a button.

Since dog boarding would constitute the largest portion of our business, most of the innovations were directed toward dogs.

To further reduce stress and to permit the kind of care we wanted to achieve, the plans included dividing the dog facilities into five separate kennels with no kennel containing more than fifty dog runs. The Imperial kennel was further divided into three areas. A center section with four extra-large rooms measuring six feet by seven feet was called the Regency Suites. The areas on either side, the Imperial Suites, each contained only nineteen suites. Each suite contained wall-to-wall carpeting, a miniature brass bed, a specially made Sealy mattress and fresh sheets every day. Because each attendant would have only a few dogs to take care of, extra time could be allocated for brushing and spending time with each dog. While all the dogs would receive a treat of Milk Bones before being locked in at night, dogs in the Imperial and Regency suites would receive an extra "cookie break" in the afternoon.

The idea of a two-tier level of care was not part of any original planning but was incorporated after a number of prospective customers persuaded us that some people would never board their dogs in a conventional kennel. If we had known how many people would desire and pay for this kind of care, we would have provided more Imperial and Regency suites than Deluxe suites. The additional charge of two or three dollars a day was no barrier, regardless of the pet owner's economic status. Love and concern for their pets were their criteria. In later years, the Imperial and Regency suites would be booked as much as a year in advance for summers and major holidays.

The demand for additional services eventually led to the installation of telephones and televisions in the Regency suites so owners could call their pets and their pets could watch television during the day.

Although our pets received telephone calls from all over the world, the distinction for the most expensive telephone call has to go to a Chicago businessman who, while aboard a cruise ship in the Mediterranean Sea, telephoned his dog every day. Each time he telephoned he would urge the receptionist to hasten the connection because the call was costing him eighteen dollars and fifty cents a minute. Only a pet owner can justify these amenities. For those with doubts, let me assure you that dogs definitely recognize their owner's voice over the telephone or on a taped recording. I have seen the proof.

In almost every instance, the dog will get highly excited and begin looking around for the source of voice. You can even note the excitement in some dogs when they see the telephone being brought back into their room. They behave like a young child awaiting an expected call from a parent.

An option for every pet owner was the playing of his or her taped voice recordings. Many pet owners would pre-record messages and have us play the taped messages for their dogs. Judging from the cassette tapes we have played, I suspect most telephone conversations are filled with tender expressions of affection, although in one instance I'm not quite sure what the owner might have told her pet to evoke the kind of response we got. After hanging up the receiver, our attendant left the room for a few minutes. When she returned, she found that the dog had jumped up and pulled the telephone receiver off its hook. The dog had chewed the cord into a dozen pieces and was working on the receiver. The Bell Telephone repairman was quite understanding when we explained what happened. Removing all the telephones from the rooms and just having a jack in the room eliminated this hazard. From then on, when a call arrived, the attendant just carried the telephone into the room and plugged it into the jack.

Telephone calls and tape recordings just didn't impress our cats. Apparently they don't associate a phone message or a recorded message with the actual speaker. Maybe it's just as one cat owner assured me: "Cats couldn't care less. You call a dog and it will come to you. You call a cat and it will send you a fax."

The establishment of different classes of boarding accommodations, with their varying charges, might appear to conflict with our original desire of offering only inexpensive boarding to the public, but it didn't. To the surprise of most people, and especially our competitors, a lower boarding cost was one of the virtues of the mass-boarding concept. By boarding large numbers of pets we were able to offer better care and facilities and provide our employees superior wages with overtime pay, medical insurance, paid vacations, a college tuition program, and a host of other benefits never before offered by a boarding kennel.

Mass boarding offered other benefits also. For one thing, having up to fifty-two employees assured that no employee would be overworked because someone didn't show up. We wanted our company to be a responsible corporate citizen and we wanted our employees to enjoy working for us. This program included annual Christmas parties where thousands of dollars worth of gifts were given out. Each year's party was different and we always included the employee's spouse, or "guest" if he or she was engaged. One year we had a Broadway play staged at the Wyndham Hotel. Another year we brought up an act from Nashville's Grand Ole Opry. To thank the many veterinary clinics that worked with us, we included all the veterinarians, their wives, and their staff. It was nothing to have 200 or 300 people at these parties. We would be a different kind of boarding kennel.

When the first lobby was designed it included a mailbox for every pet's room. Pet owners' children would be invited to write to their pets, being assured that the postcards or letters would be read to them. Over the years, we have received thousands of cards and letters from all over the world, and in every case, one of our animal attendants sat down and read the message to the pet. We always advised the owners to sleep on the letters to give the letters their scent. Although this was intended for children, ninety percent of the cards and letters arrived from adults. It made no difference to us, but it was another indication of the affection owners assign to the family pet.

In some cases, the pet owners used the occasion to advise us of changes in their plans, giving new pick-up dates or requesting that the animal be bathed or groomed on a different date. Some of the letters were quite serious, expressing deep affection and concern and reassuring the pet that it had not been abandoned or was not loved any less because its owner had to leave it behind. Other letters were hilarious and exhibited the unique composing talents of the authors.

A classic letter consisted of a series of clippings glued to the paper, like a kidnapper's ransom note.

"Porkchop," the note read, "our plans have changed. Get your hair cut on Monday. Will spring you February 11th. Be at main gate at 9 a.m. Getaway car will be in parking lot. (Signed) You Know Who."

In addition to giving all of us a good laugh, the note let us know the dog was going to be picked up one day later than originally scheduled and permitted us to have the dog groomed by nine o'clock.

We had our fun too. When the owners called for Porkchop, the receptionist played along and said something to the effect of, "Gee. I don't know how Porkchop knew you were coming today, but he has been all dressed and standing by his gate since eight o'clock." We all had a good laugh with nothing more said.

Of course, there have been times when a pet receives three or four scribbled letters every day it is with us from one or more children of a family, and we always wonder if the parents are as amused with the postage cost as we are with the letters' contents.

One of the extra things we had occasion to do, but never advertised, was to answer some of the letters the dogs received. Either Marc or I would sit down and draft a letter, written as if it came from the pet. Sometimes it was to a child whose letter begged an answer and sometimes it was to an elderly person who was hospitalized for an extended period. These letters often included a Polaroid picture of the pet.

From the very beginning, these were the kinds of amenities that distinguished our pet motel from a typical kennel.

Another feature of reducing stress was to build an attached outdoor run for every indoor dog room. In the morning, a sliding guillotine door could be raised and the dog, passing through a hanging flexible rubber flap, could go in and out by itself. At night, or during periods of extreme temperatures, the dog could be locked inside when the sliding door was lowered. We considered this ability to go inside or outside at its own volition one of the most important considerations to a dog's health. With few exceptions, every dog is a clean animal and is housebroken by its own natural instincts.

Many boarding facilities that keep dogs in cages or inside pens will tell you that the dogs are taken outside when they have to eliminate. Perhaps they only employ psychic employees. Unless they board only a few dogs, or have several attendants who do nothing else than take the dogs outside, this is not true, nor is it possible. No kennel operator in the world knows when each animal has to eliminate. The result is that the animal restrains itself until it is ready to burst and then eliminates in its cage or pen. There are many times during the year when distinct outside toilet areas are inaccessible due to long periods of rain or snow, and it is obvious that the animals in these boarding facilities are being forced to eliminate in the same cage or pen in which they eat and sleep.

To protect our dogs from inclement weather and heat prostration, the outdoor runs were covered with heavy gage aluminum awnings that extended five feet past the end of the run. It also allowed us to lock a dog in the outside run when we cleaned its inside run so they would never be accidentally struck by the high pressure cleaning hoses.

With our system of indoor-outdoor runs, we were able to board puppies, and on most occasions send them home housebroken. It required no training at all on our part. The puppies only needed the ability to go outside whenever their systems required it.

An obvious fault of many kennels is the separation of areas by only some form of wire fencing. Many times I have observed a male dog lift his leg and urinate through the wire partition onto the dog in the next run. This is one of the reasons some dogs go home reeking of urine and the reason many kennels insist that you have your dog bathed before it goes home. Of course most kennels charge you for the dog's bath, so in the end, the kennel profits from a bad situation.

To avoid this problem and also to diminish the amount of barking, we designed the walls of the runs to be solid masonry to a height of forty-two inches high with nine- gauge chain-link fencing going up another three feet. This design offered each dog the security needed while still permitting good ventilation.

Drawing on the material gathered during my five years of research, many industries were called upon to contribute their expertise for the problems we were aware of.

One of America's leading paint manufacturers offered us

a special epoxy paint for our concrete walls, one that would not absorb urine or succumb to acid erosion. The fact that it was available in beautiful pastel colors was a plus but, more importantly, it formed an impenetrable shield over the concrete so bacteria, fleas, and larvae could not germinate in the millions of tiny crevices. Since this was a vital concern of ours, the epoxy was included in our specifications.

A high-tech firm in California offered us some newly developed units that, when installed in our incoming air ducts, would charge the particles in the air with a negative charge.

This was an interesting proposal. We were sure that our special high-pressure sterilizing system would minimize the risk of bacterial infection, but viral infections were something else. We could kill the bacteria, but viruses tend to float in the air, carried by dust or other airborne particles.

Theoretically, if we charged all the air particles with electrons, instead of floating around from animal to animal, the virus-carrying particles would be drawn to the floor by the positively charged earth, resulting in a germ-free environment. All we then had to do was mop our floors with an effective virucide. Another benefit was that bacteria couldn't survive in a negative environment. Theoretically, we could leave moist foods in the animals' rooms all day without fear of spoiling.

A further purported advantage being claimed at that time in some of the medical journals was that mental patients placed in a negatively charged environment tended to be more relaxed. If we could achieve the same results with animals, it would support our efforts to reduce stress. The units were added to our plans

More common hazards were easier to deal with. Every year hundreds of dogs suffer broken teeth, lacerated jaws, and even broken jaws by getting their teeth enmeshed in the chicken wire or narrow-gauge chain link fencing most kennels use to separate one dog area from another. Chicken wire, hog wire, and most kinds of farm fencing are treacherous for commercial boarding facility enclosures.

To prevent these types of injuries, special nine-gauge, one-and-one-half-inch mesh chain-link fencing was specified for our partitions and gates. In theory, it should have worked. In practice, our canine adversaries proved it wasn't a sure thing.

Several times over the years, certain dogs have been able to twist, tear, and distort the chain link portions of their gates into unbelievable masses of twisted and shredded wire. The replacement of fencing became an ordinary recurring expense. Fortunately, the two additional chain link fences that surrounded the kennels proved to be an obstacle to escape—except in one case.

He was not the kind of dog you would expect to be the exception. While we were closed for lunch one day, a small, thirty-pound mixed terrier literally chewed a large hole in the nine-gauge wire fence to gain his freedom. When he came to the seven-foot-high perimeter fence, he dug an escape tunnel in the frozen ground and went under the lower steel bar. We saved the broken strands of steel because we doubted anyone, especially the owner, would believe a dog could perform such a feat.

Fortunately for everyone, the story had a happy ending. The dog defied capture and continued to elude us by hiding in the fields surrounding the motel. During this time, the temperature dropped below freezing, but he refused to allow anyone to come near him, nor would he come into our fenced area for food or shelter. Four days later, the owners found the dog sitting on the front steps of their home, some six miles from the pet motel. He was a remarkable dog!

The constant availability of water is another important consideration for most animals and it can be a matter of life or death for older dogs whose kidneys are beginning to deteriorate.

Our solution to this concern was the installation of a special watering device manufactured by a company on the East Coast. It was a stainless steel bowl that was connected to a separate water system. As a dog drank from its bowl, the water would be continually replenished. Every dog would always have as much fresh water available as it desired.

Because most dog owners object to having their dogs sleep on bare concrete, we decided to place a special perforated, pure vinyl matting in every dog's room. The matting we selected had risers molded into the lower surface to permit the circulation of air so the floor beneath it would dry rapidly. At a later date, we decided to add fiberglass-resting pallets in the deluxe rooms, where brass beds and mattresses weren't available.

Recognizing that some dogs would use the carpets to satisfy their urge to chew on something, we had to be careful to select a carpet that was impervious to urine and bacteria and that was also non-toxic if swallowed. These parameters narrowed the alternatives and substantially increased the cost of the material selected.

Whether outside dog runs should be poured concrete or gravel is an age-old controversy that has been argued at length by persuasive advocates of each. Although it is much cheaper to use gravel, we chose poured concrete slabs, as concrete can be cleaned and sanitized, eliminating the harboring of residue that can cause disease and infection.

The inside room sizes were a special concern of mine. I had always hated to see any kind of animal cooped up in a constrictive cage. To me, it always seemed the animal was being imprisoned or punished, rather than humanely housed. I insisted that every animal have plenty of space to move around in. That meant a sleeping area for dogs of from twelve to thirty-six square feet and an adjoining outdoor run of twelve or sixteen feet in length, depending upon the size of the dog.

The threat of viral infections also had to be coped with. A single outbreak could jeopardize the health of every animal in the facility. For this reason, our heating and cooling systems had to take this risk into consideration.

Radiant heat offered the advantage of warm floors, but it failed to provide the necessary air movement we desired. To meet the Academy of Science's recommendations, we had to be able to provide up to twenty air changes an hour. In addition, we had to be able to switch to 100 percent fresh outside air if a viral infection broke out. Only a forced air ventilating system could meet these requirements.

As an added safety factor, separate heating and air-conditioning sources were installed for each animal area. This meant that we could maintain different temperatures and percentages of fresh air for each different species of animal. If an infection broke out in one kennel it could be isolated without contaminating pets in the other areas.

The boarding of cats presented a unique set of challenges. Because of their susceptibility to viral infections, many kennels even refuse to board cats. The problem is that cats can appear perfectly healthy but still be carrying one or more viruses in their systems. When they get into a stressful situation, such as when they are boarded, the stress causes changes in their metabolism and the next thing you know, you have a sick cat that can spread its illness to every other cat in the area.

The seriousness of the hazard was heightened for me when I visited the Purina research facilities just outside St. Louis. Our guide at Ralston Purina's research facilities was Dr. Jim Corbin, the director. It was he who had been primarily responsible for the development of pelletized dog food and for Purina's dominance in the pet food industry. At one time his picture graced the front of every bag of Purina dog food.

He turned out to be one of those individuals who possess the unique talent of being genuinely liked and respected by everyone who met him. Rarely have I met anyone in the pet industry who doesn't know Jim Corbin, and I have yet to meet anyone who doesn't respect and admire him.

As he guided Peggy and me through the research facilities, it was easy to understand why he impressed people. At that time I was still a novice and had a great deal to learn. Despite a heavy schedule, Dr. Corbin took the time and effort to explain every little detail he thought would contribute to our success. In addition to the tour, he ran several research films for us on nutrition, diseases, and the general care of dogs and cats. When we finally departed, we were loaded with pamphlets and research results that would help us in our future efforts.

When we finally came to the research cattery he was honest enough to tell us about their recent viral outbreak that had just ravaged their feline research colony resulting in the deaths of numerous cats.

It was a devastating blow to the world's largest pet food manufacturer. In developing its foods, Purina had kept detailed records on the type and quantity of food each cat and its succeeding generations had eaten. The continuing history of every imaginable breed had been carefully documented to reveal any relationship between various health problems and the cats' diets. Taste preferences and consumer attitudes had all been factored into these years of research to permit Purina to try and produce the highest quality cat foods available.

Now, with one single outbreak, the entire population had been ravaged. Years of study and scientific observations were hopelessly interrupted. Those cats that survived the disease were no longer suitable for research and had to be replaced by an entirely new generation of specially bred felines.

A totally new population of disease-free cats was flown in from England on specially chartered aircraft. Once the cats entered the new facilities, they would live the balance of their lives within those walls. Every ounce of food and water would be measured and documented. When their lives ended, veterinary doctors would perform a thorough examination to determine any characteristics that might indicate a benefit or a deficiency attributable to their diet. Few pet owners realize the extent of time, effort, and money major pet food manufacturers expend on perfecting the nutritious diets available to our pets. It was our experience at Purina that convinced us to use only the best brands of pet foods for our pet motel.

Since Purina could never be sure whether the virus that wiped out its cattery had been carried in by a visitor or contracted via air while the cats were in an outside run, both potential hazards were eliminated when they planned this new cattery. Purina's new building had a totally enclosed cattery and admittance was restricted to only those employees who worked there.

Although I was primarily interested in the construction of this new cattery, Purina's recent experience led me to require several new safeguards for our own catteries.

For one thing, Purina stopped letting visitors tour its cattery. No material and no employee went in or out of the facility without special safeguards being enforced. Employees even had to change into sterile white gowns each time they entered the cattery, and the gowns were disposed of when they left.

This presented a challenge to our plans because we wanted people to go through our animal facilities. We wanted people to see how well they were designed and maintained and how vastly we differed from an ordinary kennel. In the end, we compromised. We built a large window through which cat owners and others could observe the cattery. Looking at your pet's quarters through a window, however, does not tell you the level of odors in that room, the temperature, the general conditions of the boarded animals, or the level of housekeeping in the areas you can't observe.

During the time I was visiting different kennels, I found the majority of kennel owners extremely reluctant to show me the inside of their kennels. In some cases they did provide a single window through which I could see only a small portion of the boarding facilities, but the real reason for keeping people out was their reluctance for anyone to see and smell the conditions that existed. From the very beginning we had planned to encourage pet owners to tour our facilities. I knew that I would never again board one of my pets in a facility that didn't let me inspect it. When we did open the pet motel, we found that while most cat owners were satisfied with a window, many others were not. Finally, to alleviate their concerns, we changed our policy, but only the owners of a boarded cat could enter the cattery and then, only if they requested it. If they did enter the cattery, they were not allowed to pet any cat except their own.

Purina's new cattery also incorporated a system of 100 percent fresh air. This meant that there was no re-circulation of air at all. Regardless of the outside temperature, fresh air was brought in, heated or cooled to the desired temperature, and then exhausted directly to the outside. Considering the temperature extremes of the St. Louis area, this had to be a very expensive alternative to any conventional ventilating system. Still, it was the only system that could ensure that a virus would not be re-circulated through the ventilating system over and over again until every cat was infected.

The concept made such sense that we incorporated it into our plans. We would be able to boast that ours was the only commercial cattery in the world with a negatively charged, 100 percent fresh air system, with all incoming air sterilized by ultraviolet light.

Unfortunately we didn't foresee the staggering increases in natural gas and electric rates that would increase our utility bills to over $6,000 a month and threaten our very survival.

The use of stainless steel cages gave the room a sterile hospital appearance, which was not what we desired. We wanted it to be sterile, but we didn't want it to look like a laboratory or research facility. Instead of using standard eight cubic-foot steel cages, we elected to design our own cat apartments ranging from sixteen-cubic feet to thirty-two cubic feet, up to four times the space normally provided. Although made of plywood, the surfaces were coated with two layers of our special epoxy paint. The surfaces were like glass and totally impenetrable by bacteria.

To eliminate even the suspicion of putting dogs into crates or cages, a policy was instituted that cages were not even to be stored near our boarding areas. The only place we would ever use cages would be in the grooming parlor, where they were used for drying pets, or in one of the small-animal rooms, where they were appropriate for holding small rodents.

We never expected to board many birds but still we included a special room for birds. An aviary dictated a different set of considerations. The most important one was good ventilation without any drafts or fluctuating temperatures. As a safeguard, we also installed electric baseboard heaters since warmth was critical. As an afterthought, we added a row of heat lamps suspended from a track running across the top of the room.

This innovation proved most amenable for Charlie, a large Amazon parrot who became one of our many regular boarders. Charlie suffered from arthritis, and we found that by pointing one of the heat lamps toward a corner of his cage, we provided him with some relief for his pain. Charlie appeared to find this accommodation most welcome and basked in the extra heat during his numerous visits.

Because we thought the aviary, with its many brilliantly plumed birds, would be a decorative feature, we located it right off the main lobby with a floor-to-ceiling glass wall through which visitors could observe the birds.

Two smaller rooms were planned for the boarding of small animals and reptiles. It was a mistake for us not to anticipate fully how many rabbits, ferrets, raccoons, monkeys, lizards, turtles, and other small animals are kept as household pets. During holidays and summers these rooms would be filled to capacity.

A special area was designed for the boarding of fish and other aquatic guests. Space was provided for ten thirty-gallon glass aquarium tanks that could have their temperatures and filtration controlled either individually or from a central source.

Another feature that we had to offer was a bathing and grooming salon. Not content just to have another damp cement area with someone's cast-off bathtub, I asked the architect to design a room that would have the same appearance as a beauty salon. This he did, with walls that sported red and gold flocked wallpaper and oval gold-framed mirrors. Outside the doorway was an antique illuminated barber pole with the rotating cylinder featuring dancing poodles. Above the doorway, in large white letters, we placed the admonition, *"IF YOUR DOG IS UNBE-COMING TO YOU, IT SHOULD BE COMING TO US."*

One minor addition we insisted on was a master temperature controller on the dog's bathwater lines. This request came about out of my own contempt for every home shower system I had ever owned. It seemed that whenever I got my shower water just the right temperature, someone, somewhere, would flush a toilet or open a faucet, resulting in my shower water temperature alternating between scalding and freezing.

I had the luxury of being able to scream out at someone, but the poor dogs and cats were at the mercy of the groomer, who might not always notice the rapid change in temperature. With the automatic temperature modulating valve, the temperature of the bath water never varied by more than one or two degrees from a very comfortable 100 degrees.

After seeing the system in operation, I vowed that if I ever could afford it, I would have a similar convenience installed in my own home.

Since the process of grooming dogs holds a certain fascination for pet owners, I asked that the grooming salon, with wall-to-wall glass partitions, be located adjacent to the main lobby. Despite the groomers' objections, this was done. This was not only for the sake of appearance, but would serve as an additional assurance to pet owners, since dog grooming is another business whose reputation has suffered from bad practices, both real and imagined.

I decided that one way to totally eliminate the chance of a groomer abusing an uncooperative dog was to expose the process to the public. This is a good idea in theory, but on a few occasions our image was tarnished by the unanticipated outbursts of frustrated groomers while a lobby full of people was looking on in dismay. Needless to say, another strict policy forbade using profanity, or ever yelling, or striking a dog. If you doubt this happens in most grooming shops, visit a few and stay there for a while.

A spacious three-stall horse stable and a large training barn completed our design.

When we had finished our final building plans, I was satisfied that they offered the finest option in pet boarding in America, and perhaps in the world. The buildings would not only be attractive and functional, but they would include the systems necessary to meet or exceed the recommendations set forth by the American Academy of Sciences for an animal research facility.

It was an impressive dream, but its price would be even more impressive.

Prologue to Chapter 5

THE SAUSAGE COLORED DOG

Joseph J. McDonough

The rain was pouring down that day
As I arrived at work.
The lightning flashed; the thunder clashed;
The world seemed all berserk.
Wind whistled through the building's halls
As I made my way past art-hung walls.
Then, through a storm-streaked door I saw
A Sausage-Colored Dog.

He stood there looking in at me,
That Sausage-Colored Dog.
His brown and darkly-speckled fur
All dripping in the fog.
His eyes looked out so sorrowfully
As though accusing me:
"Please let me in!" he seemed to plea,
That Sausage-Colored Dog.

My company is rich and strong
With corporate power to spare.
But, for a Sausage-Colored Dog,
There's no room anywhere.

The executive suite's replete with men
Concerned with the quarterly dividend.
Earnings, profits, ten times ten,
But not a Sausage-Colored Dog.

This dog no assets has, nor will.
This dog from who knows where?
He buys no stocks or couponed bonds
Nor has a market share.
He probably sneaked out that day,
A harmless jaunt across the way,
But, alas, got lost – got lost at play,
That Sausage-Colored Dog.

And there but for the grace of God
Goes someone you might know,
Another time might we not find
The indifference that we sow.
For there but for the grace of God
We all shall lose our way
And once outside will we abide
That Sausage-Colored Dog?

I turned the dog away that day,
That Sausage-Colored Dog.
I thought I could escape the eyes
And lose him in the fog.
But every night this dog I see.
In piercing shrieks I hear his plea.
"Cannot you invest one moment for me,
A Sausage-Colored Dog?"

5

THE QUEST
FOR FINANCING

"A quarter of a million dollars?" I gasped.

"If you compromise some of the design and don't start adding or making changes."

"My God," I intoned irreverently. "A hundred thousand. Even a hundred and fifty thousand. But two hundred and fifty thousand dollars?"

My enthusiasm was suddenly dampened by the cold realism of financial inevitability. Figuring in another $50,000 for land and site work, we were talking $300,000 . A third of a million dollars for a dog kennel. In 1969 this was a lot of money. It's not an insignificant number even today. When I told my friends, even my best friends advised me it was a ridiculous prospect.

I went back to my financial projections. The price tag of $300,000 appeared staggering, but when the bottom line was in place, the concept still showed I could earn a return of more than thirty percent on my investment. As an engineer, I had confidence in the empirical data I had collected during my years of research. I was not about to be swayed by the logic of those less familiar– or, for that matter, those more experienced.

Despite the fact that there were eighty-one boarding kennels serving the Detroit area, grossing $1.6 million each year, 95 percent of these kennels had to turn away business during the summers and holiday periods. Many of these kennels required reservations weeks in advance. The demand for kennel space was there.

The facts seemed so clear. All I had to do was lay them before my friendly neighborhood banker and walk out with the necessary funds.

With a briefcase full of statistics, I began making the rounds of Detroit's major banks. I went to one that had large billboards all over the city proclaiming, "Come to see us for your next million." Either it was because I didn't have my first million or possibly because they didn't have a pet motel in mind when they thought up that slogan, but in any event I came away empty-handed.

After many refusals, I felt a little sorry for the bankers. After all, they were going to miss out on the opportunity of a lifetime. Then, when I ran out of banks, my sympathies lay a little more with me than with them. I began to wonder what it would take to get a bank loan. Obviously, it was something more than a pet motel.

There were three formidable obstacles that I couldn't overcome. First, the idea of a pet motel was new. No one had ever attempted to build one, let alone succeeded. Second, if the business failed, the banks felt they would have trouble finding a buyer for the unusually shaped, specially designed buildings (unless the buyer had friends who liked to bowl.)

The last obstacle was my lack of collateral. I was still employed by General Motors, but research and architects' fees had eaten up most of my wages and savings. The only property we owned was our house in Bingham Farms and that already had a sizeable mortgage. Obviously, a bank wasn't going to be the solution to our financial dilemma.

Mortgage companies were no more perceptive than banks, and after canvassing them in vain, I began the long and exhaustive march to the venture capitalists. For two more years I walked from office to office, extolling the financial and humanitarian virtues of a new concept in pet boarding.

Almost without exception, the response was the same. They were impressed and congratulated me on the thoroughness and detail of the presentation. They called their associates in to see this wonderful, revolutionary concept–so revolutionary that they didn't want to invest their money in the first unit. It was of little comfort that each one gave me the same assurance. "You build the first unit and, if it's as profitable as you predict, we'll loan you the money to build a second."

(Hello! Didn't you hear me? I'm here because I don't have the money for the first unit!)

Hell, if I'd had the money to build the first pet motel I wouldn't have been wasting my time talking to them. My confidence never wavered. With every rejection, my own belief in the concept grew stronger. There was only one alternative left: private financing.

Wealthy people don't have to take risks, but some do. Some do it for the prospect of exceptional monetary gain. And some do it for the excitement of creating a success out of nothing more than a bare idea. Unfortunately, the latter are few and far between.

One attribute seemed common to both types. Having achieved financial success, they presume a divine right to alter, amend, and/or revise anything they touch. Research, market studies, and facts are set aside, and their intuition has to shape your concept. Holding the purse strings conveys this right.

A perfect example was my negotiations with a group of six businessmen in Southfield, a wealthy suburb of Detroit. Two of the group were brothers who had a very successful law practice. After spending months of reviewing documents and making compromises (mostly on my part), everything was agreed upon for a group venture. The contracts were to be signed as soon as the two lawyers returned from a vacation in the Bahamas.

Two weeks later I showed up for the signing only to find an almost deserted office. Only the two brothers were present. Surprise must have registered on my face, because one of the brothers immediately started explaining.

"We thought it over and since we only need $300,000, my brother and I are going to finance the project alone." He added that since they were putting up the money they would be taking eighty-six percent of the stock and would be the ones who operated the company.

I didn't mind their taking 86 percent of the profits, but giving that much voting power to two brothers, and attorneys at that, raised certain apprehensions about my future prospects. This was especially so because these two men had been the most difficult to deal with of the original six investors.

Fortunately, or unfortunately, as the meeting wore on, it became more and more apparent that the two men had different ideas about what American Pet Motels should be.

"Look here," the older brother began. "There are some things we're just not going to do. I just got done spending two weeks in Nassau, and I met this veterinarian that made a lot of sense. There's no way we are going to board cats! They're just trouble. Also, it's stupid to spend money on stables and aviaries. The money is in dogs. That's what we're going to board. Dogs!"

After having spent months discussing the concept of all-pet boarding, I wasn't sure I heard him correctly. Over and over, I had stressed that if it walked, crept, crawled, swam, flew, slithered or hopped, American Pet Motels would board it. It was the major marketing advantage in this industry and a major difference between a regular kennel and us.

The younger brother picked up a thick set of prepared contracts and set them down in front of me. Then he offered me his pen.

I just sat there not believing what was happening.

"Look," his brother said. "We've got the money. With us you'll get your pet motel. Without us you've got nothing."

In that brief moment I knew the chemistry was totally wrong. No deal at all was better than a bad compromise. Why trade a headache for an upset stomach? If they were willing to display their muscle this early in the game, I knew what I might expect every time a tough decision had to be made.

I shook my head back and forth and began stuffing my documents back into my briefcase. Out of the corner of my eye I could see the smiles disappear from their faces. At the doorway, I turned around to see two men staring at me in seeming disbelief. The younger brother still held the pen in his outstretched hand.

"I'm sorry," I said. "It has to be a pet motel. I really haven't any interest in running another dog kennel."

The next year was spent in negotiations with the owners of Stroh's Breweries. At that time they were one of America's largest breweries. The process might have been expedited if I could have met with them in person. Instead, all of our correspondence and discussions had to be conducted through their attorney. They would send their questions to their attorney and then he would forward them to me. Then, I would send the answers to the attorney and he would forward them to his clients.

The financial ping-pong went on for more than a year until, just when I thought everything was all set, their attorney called me with the bad news. "With the stock market down so much, now would not be a good time for my clients to sell any stock so they could invest in your concept. However, as soon as the stock market comes back, my clients would be interested."

My experience in the brokerage business led me to believe that there were only two kinds of people who keep all their money in stocks: the kind who will never sell in a declining market because they don't want to take a loss, and the kind who will never sell when the market is going up because they expect more profits.

What I needed was someone who had all his money tied up in cash.

Prologue Chapter 6

WITHOUT A DOG

Douglas Malloch

A man may have his share of gold,
>Though hard to get and hard to hold,
May even have a little fame
>Although they soon forget your name.
May even have a little bliss,
>The rapture of a faithless kiss,
And yet, the while the world you jog,
>Life isn't much without a dog.

Life gives him friends a-plenty,
>Friends as many as the coins he spends,
Yet, when he has a trail to go
>Up hill, down dale, through rain or snow,
One, only one, will rise and leave
>The good red fire, grieve when you grieve
Go where you go, the peak, the bog —
>Life isn't much without a dog.

Unless a man can say, "Come, Jack,
>Come Sport or Scotty," life will lack.
The only love man ever knew
>That would not vanish like the dew.
To ev'ry man must come a day
>When he must walk some hurt away,
And in that hour of doubt, of fog,
>Life isn't much without a dog.

6

CHICAGO,
THE PROMISING LAND

By December 1970, I had exhausted my list of capital resources in Detroit without success. There were a lot of compliments on a fantastic idea and an outstanding presentation, but nobody wanted to be first.

Working six and seven days a week at General Motors didn't leave me a lot of time to devote to raising capital, and I began blaming my failure on my lack of free time.
As the Christmas season approached, I came to the conclusion that I was going to have to leave General Motors. Persuading Peggy of this was not going to be easy.

I began the softening-up process at once. Chicago suddenly became the only solution to the dilemma of raising the capital we needed. Every opportunity that presented itself, I pointed out that Chicago was the best source of venture capital. She learned that it was the hub of commerce and the treasury of venture capital. It was the Promised Land. I did everything except hire the elephants and a marching band to build up the necessary enthusiasm to overwhelm her ties to our present circumstances.

By the end of the year, we were both psyched into selling our dream house and striking out for Chicago, and in December 1970, I tendered my resignation to General Motors.

Our daughter, Leslie, was attending Flagler College in Sarasota, Florida, while our son, with the support of our neighbors, prevailed upon us to let him remain with them so he could graduate from high school with all of his old friends. He neglected to mention that he and his friends planned on enlisting in the Air Force upon graduation. Peggy and our daughter, Gail, decided to stay in Michigan until our home was sold, so only I would be moving to Chicago at the time.

Instead of purchasing a comparable home in one of Chicago's prestigious suburban communities, we decided on a small, unpretentious house in a Leavitt-built subdivision some thirty miles northwest of Chicago's Loop.

Our new home was a great disappointment to Peggy. She had grown accustomed to the privacy she so much enjoyed in Bingham Farms. Even though this new house was on a cul-de-sac, with an extra large lot, it seemed as if we could reach out and touch our neighbors. The neighborhood swarmed with children who appeared at the first dawn of light and who disappeared just as mysteriously with the setting sun. They spilled over into our yard and when they were gone, they left a trail of tricycles, toys, and clothing that sometimes remained for several days before being reclaimed.

Instead of awakening to the sounds of birds, it was the honking of horns from neighbors' car pools. Each day brought a parade of little cherubic figures collecting for this cause or that. With frequent regularity, neighbors who never spoke to us when we passed them on the sidewalk accosted us at our front door, urging us to sign petitions against every conceivable evil except that of distributing petitions.

We were in the suburbs, but it was not the peaceful nature center we had enjoyed in suburban Bingham Farms, and even my constant assurance that it was only a temporary situation did little to mollify Peggy's growing disappointment.

To compound matters, Chicago did not turn out to be the financial wellspring I had anticipated. In most instances, pleas for start-up capital brought the same response I had encountered in Detroit: "You build the first pet motel and if it's successful, we'll furnish the capital for the second one."

During these months I met several people who expressed an interest in putting money into the project but I still could only account for half the monies needed. The problem was where to obtain the balance.

What happened next was one of those acts of providence.

While sitting in a friend's office one afternoon, my eyes were drawn to the cover of one of his marketing magazines. On the cover was a picture of a handsome executive and the bold headlines above the picture proclaimed, "AMA Chicago Chapter Names McDonald's Kroc Marketing Man of 1972."

"Who's Ray Kroc?" I asked

My friend, Nort Beckerman, looked at me in surprise and then told me. I was flabbergasted to learn that this man had parlayed a mundane thing like a hamburger into a $700 million chain of fast food restaurants.

I had never heard of McDonald's or Ray Kroc, let alone eaten in one of his restaurants. Peggy and I had our favorite restaurants and dined out frequently, but our choice never included fast food. Perhaps living in Michigan, instead of Illinois, partially accounted for my ignorance. However, one thing occurred to me. If anyone should be able to tell me how to take a concept from the drawing board to reality, this had to be the man!

I took the magazine back to my house and read the article on Ray Kroc several times.

"What the hell," I thought. "What have I got to lose by asking?"

I sat down at a typewriter and began typing, "Dear Mr. Kroc . . ." On a single sheet of paper, without actually revealing what my concept was, I told Ray Kroc a little bit about my personal history and a lot about my problem of obtaining venture capital for a unique and worthwhile concept. I closed by asking for twenty minutes of his time to get his advice.

I all but forgot about the letter until I was summoned to the telephone the following week.

I picked up the receiver and answered, "Leeds."

The other voice came across clear and crisp, "Bob, this is Ray. What can I do to help you?"

I paused and tried to think of whom I might know by the name of Ray. Except for a friend in Detroit there was no one. I drew a blank.

After an embarrassing pause, the voice began again. "This is Ray Kroc."

I still couldn't place the name.

"I'm Ray Kroc, from McDonald's!"

"Jesus Christ," I said to myself. "It's the guy from the hamburger place!"

Within a few minutes, the tone of Mr. Kroc's voice had me at ease, and his apparent sincere interest in my problem was confirmed by an appointment to meet with him at McDonald's Oakbrook headquarters the following week. It was to be one of the longest waits of my life.

The appearance of the eight-story McDonald's home office was intimidating, but the impression of the man who made this enterprise happen was nothing less than overwhelming.

His office was laid out similarly to all the offices on the eighth floor. It was a very contemporary arrangement with wide-open spaces and no permanent interior walls. The work area of each employee, from the chairman on down, was at least partially exposed to all the other employees. Only informal, moveable partitions gave a loose definition of each individual's work area.

By being tucked away in the far corner of the floor, Kroc's office enjoyed a small measure of privacy. There were a few executive trappings of the type one might expect to find in the office of a man who headed a multi-million dollar enterprise.

He appeared older than the magazine picture I had seen, but his actions and exuberance were those of a young man. His handshake was warm and friendly. His greeting put me immediately at ease.

After a brief exchange of trivia, he invited me to reveal my mysterious concept to him. I started to open my charts on a nearby table, but with a wave of his hand he insisted that I place everything on his desk. Nothing he could have done would have made me feel more comfortable.

I pointed to the artist's rendering of the buildings.

"This is a pet motel, Mr. Kroc. It's a facility specifically designed for the boarding of pets when a pet owner goes on vacation."

A big smile spread across his face. I think he was trying to suppress a laugh. "A pet motel?" He asked.

"A pet motel!" I replied emphatically. "Mr. Kroc, there are over twenty-six million dogs and twenty-one million cats in American households today. And, in addition to these, there are another fourteen million other types of animals being kept as household pets. Up until now, no one has designed, built, and operated a facility that would really deal with all the inherent problems of boarding pets."

As I talked on, his eyes kept wandering back to the artist's renderings. The smile never left his face, nor did he once interrupt me. When I was through, there was a brief pause.

Kroc looked around at all the charts and supporting documents covering his desk. "How much would all this cost?" He asked.

"Land, sixty thousand. Buildings, two hundred, sixty-nine thousand, five hundred. Equipment, twenty-nine thousand, five hundred, Non-variable, non-recurring start-up expenses, fourteen thousand, six hundred dollars. A total of three hundred seventy three thousand, six hundred dollars."

He began shaking his head from side to side. Finally he said, "This is the God damnedest thing I've ever seen since I thought of McDonald's!" He turned his head toward the front office and called out.

"Fred?" Fred! Come here for a minute."

A tall good-looking man appeared from the other side of the partition.

"Fred, this is Robert Leeds." Fred Turner, the man Ray Kroc had plucked from behind a grill in a McDonald's restaurant and hand-groomed to be his successor, acknowledged the introduction with an abrupt nod of his head. Then, almost emotionless, his eyes darted to the renderings and the mass of statistics on Kroc's desk as Kroc explained my concept to him. There was an awkward silence when he finished.

It was obvious to me that Turner wasn't impressed. I felt a little embarrassed, wondering how many times Kroc invited people like me to his office for similar shows. Turner simply nodded his head and disappeared back behind the partition. I felt it was an awkward moment, but if it was, Kroc didn't seem to notice.

"Have you got any plans for lunch?

Before I could figure out an answer, Kroc took me by the arm and marched me through the labyrinth of office modules to the elevator.

Arriving on the first floor we entered the unpretentious restaurant where the manager immediately seated us. Within a few minutes, several McDonald's executives joined us. I was disappointed that the menu did not list any McDonald's fare. Here I was sitting next to the man who had made the Big Mac a phenomenon, and I had never seen or tasted one. I settled for a bacon, lettuce and tomato sandwich.

Kroc began by telling me he was a self-made man and then went on to tell me the story of how he had started McDonald's. Like so many others, his climb to the top was not without trials and adversities. It began when he was a partner in a company that had the rights to the multi-spindled malted milkshake mixers.

He recounted how he stood in a small California fast food restaurant and was fascinated to see hundreds of people lining up to buy identically prepared meals of hamburgers and French fries. He had just sold the McDonald brothers their second five-spindle milk shake machine and they still couldn't keep up with the demand.

Ray became obsessed with the potential of that business and became determined to buy out the McDonald brothers. Unfortunately, the McDonald brothers were not that anxious to sell that they would just give the restaurant away and they asked more than Kroc could afford.

Although the exclusive sales rights to the multi-spindle milkshake machines promised to be worth a lot of money, without any other resource for money, Ray approached his partner and long-time friend to buy him out. Realizing that Ray had no other alternative, his partner made him a ridiculously low offer for his interest in their company. It was only a fraction of what Ray felt his interest was worth, but it provided Ray the money he needed. He accepted the terms.

Although Ray accepted the offer, he vowed that he would one day get even. He was smiling at me but his message was deadly serious. "I don't get mad. I get even!"

Much later, Ray's friend became the president of one of America's largest paper products companies, and although McDonald's was using millions of dollars worth of paper dishes, cups, and napkins, not one penny's worth was bought from his former friend's company. "I got my satisfaction!" he said with a smile. Not until his former friend died did Kroc lift the ban, even though it might have meant paying a little more to someone else.

There was a message in his story, and I didn't miss the point.

When we returned to his office, Kroc straightened out my papers on his desk. He looked again at the artist's renderings of the building, and the broad smile returned to his face.

"I'd like you to leave these with me for a few days. O.K.?"

"Certainly," I agreed.

Shortly after, I was on my way back home. I thought about how many times before I had been full of hope and confidence. The feeling was different this time, but I had mixed emotions. I could feel that Kroc's genuine interest and appreciation of the concept, but, on the other hand, I was uncertain just how he could really help me.

He couldn't very well have his company own a pet motel. There wouldn't be enough newspaper or airtime to carry all the jokes that would have been made. On the other hand, Kroc had many friends. Many wealthy friends. His personal interest could be the ingredient necessary to put the investment package together.

Prologue Chapter 7

A DOG WAS BORN

Author Unknown

Ages ago a heartfelt prayer
Arose from a man in deep despair.
"Oh God," he pleaded, "hear my cry,
A weak and selfish sinner am I.

Deserted alike by friend and foe,
No way to turn, no place to go.
Though I deserve such misery,
Oh God, restore some hope to me."

The Father heard, "His need is great,
For such poor mortals I'll create
A loyal friend, who'll stay close by,
To love, to share, to live and die.

His willing slave, who'll ask no more,
Than just to worship and adore,
A friend who'll never criticize,
Will never question or advise.

"Who cannot speak or lift a hand
To help — but will just understand."
And so it came to pass, at morn,
An answered prayer
A dog was born!

7

THE OFFER I
COULDN'T REFUSE

The next several days were pure torture. I waited impatiently for some word to arrive. I wanted something to happen, but at the same time I remained skeptical that my meeting with Kroc would actually lead to anything.

I spent the next week typing out resumes. If I was going to keep trying, I was going to have to get some kind of job and get some money coming in.

Just when my spirits were flagging, I received a telephone call from Kroc's secretary. Mr. Kroc wanted me to make my presentation before the board of his executive committee.

A few days later I was set up in the conference room at McDonald's headquarters. A half dozen executives strolled in and introduced themselves and sat down. A few minutes later a few more sauntered in. When it appeared we had a quorum, they asked me to start.

"My vet told me that it's impossible to board different animals in the same building," came a voice out of the dark.

I stopped the presentation and spent fifteen minutes telling them how it could be done and then went on with the presentation.

"Where did you get your building cost from? If you used wood instead of masonry, you could save fifteen percent." It was another voice this time.

Once again I interrupted the talk to explain the advantage of fire-resistant construction. I began again only to be stopped again by another voice declaring it would be impossible to even buy farm land for ten thousand dollars an acre. "How are you going to buy a site for sixty thousand dollars when we can't find a small parcel for under a hundred thousand dollars?" This time I recognized the voice of Luigi Salvaneschi, McDonald's vice president of real estate. Apparently Mr. Salvaneschi had done his homework and had prepared a site survey showing seven sites he had checked on. Three of the sites were over $450,000 while the other four ranged between $90,000 and $255,000. (None of the sites were close to the ten-acre site I ended up purchasing for only $65,000.)

Another interruption and I explained that I didn't need a prime location at the intersection of two major cross streets. I intended to use vacant land in rural locations. "It isn't like the convenience food business. People will travel to take their pets to a good boarding facility!"

More starts and more stops as people without any knowledge of the pet care business proceeded to tear my presentation apart. Worse still, as the meeting stretched out, more and more of them were getting up and walking out.

I didn't have to wait until the end to know that I had failed miserably. I packed up my things and went home. It's hard to remain enthusiastic when no one in your boat wants to row.

I think I had just about hit rock bottom when another call arrived from Ray Kroc's secretary. Mr. Kroc wanted me to meet with his attorneys at their office in Chicago.

The law offices of Sonnenschein, Levinson, Carlin, Nath & Rosenthal occupied an entire floor of 69 West Washington Street. On their stationery were listed the names of ninety-seven attorneys. In addition to handling the legal matters for some of the largest companies in America, including McDonald's, at least two members of the law firm also represented the personal interests of

McDonald's founder, Ray Kroc. I was impressed.

Three lawyers were present. Two of the lawyers, Don Lubin and Ed Lembitz, were much older than the third man and, since he never participated in the conversation, I assumed he was just sitting in to watch the two pros perform.

When we had finished the introductions, Don Lubin paused and looked directly into my eyes.

"Mr. Leeds, McDonald's doesn't want to get involved with your pet motel; however, Mr. Kroc would like to become involved personally."

I tried to take in a deep breath without being obvious.

"Would you be interested in this arrangement?"

"I suppose so," I replied. It was an opportunity I hadn't even considered.

"All right," Lubin went on, "let's go over to the club and discuss it over lunch."

The club turned out to be the Chicago Athletic Club on Michigan Avenue. When we were seated, a round of drinks was ordered and Ed Lembitz turned to the young attorney next to him. "You should feel honored," he said. "Only a short time ago they wouldn't have let a Jew in here." I felt uncomfortable at the remark. I almost wanted to cap it off by adding the old cliché, "Gee, he doesn't look Jewish."

If the remark bothered Don Lubin he didn't let on. Instead he looked at me and said, "Mr. Leeds, you may be a very lucky man. Ray likes you and he thinks you have a terrific idea. He wants to help you himself. Now, you tell me what you want in order for him to become involved."

"Well," I replied slowly. "I need equity capital. I think I have investors who will put up half the money. That means I need another $187,000–"

Before I could finish, Lembitz cut in, "No!" he said emphatically. "If Ray gets involved, there can't be any other investors! He's got to do the whole thing himself. He doesn't need any other investors. He doesn't even need a bank. If he does this thing, he'll do it all by himself."

I had to think about this for a while. Although I had other interested investors, no one had offered to put in a major chunk of the money needed, nor had I made any commitments to anyone. There could be a lot of advantages to a single investor with Ray Kroc's stature. I failed to see the potential hazards of such an arrangement.

Finally, I spoke up. "If it's investment capital, I don't see any problem. The one thing I don't want is debt capital. I won't borrow money to get this first unit off the ground. If I borrowed this much money, the interest payments would eat me up alive." Lubin and Lembitz nodded in understanding.

"Good," Lubin replied. "Ray's worth six hundred and eighty-five million dollars. He doesn't need anyone else's money."

There was one other condition I wanted. It was the one thing I had held out for from the very beginning. "I also want 51 percent of the stock. We can structure the company so Mr. Kroc's investment is protected, but I want to be able to control the company's operations." I wanted to be sure that the pet motel would never be turned into another dog kennel.

Lubin and Lembitz were both shaking their heads from side to side.

"That's not possible, Mr. Leeds. You have to understand that a person in Mr. Kroc's position has certain obligations due to his tax requirements and also because of his arrangements with McDonald's. There's no way Mr. Kroc could participate in any venture unless he owned controlling interest."

I didn't understand what those requirements could be, but I had no reason then to believe it wasn't so. Both lawyers began assuring me that I was about to become one of the luckiest persons in the world, and my reluctance started to weaken.

"If you go along with Mr. Kroc, you could be a millionaire in five years. Maybe a multimillionaire." Lubin's voice was soft and sincere. I had, and still have, no doubts that at the time he believed what he said.

Then came a succession of stories about people who had

cast their lot with Kroc, stories about people who had trusted Ray when he started out and who were now worth millions. To hear them tell it, no one had ever been disappointed. Not only was he a man of unquestionable integrity, but also he was one of those rare individuals who rewarded his associates generously. He never forgot favors; he also never forgot those who crossed him or took advantage of him.

Together, the lawyers spelled out the terms of what they thought were a fair arrangement and one that might be acceptable to Kroc.

Mr. Kroc would put up the money to build the three pet motels planned for the Chicago area. We would build only one pet motel in the beginning and if the concept proved economically feasible, we would build the other two. No bank monies or outside investors would be taken in. Ray could and would do all the financing necessary. I would be president and have total operating control. Joan, Ray's wife, would be vice president and would become actively involved in the company because of her interest in animal welfare.

The fact that Mr. Kroc had more than $685 million to back the growth of the company kept coming up over and over again in their conversation. If it was meant to influence me, it worked.

In exchange for putting up all the money, Ray would retain title to the land and buildings and take all the depreciation. I had no trouble with that. He was going to make this thing happen and deserved this protection and reward. Also, after the company was financially sound, it would buy the land and buildings from the Krocs at a price we would negotiate at the time. I thought I knew what that meant and I didn't object. Anyone who stood the initial risk deserved to make a good profit on his investment. Besides, I would surely be a millionaire by then and it would all be due to him. I agreed to every thing they asked.

Unfortunately, there was more. "Of the one thousand shares of stock to be issued, Ray would own eight hundred and fifty and you would own one hundred and fifty."

"One hundred and fifty?" I said. That's only 15 percent.

I don't think I had to do the math for them. Apparently they had everything worked out before we ever sat down. A second round of martinis and a great lunch also was doing nothing to fortify my resolve.

Perhaps if I had been more worldly wise, I would not have been so surprised. Venture capital has a price the average person would not understand. The best idea in the world isn't worth a plug nickel if it isn't brought into being. My rounds of the venture capital companies should have prepared me for this kind of demand. I used to teach my graduate students the same thing. Now it was time to test my own preachments.

Lubin began speaking again and the offer took on a more positive glow.

"We'll start you out at twenty-five thousand dollars a year and, of course, your expenses. You'll get a company car, a health insurance program, and all the regular perks. If it will make you feel better, we'll also give you a five-year employment contract. That should be plenty of time for you to prove yourself."

When he had finished, the whole deal didn't sound bad at all. Maybe it was the content. Maybe it was the martinis.

"O.K." I said. "We've got a deal."

"Well, wait a minute," Lembitz cautioned. "We can only recommend these terms to Ray, but it's up to him whether or not to accept them."

I doubted that, but I let it pass. I finished my second martini but had barely disturbed my food. For the balance of the meal I listened to them tell me how lucky I was and how rich I was about to become. I listened and I loved it.

I lived the next week in ecstasy and agony. Ecstatic at the prospect of becoming Ray Kroc's partner in the pet motel business, and agony at hearing Peggy upbraid me for agreeing to give away controlling interest in the dream that we had sacrificed so much for. Despite all my assurances that we could be millionaires in five years, she refused to be swayed. The eighth wonder of the world: A wife's intuition!

I had an attorney review the contracts to make sure all the important items were covered and our own interests properly protected. At first he flinched when I told him I was giving Kroc eighty-five percent of the stock in exchange for putting up the construction money. However, after hearing me recite the history of my capital-seeking exploits, he reflected that a bird in the hand was worth two in the bush.

The following week, in the Kroc's Lake Shore Drive mansion, amidst cocktails and hors d'oeuvres, Peggy looked on as I signed the contracts that made me a partner with one of the world's richest men. Joining us on this festive occasion were his attorneys, Don Lubin; Ed Lembitz; Al Doty; Ray's personal accountant; and Burgy, the Kroc's miniature schnauzer.

For me it was the culmination of a long struggle, long sieges of hopelessness and brief periods of misguided elation. It had been years of dreaming and false beginnings. In that single evening, Ray Kroc and his lovely wife, Joan, made it all worthwhile.

His attorneys had not misled me. Again and again Ray and Joan told Peggy and me how enthusiastic they were about the whole concept for improving pet care in America.
Watching the way Ray picked up and fondled his dog only fortified the instinctive feeling that I had about the man. It was truly a joyous occasion for all of us. Perhaps it was only one of many for the Krocs, but to us it was the moment in our lifetime.

At the end of the evening, we were treated to another example of Ray's generosity. As we were getting ready to leave, I brought up the subject of the company car. I told him that we had always driven a Cadillac and if there were no objections, I would like to have one as a company car. I started to tell him that the difference between leasing a Cadillac and a Chevrolet would be paid for out of my salary, but before I could get the words out, Ray raised his voice.

"Hey! Listen here. We're going to make a lot of money together. You want a Cadillac? Get a Cadillac! You're president of the company, you do any goddamned thing you want!"

I could feel the shudders run up and down his accountant's

spine. (I got my Cadillac but I always paid the difference between its cost and that of a Chevrolet out of my own pocket.)

When we left their apartment, I turned and swept Peggy into my arms and hugged her. "Well, was I right?" I asked.

Although her eyes were sparkling, and she stood there holding me tightly, she whispered, "Remember, I don't trust anybody!" I wrote her remark off. Years of living in Finland, first under the Nazis and then under the Russians, had endowed her with mistrust for anyone she didn't really know.

I dismissed her pessimism as a typical feminine characteristic. In a few years I would call her prophetic and wish I had heeded her instincts. It would be the last time I would ever fall prey to the adage that a bird in the hand was worth two in the bush without knowing what kind of bird I would be holding.

When we arrived home, we sat down and reflected how far we had come since I had brought Peggy to America from Finland. We literally started with nothing and even had to borrow money to get from New York to Detroit. Jobs were so scarce that our salvation lay in my ability to get into college on the G.I. Bill.

In those early days of marriage, we had taken a cigar box and divided the inside area into twelve small spaces. Each month, I would cash my government check for rolls of coins, and together, like a ritual, we would sit down and divide the change among the different compartments: rent, electricity, water, coal, food, medical, insurance, clothing, entertainment, and miscellaneous.

Somehow, the money always ran out before we got to the entertainment compartment. More often than not, one crisis or another required more than we had budgeted and Peggy reluctantly took the additional amount from the space marked "food."

I remember once when my parents and my two brothers and their wives kind of invited themselves over for dinner. We spent more than we should have but still ran out of food. It was my brother, Henry, who noticed that Peggy was walking around in a pair of shoes with almost nothing left of them. The next day he showed up with a pair of brand new red shoes. We will never forget things like that.

Odd jobs and hand-me-downs scarcely carried us from one crisis to another. Being able to sell a pint of my rare O-negative blood to the local blood bank every eight weeks was something we counted on to make it through. From time to time, when my mother wasn't looking, my father would slip a dollar bill into my hand and whisper to me to take Peggy to a movie show. It was a luxury he rarely, if ever, bestowed upon himself.

If I was now cautious about spending money, it was a reflex conditioned by a lifetime of struggling to just exist. Being partners with a free-spending multimillionaire would be a new experience and one that I would have a problem getting used to.

When Ray called and suggested that I interview the McDonald's architect for the job of designing our first pet motels, I thought it prudent not to refuse. Although I had already completed several architectural designs, the least I could do was talk to Ray's friend.

I readily understood why this young man enjoyed such popularity with Ray. Not only did he impress me as being personable and highly qualified, but also he radiated the kind of enthusiasm I enjoyed being associated with.

Taking up a pad and pencil, the young man began sketching exterior wall treatments and building shapes that added whole new dimensions to the concept. His talent and Ray's not-so-subtle coercion resulted in my awarding him the Design and Build contract for America's first pet motel. More than ever, I am convinced that having your architect also build your facility is like letting foxes build your chicken coop.

I turned over all my preliminary plans together with the recommendations of the National Academy of Sciences-National Research Council. By following these recommendations, we could build the finest commercial pet care center in the world.

There were two considerations that I insisted had to be met. Every year, I read about some animal facility burning down with tragic loss of animal life. I never wanted to be responsible for such a tragedy. Our buildings would have to be constructed to meet the county's fire resistant code requirements.

The second requirement was vital to the future of all our plans: The entire project could not exceed $375,000!

"As long as I can control the construction, I don't see any problem with that figure," the architect said. "Trust me!"

Prologue Chapter 8

BUYING LOYALTY

Anne Campbell

You can't buy loyalty, they say.
I bought it, though, this very day!
You can't buy friendship, firm and true.
I bought sincerest friendship, too.

And truth and kindness, I got,
And happiness, oh, such a lot!
So many joyous hours-to-be
Were sold with this commodity!

I bought a life of simple faith
And love that will be mine till death.
And two brown eyes that I could see
Would not be long in knowing me.

I bought protection. I've a guard
Right now and ever afterward.
Buy human friendship? Maybe not!
You see, it was a dog I bought.

IT'S ONLY MONEY

Although Ray offered the services of McDonald's staff, I learned very early that it would be to my best interest to proceed on my own. My intuition was reinforced when I received a copy of a two-page departmental communication from Ray's vice president of corporate real estate. In the communication, he listed several reasons why my projection of land costs was unrealistic and predicted we would spend two to four times what I had allocated.

My research was correct. I found an ideal site of 8.5 acres in Prairie View, Illinois, for only $65,000. The cost was 30 percent below my estimate.

With each contact, I came to realize that the McDonald people were spoiled by their financial success. Their company was making a lot of money, and they could, and would, spend a lot of money.

It also became apparent to me from the beginning that my budget of $375,000 would not be met unless I monitored every facet of the design and construction.

Despite the architect's denials, when I looked at the blueprints, I could tell immediately that the construction cost would be double or triple our original budget. Neither my dedication to fiscal responsibility nor my increased warnings that the architect was the wrong man for the job received any sympathetic response from Ray. Each time I called him to complain, Ray would launch into a tirade and order me to let the architect do his work.

Finally, after several months of frustration, Peggy and I were summoned to a luncheon meeting with Ray's wife, Joan. We met at the plush Tavern Club, an exclusive restaurant in downtown Chicago.

Joan was waiting for us at her table, looking like she had just stepped out of a fashion magazine. She appeared much younger than Ray and was exceptionally attractive. It was easy to understand why Ray was so proud of her.

She greeted us warmly and ordered each of us our choice of drinks. We began by talking about the pet motel and our progress, or lack of it. I knew she was familiar with some of the building problems.

She listened patiently while I tried to emphasize that the profitability of the new company depended on our holding the building cost to our original budget. I explained that the only way to prove whether or not the concept was viable was to build it the way we originally planned and then see what kind of profit it produced.

The same sympathetic smile was on her face when I finished. "Listen to me, Robert. Ray is not a well man and this constant calling him is not good for him. We don't care if the company doesn't make a profit. We don't care if the company never makes a profit. We both think the idea is wonderful. We love it. Don't even worry about its profitability!" Her eyes never left mine and she emphasized the right words to make sure I understood what she meant.

"Ray and I are worth 685 million dollars, and we'll never live long enough to spend it all. We don't care how much the buildings cost. We don't care if the company ever makes a profit. We are not doing this for the money. We're doing it for you and Peggy. Ray wants to make you rich, and if you stop fighting him, he will. So what if the architect does go over the budget? It doesn't matter. Ray wants the first motel to be a showplace. Do it right! You can build the second one within your budget and prove the economics then. The money isn't important. Believe me!"

85

I understood what she was saying, but instinctively, I felt she was wrong. The money *did* count. Their accountant, Al Doty, let me know it every time he paid a bill. It would be a monumental embarrassment to me to spend a million dollars on something I said could be built for one third that amount. More important was the indifference to seeking a favorable return on the investment.

I reminded Joan that part of our agreement included a bonus to me. I was counting on my fifteen percent of the profits. That fifteen percent was important to Peggy and me. If there was no profit, we would be the ones to do without. I was reluctant to say this to Joan. I knew that if I did, she would probably go back to Ray, and he would just increase my wages. I didn't want charity; I wanted to prove the concept on its own. I wanted to earn my money the old-fashioned way.

"I'll tell you what we'll do," Joan said. "We'll figure the return on investment based on your budget figure and not on how much is actually spent. That way, everyone will have what he wants."

All my major objections were quashed. I didn't ask her to confirm it in writing. I didn't have to. I was dealing with a lady, and her character spoke for her.

In a final gesture, Joan raised up her glass to toast the arrangement and I lifted mine to hers. Suddenly, my glass slipped from my grasp and fell to the table, spilling its contents down the front of her beautiful dress.

I was mortified. Before I could recover, Joan blotted the excess moisture with her napkin and ordered each of us a fresh drink. The waiter directed us to a clean table, and Joan continued talking as if nothing had happened. That's the kind of lady she was.

When we parted, we agreed that I would not question anything the architect did and I would not bother Ray about such frivolous concerns as cost overruns. In exchange, the profitability of the pet motel would be based on an investment of $375,000 regardless of how much was spent.

I had the feeling that Ray had already told the architect not to heed my objections. I really do not believe the money or profitability was a paramount consideration to him. He was a man who delighted in innovation and thrived on success. He enjoyed being the first with the best and he wanted his pet motel to be the best. Once he committed himself to building the world's first pet motel, cost was not a consideration.

Over the next several months, I watched as earlier construction mistakes resulted in more costly remedial efforts. Foundations had been poured in the wrong places and now certain prefabricated equipment could not be accommodated. By reducing the height of the building by one building block, there no longer was room to run the ventilating ductwork. Flexible fiberglass ducts were chosen so they could be squeezed into an oval shape in the shallow ceiling. As a result, the plastic wrapping ruptured in numerous places and our heat and air conditioning poured out into the ceiling areas. Major electrical terminals could not be found and additional electrical lines had to be re-run through the ceilings. Lobby walls were built and then torn down and rebuilt to mask the results of ineptness. Even the manager's residence wasn't exempt. When the refrigerator arrived, the kitchen counters were too long to permit opening its door. Where possible the defect was corrected or at least covered up. However, all of the additional costs became our cost.

Although I knew we were over our budget, I kept my word and didn't complain to Ray. Not until the middle of June 1972, did I learn that our construction costs then exceeded $1 million. Ray never voiced one word of complaint. Instead, he seemed to take pride in how much we were spending on the facility, as if cost were synonymous with quality.

Although we tried to keep the project secret, it didn't take long before visitors started showing up at our building site. While I did not reveal our trade secrets, I was not reluctant to tell them what our objectives were. On one occasion, Dr. Corbin showed up with three other gentlemen. He introduced one of the men as Mr. Danforth and another man as a representative of the Seeing Eye Dog Association from New York. The other gentleman was an architect and was looking for ideas to build a modern kennel for The Seeing Eye Association of Morristown, New Jersey. This association is the one that trains seeing eye dogs for the blind.

While I had always guarded our plans from suspected competitors, I was always very open with non-profit animal shelters and groups like the Seeing Eye Association. I took them everywhere and showed them everything based on the information they had given me. It was only months after we opened that Danforth opened a similar pet boarding operation in St. Louis, Missouri. It turned out that the "Mr. Danforth" was the brother of Senator John Danforth and a member of the family that owned Ralston Purina.

I doubt that anyone was even connected with the Seeing Eye Association or ever intended to build a kennel for them. However, although the Missouri people had immense financial resources at their disposal, like the majority of kennel owners, they cut costs where it mattered most.

One of these savings was by building their pet motel out of flammable wood instead of fire-resistant materials. A few years after they opened, I picked up a paper and read that their kennel had burned to the ground with the tragic loss of many animals. The cattery, which was in the rear of the facility had only one interior entrance. While the details were never made public, an employee confirmed that every cat in their cattery died from smoke inhalation or burns.

The surviving animals were moved to a vacant building where they were held in crates and cages. Even though these animals could not receive the kind of care promised, those people who were able to get a pet back were charged the normal boarding rate. This was the prevailing pet care mentality.

Shortly before the scheduled date of our grand opening, Ray called me with another offer I couldn't refuse. A lady who operated a non-profit animal shelter had been asking him to donate some money to it. Ray explained that he'd like to give the woman $5,000 or $10,000, but thought it would be a good idea to do it through American Pet Motels. That way, the woman would get the benefit of the money and we would get the benefit of the publicity. Ray had already talked to Al Golin, a friend of his who ran a public relations firm. I was to call him because he had some good ideas he wanted to discuss with me.

The lady was Gertrude Maxwell, a retired schoolteacher who had dedicated her life to rescuing abandoned pets. What made her Sav-A-Pet Animal Foundation unique was that she took in stray and abandoned animals and would never let one be euthanized. If it was sick, she had a veterinarian heal it. Regardless of the pet's age or condition, if she couldn't find someone to adopt it, Gertrude kept the animal at her decrepit shelter, where it was fed and cared for. It was a formidable challenge for a compassionate senior citizen already approaching her seventies. I welcomed the opportunity to help.

Not until our construction was hopelessly behind schedule did Joan Kroc intercede. I don't know what action she took, but the architect finally gave a completion date of June 23 and our grand opening was scheduled accordingly.

As a commercial pet-boarding facility, our motel's appearance was a marvel. Brilliant red mansard roofs highlighted the low gray buildings. When you stepped through the glass double doors into the lobby, you had to remind yourself that you were entering a pet-boarding facility and not some first class luxury hotel. The simulation was excellent. The architect's minor oversight of not providing space for the reception desk had to be worked out by deleting two feet of space in the foyer. However, only those customers who have gotten caught in the swinging doors had any adverse comments to make.

The problem of obtaining mattresses for our miniature brass beds was resolved with a single telephone call to the local Sealy Mattress Company with an explanation of what the mattresses were needed for. A week before we opened, our driver pulled up to the Sealy loading dock and picked up a truckload of specially constructed two-inch thick foam rubber, waterproof mattresses. The Sealy nametag had even been sewn onto each mattress. For our canine guests, sleeping at the pet motel would be, in Sealy's phrase, "like sleeping on a cloud."

The grand opening was a memorable black-tie affair. A huge pink-and-white-striped circus tent was set up on our front acreage and an orchestra played popular melodies while guests glided to and fro on the specially installed dance floor. A huge buffet offered all kinds of delicacies, and uniformed waitresses darted from table to table to oblige the guests' special wishes. At each corner of the tent, a bar had been set up to provide liquid refreshments.

Except for our neighbors, each guest was required to purchase a ticket, and all the proceeds were given to the Sav-A-Pet Animal Foundation. Smartly uniformed employees escorted the guests on a guided tour of the facilities.

The event was capped off with the appearance of Ray, Joan, and Burgy, their miniature schnauzer. Even Burgy had dressed for the occasion. He was wearing a stiff white pointed collar with a black bow tie. I submit he was as appropriately attired in formal wear as any one of our guests.

A minor embarrassment occurred when Ray asked for his special brand of bourbon and the bar didn't have it. No one had even considered such an occasion. It was readily remedied by dispatching one of our employees to the nearest liquor store.

It was a joyous afternoon and evening and I was not about to cast a pall on it by telling Ray that only thirty-four of the two hundred and sixty-eight dog runs were usable, or that one hundred and eighty kennel gates, built according to the architect's drawings, were inoperable. No one would notice that the quick disconnects for the sanitizing hoses had been anchored flush with the concrete, making them unusable, or that all of the electrical outlets in the kennels had been covered by the fencing posts so they were completely inaccessible.

For one glorious day all the problems were set aside. This was a day to let my partner savor the potential of our aspirations, and I would let him do so without recrimination. He was delighted with what he saw and I let him depart with those feelings.

The following day, the entire process was to be repeated for the members of Chicago's veterinary profession. This was a most important occasion because we anticipated a large number of our referrals to come from the veterinary community.

To our dismay, the swarm of veterinarians failed to materialize. The orchestra played to an empty house and trays, heaped with fancy foods, went uneaten. By the end of the day only a handful of veterinarians had made an appearance and no one could explain why.

It wasn't until Monday that we began receiving calls from some very irate veterinarians. Then it was evident what had happened. Apparently someone at the public relations firm had neglected to mail the invitations until the day before the party. Only a dozen veterinarians received their invitations in time to attend the opening. The rest received their invitations the following week. When I brought the subject up, someone dismissed it by saying we could do it some other time just for the veterinarians. That time never came.

Prologue Chapter 9

I PITY THE MAN

Author Unknown

I pity the man who never has known
The pleasure of owning a pup,
Who never has watched his funny ways
In the business of growing up.

I pity the man who enters his gate
Alone and unnoticed at night,
No dog to welcome him joyously home
With his frantic yelps of delight.

I pity the man who never receives,
In hours of bitterest woe,
Sympathy shown by a faithful dog
In a way only he seems to know.

I pity the man with a hatred of dogs;
He is missing from life something fine;
For the friendship between a man and his dog
Is a feeling almost divine.

THE GUESTS ARRIVE

The following Monday, June 25, 1973, American Pet Motels was opened to the public.

To say that we were overwhelmed would be the understatement of the year. Not only from the Chicago area, but also from as far away as Michigan, Indiana, and Wisconsin, people brought their pets to a facility that, for the first time, offered them the safety, security, and care they sought.

There was only one problem. With only forty-two of our dog runs usable, we occupied our time inventing reasons for declining business. Not until after the peak boarding season had passed would most of the facilities be suitable for use. In appearance, our operation was a huge success. Financially, it was a disaster. A kennel makes almost all its money during the summer months, and this was the period we missed.

The construction repairs continued for several more months and as more accommodations became available, we readily filled them with the clientele I had predicted would come.

Dogs, cats, rabbits, horses, goats, mice, olingos, coatimundis, foxes, wolves, raccoons, squirrels, ducks, mink, fish, ferrets, birds, snakes, lizards, skunks, monkeys, apes–you name it, and we boarded it. It was only a short time before we lived up to our slogan, "If it walks, creeps, crawls, swims, flies, slithers, or hops, we will board it." We did!

There were conditions under which we would refuse a

pet. We would not board a vicious or poisonous pet, or one with a contagious illness. In addition, each owner had to show written proof that the pet's vaccinations were up to date. We would not expose either our employees or other people's pets to these hazards.

From the beginning we realized how provincial many pet owners were in their attitude toward other types of pets. The most compassionate dog owner may abhor cats, while a doting cat owner failed to find any virtue in owning a dog.

Perhaps pet owners should be classified by the species of pet they own. We have seen people spend more money on the care of a common pet house rat than they would feel justified for someone else to spend on their beloved dog or cat. Many pet owners fail to extend their compassion beyond their own particular pet.

An example of this attitude occurred while I was at the front desk one day. A woman who had just paid a boarding bill of more than $200 for a plain old nondescript cat was waiting for her pet to be brought to her. As the attendant placed the undistinguished feline on the counter, a man standing nearby, waiting to check in his dog, took one look at the cat and blurted out, "Why would you pay two hundred and fifteen dollars to board a cat like that? You could have gotten another one for less than five dollars!"

She glared at the man as if she couldn't believe what she had heard. Her lips quivered, but she repressed whatever it was she wanted to say. Instead, she clutched her cat close to her and stormed out of the building. This same man then boarded his mangy mongrel dog in our finest and most expensive suite. The value of a pet lies in the heart of the owner.

Such an attitude was responsible for one of my most trying experiences with a dog owner. The woman suddenly realized we also boarded reptiles and, apparently, she did not consider eight and a half acres of space, with carefully constructed security areas, adequate protection for her dog. I showed her the security tanks with their locking lids and the solid door that stood between the serpentarium and the rest of the building, but nothing would assuage her concerns. Before she finally agreed to leave her dog, I had to guarantee that no attendant who touched a snake would ever feed or touch her dog. I doubt that this lady really enjoyed her vacation worrying that somewhere within our boundaries there might be a harmless snake, even though the snake would undoubtedly be more afraid of the dog than her dog would be of it.

Snakes are more common pets than most people presume and are owned for a variety of reasons. For children and many adults, it appears to be a mixture of curiosity and fascination. For one of our enterprising clients, the reason was strictly business.

I recall coming in one day and seeing a huge boa constrictor in a monkey cage, which had been moved into the Serpentarium. Obviously, it had been placed there because no aquarium tank we had was large enough to hold it comfortably. As I was watching, a buxom young lady entered the room with our attendant and began rearranging the cage. The lady's male companion proudly informed me that his wife was the famous exotic dancer who was performing nearby in a local all-nude cabaret show.

"When we get back, you gotta come over and see her do her snake dance. Just ask for me and I'll get you in free," he invited.

"Thanks a lot," I said. I smiled as a picture came into my mind of Peggy tying the snake in a knot around my neck if she ever found out I visited a place like that for any reason.

On another occasion I received a telephone call from a public relations man at the Palmer House hotel in downtown Chicago. The opera star, Patrice Munsel, was staying at the hotel and traveling, as she always did, with her pet boa constrictor.

The agent thought it would be a good publicity gimmick if we sent our specially designed twenty-eight-foot Travco pet limousine to the Palmer House and Ms. Munsel permitted the press to photograph her sending her pet boa to the pet motel.

We are usually happy to participate in these events because the publicity is as good for us as for the celebrity. However, the arrangement was cancelled at the last minute because Ms. Munsel objected to parting with the snake for even a short time. She cared much more for her pet boa than she did for any publicity the story might generate.

Although we had boarded hundreds of snakes, it was always a problem for me to reconcile one aspect of it. With few exceptions, most snakes will not eat anything that is not alive. In my own mind, I found the thought of feeding one live animal to another repugnant and a contradiction to my beliefs. I do not abide the unnecessary taking of any human or animal life. I have been involved in three wars and I will not begin to defend my actions in war. I know about the laws of nature and the different requirements of balance that exist. I can abide with it in nature where it occurs without my knowledge or participation. But, in my own animal shelter I consider the needless taking of any kind of animal life as impugning of my beliefs. While many may not agree, I am sure that those who have raised common field mice, turtles, and lizards as pets would concur.

I suppose we all share some ambivalent attitudes toward different forms of life, and I am no exception. Although I loathe poisonous snakes and many types of insects, Peggy would be the first to confirm that I harbor strange respect for some lesser life forms. I will not harm a cricket or beetle that has found its way into our home. To her everlasting consternation, I absolutely forbid harming or even disturbing some little spiders (and some pretty big ones as well) that have decided to share our home. When we lived in the south, disagreements over spiders became an increasingly familiar occurrence. If you have never lived in Florida, you can't even imagine what I mean.

The longer I was in the business, the more I began to worry that my attitude might be reaching the borderline of senile benevolence. Fortunately, the more people I met, the more I realized that, although we are a minority, we are many.

My confidence received a major boost when I met the new general manager of the Kasco Dog Food Company. It was a warm spring morning, just after a long period of rain and the walk-way to the pet motel was littered with floundering earthworms.

As I stepped from my car, this man introduced himself and I invited him in to discuss his line of foods. I began walking toward the front doors, being very careful not to step on any of the worms littering the path. As I reached the lobby door, I suddenly realized that I was alone. I turned around and, to my surprise, I saw this well-dressed stranger stooping and picking up earthworms and depositing them in the safety of the nearby grass. It was an act of consideration that pleased me immensely, and I promptly joined him until the very last worm disappeared into the safety of the tall grass.

At the time, I thought we were probably the only two people in the world crazy enough to do such a thing. Since then, I have met many people who perform the same ritual acting as guardians of the lowly worm. I like to think that the good Lord reflects kindly upon such acts.

Soon after I initiated a new policy. We would no longer board any animal that had to be fed another live animal. This new policy almost eliminated our reptile trade but we continued to grow and prosper despite it.

I met another kind of pet lover also. Early one morning, a well-dressed man drove up to our entrance just as my son, Marc, was unlocking the doors. Holding a brown paper bag in one hand, he stepped out of his Mercedes 560SEC and approached Marc. The man explained that he had been driving to work when a sparrow struck his windshield and fell on the roadway. Not wanting to leave the bird lying there, he had pulled his car onto the shoulder and got out to move the bird's body off the road. However, upon picking up the bird, he found that it was still alive and so decided to bring it to us for veterinary care. When Marc explained that we were only a boarding facility, the man requested that we have one of our visiting veterinarians treat the bird and that we board it until it was well enough to return to the wild. He offered to leave an adequate deposit to guarantee covering the costs.

A few hours later, the bird was alert and walking around

its cage and by that evening it was flying as well as it ever had. We took the cage outside and watched the little bird fly off into the sunset. It was a pleasure to return the man's deposit along with a little note thanking him for his concern for our feathered friends.

On another occasion, an elderly couple brought in a squirrel that had been injured by a BB pellet. They had paid a veterinarian to treat the wound, but now they were going to visit their children on the Coast and needed a safe place where the squirrel could recuperate. The squirrel was with us for almost two months before the couple returned to claim it and by this time had completely recuperated. They gratefully paid the boarding bill of more than fifty dollars and took off for the Wisconsin border where the dense woods and lack of human habitation offered the animal the safety the old couple sought for it.

Each succeeding day, the elderly couple climbed into their old Chevrolet and drove the thirty-five miles just to check on the squirrel's well being. The first few days, the squirrel came down from the tree and accepted food from them but on the third day it just stood on a branch and looked at them until it turned and disappeared. From then on, it never came to them again, but the old lady assured us she could hear the chattering of another squirrel nearby and was convinced her squirrel had found a mate. I would like to think so.

I suspect there are more individuals secretly operating private animal shelters than we could ever imagine, and I can't think of a better way to spend one's retirement. It is a shame that hastily initiated city ordinances and anti-animal individuals sometimes impose cruel and unreasonable penalties on these well-meaning individuals.

One of the most unusual pets we ever boarded was a six-foot-long iguana. It was so long that we had to procure a bathtub in which to contain it. It wasn't only ugly; it was downright mean and disrespectful. When it wanted to show its displeasure, the iguana would lurch its body sideways and spit a bolt of black substance across the eight-foot room at its target. I was never so glad to have a guest leave as I was that one.

Not too many months after, another iguana was boarded

with us. It was the same size but had a totally different disposition. It arrived in a limousine and was led in with a harness and leash by a uniformed chauffeur.

"If you let anything happen to Peter Pan here, the lady will kill you," he warned.

This iguana loved attention and especially enjoyed having its stomach rubbed. Never did it exhibit the barbarous demeanor of our earlier guest.

Another of our regular guests was a fifty-two-year-old Greek land turtle owned by the wife of the German consul in Chicago. She had found it many years before and had adopted it as a pet. As they traveled around the world, her pet turtle went with her. Now they were being transferred to Washington, D.C., and had brought the turtle in for boarding and for later shipment to their new location. I remember watching the woman break down and cry because she was worried the turtle would be exposed to the cold weather and not survive. He did survive and made the trip just fine.

There were as many strange people as there were strange animals that came to this strange pet motel where strange people went to all kinds of extremes to care for their pets. In retrospect, I think most pet lovers would call these people extraordinary rather than strange.

One of our extraordinary patrons was a very well dressed lady in a full-length mink coat who entered the pet motel leading a goat on a rope lead. It seems that her husband, having forgotten their wedding anniversary, had slipped out of the house and driven to the nearby shopping center in her brand-new Lincoln. Unable to decide what to buy her, he went into an establishment that offered alcoholic beverages and camaraderie. Fortunately, or unfortunately, the gentleman occupying the seat next to his turned out to be the owner of a traveling petting zoo, and he offered the husband a solution to his quest. The more the husband drank, the better the option sounded, and in the end, he loaded this rare Nubian goat and two prize Peruvian roosters into the back seat of the Lincoln and returned home to their country estate.

"Can you imagine?" the lady asked with a smile. "He brought this smelly goat home on the back seat of my brand new Lincoln!"

She wasn't upset at having been given an old goat and two roosters for an anniversary gift. She was only mildly upset at having the rear seat of her Lincoln saturated with an odoriferous aroma.

The goat boarded with us for several days until the couple had a special fence erected to protect it from their dogs. The episode reminded me of the time I brought Peggy the coatimundi for an anniversary gift and she cried for two days.

When we opened the pet motel, we were confident that we had every kind of pen, crate, cage, or container to confine any type of pet. Time proved we didn't. We didn't then and we don't now. I doubt that anyone ever will have. The cunning ability of certain members of the animal kingdom is beyond mere man's comprehension.

Proof of this was a pet raccoon named Rocky.

Rocky Raccoon loved to roam freely or cuddle in one of the attendants' laps. Our attendants, however, couldn't always be there to watch him, so he was frequently contained in a special heavy-duty, five-foot square monkey cage.

When I entered the pet motel one morning, I couldn't believe my eyes. The doors to Rocky's cage and room were wide open. Most of the store shelves were wiped clean of products, and most of the food products were opened and their remains strewn about the floor. Tucked away on a shelf behind the front desk, amidst all our motel forms, was our culprit, Rocky, sound asleep.

During the night he had managed to unbolt the door hinges to his cage and escape. He must have had a royal time. He visited the aviary and other small animal rooms, scrounging for food, but never disturbing any of our other guests. Apparently, sampling the diets of other animals wasn't sufficient, so he decided to try the pet food that was stacked on shelves in our store. Rocky also consumed an entire bag of potato chips, part of a box of chocolate chip cookies, and several candy bars that the receptionists kept behind the reception desk.

I placed Rocky back in his cage none the worse for his escapade, and additional padlocks proved an adequate match for his efforts on subsequent visits.

Monkeys and apes presented similar problems. Simians seem to have a peculiar ability to perceive the slightest weakness in their confining structure. An ape will select the junction of two or more steel bars and, by determined shaking and twisting, all too frequently will be able to pry them apart. In an orderly sequence, the ape will then proceed to take each adjoining link of the cage apart until there is a hole sufficiently large for it to exit through.

It is a miracle that we have never lost one of these precocious guests, but that is probably due to an ever-increasing vigilance and continued efforts to anticipate what could conceivably happen next.

We learned another lesson from a monkey the hard way. Because they attract a lot of attention, we liked to board them in a room adjacent to the main lobby, where visitors could watch their silly antics. This particular room was decorated to give the appearance of a rain forest and included several artificial trees.

The first time we boarded a monkey, we made sure it could not reach and damage the plants and trees with their arms. What we failed to consider was that its tail had twice the span of its arms and could be just as destructive.

The following morning, we arrived to find the artificial trees on the floor in thousands of tiny plastic sections. Experience can be an exasperating teacher!

Prologue Chapter 10

PALS

Charles F. Doran

When you're feeling sad and lonely
  And your "friends" all pass you by,
When there doesn't seem a single thing
  But to crawl away and die,

When the world is black and hollow,
  When you're buried in your woes –
Then, there comes a bark of welcome
  And a touch of a wet, cold nose.

While two hairy paws are clawing
  To scramble on your knees,
And a bushy tail is wagging,
  Two brown eyes say, "Master, please,

Let me crawl upon your bosom,
  Let me take my rightful place,"
And trying hard to lick the tear
  That's streaming down your face.

Could you find a better fellow
  If you searched the whole world through,
Who would stand by you in trouble
  And would always be true-blue?

In his mind there is no question
        If or not the Master's right –
He's your pal if you're a pauper
        Or if you're a man of might.

Feed him then and give him shelter.
        Water when the sun is hot;
Do not be a self-made heathen.
        What would you do, if God forgot?

You're his God, friend, please be mindful,
        Do not let your memory clog.
Folk will know how large your soul is,
        By the way you treat a dog!

10

EMPLOYEES ARE SPECIAL PEOPLE

By our second year, 1974, we had twenty-six employees, an average of one person for every sixteen pets. Not only were we making money, but also our boarding rates remained competitive with other kennels in our area and, in fact, were lower than the rates many kennels were charging to keep a pet in a cage.

Mass boarding was not only profitable, but it permitted a higher level of care than was possible in most smaller kennels.

Selective hiring had a great deal to do with our early success. I was never doubtful about our potential for success, but I was equally convinced that it could only be achieved if the staff recognized a specific order of responsibility. This led to the formulation of a set of priorities that we stressed to both management and employees. These priorities became our "Hierarchy of Obligations," and I expected every employee to know them and to abide by them.

Our first obligation was to the welfare of the pet. No matter what occurred, we expected an employee to attend to a pet's needs first. No attendant was to go to lunch or go home if one of his or her animals still required attention. If an animal wasn't eating well, we expected the employee to find something the pet would eat, even if it meant coming to me for something special. If it was necessary to stay after hours, we expected the employee to do so; we would pay for the time. The welfare of the pet was of paramount importance and the primary obligation of us all.

Our second obligation was to the pet owner. Many people cannot enjoy their vacations if they are worried about their pets. We expected our employees to be sympathetic and understanding so that every pet owner left the premises confident that we would provide his or her pet the best possible care.

The third obligation was a shared one. The employee's obligation to the company and the company's obligation to the employee were equal! Neither could be greater than the other's. For our part, we tried as hard as our limited resources permitted. A huge turkey for Christmas, an annual company dinner at one of the finest restaurants, paid vacations, medical insurance, and a tuition-refund program to encourage continued education were all provided in addition to the benefits other small companies offered. All we asked our employees in return was that they take loving care of our clients.

Except for those whose sole duty was exercising dogs, employees had to be mature and older than sixteen. In addition, each one was required to take a battery of tests from which a psychological profile was drawn. We were concerned about employing someone who might abuse or otherwise injure an animal.

Later on, after a particularly tragic event, we instituted drug testing before hiring and random testing during employment. To show our commitment, we required managers and officers of the corporation to comply with the testing requirements.

We strictly enforced one rule: If a customer was told we would do something for his or her pet, it had to be done! Regrettably, our first manager was our first casualty.

Charles was brought to American Pet Motels from Hollywood, where he had operated a show kennel for a movie star. If vanity had an image, it was Charles. All day long he would strut about the premises lamenting the fact that cruel, unknown forces had deprived him of his just role as a major Hollywood movie star. On the slightest pretext, he would produce an album (which he usually carried with him) and begin showing customers old newspaper clippings and pictures of him standing beside famous actors and actresses, most of whom had long since retired from the scene.

Within a short time, it became obvious Charles was spending a disproportionate amount of his time on his past rather than on our future, and he was not inclined to change after several warnings.

One evening, I returned to the motel after the dogs had been locked in for the night, and I decided to inspect the kennels. As I suspected, there was evidence that a few of the dogs had been locked into rooms that had waste in them. In addition, I couldn't find any trace of cookies in any of the rooms. I knew that most of the dogs devoured the Milk Bones we passed out each night, but there were always several who did not eat them.

I went to the director's quarters and asked Charles about the cookies.

"You mean you really expected me to give them cookies each night?" he replied.

I just stared at the man. I was actually speechless.

"Oh, I know you kept asking me about them and talking about the dogs' 'cookie-breaks,' but I thought that was just for the customers to hear. I didn't think you really meant it. The people don't have any way of knowing."

The next day I gave him a ticket to Los Angeles and drove him to the airport.

We had spent $200 to have him interviewed by one of Chicago's best employment psychologists before hiring him and had paid all his moving expenses from California. We had trained him and tutored him. Still, it was a lost cause. He was too used to the old deceptions of the kennel industry, and he compounded the problem by having a little too much Hollywood in him.

Sometimes, when you do hire the wrong person, thanks to the malignant benevolence of modern labor laws, it takes a tragedy to resolve the situation. We've had our share of these.

One case involved a sweet young woman whom we soon

began to suspect was using drugs. Several signs were apparent, but there never was any hard evidence we could confront her with to justify discharging her. Unfortunately, some of the other employees knew she was getting high and had actually seen her go out in back of the kennels to smoke. Due to a warped sense of peer loyalty, they didn't want to turn her in.

One day, just at quitting time, this girl stopped on her way out of the building to report that one of her dogs, a small poodle, was missing. We knew it had been there when we opened the kennels because the Director of Animal Welfare had seen it in its room that morning. The girl could not remember if the dog had eaten its food that day or anything else about it. She had not even marked the dog's health card for any of the items she was responsible for checking.

A thorough search of the kennels and grounds failed to turn up the little dog. Escape was virtually impossible. The gates to its dog run were closed. There was an escape barrier over the top of the run. The entire kennel was enclosed in an additional six-foot-high chain link-fence, and beyond that was another seven-foot-high chain-link fence with an additional one-foot section containing three rows of barbed wire. With the dozens of employees and customers walking in the area all day long, it was just not possible for the dog to be running around loose without being seen.

The dog was never found. The girl was discharged but never revealed what occurred. Even the dog's owners interviewed the girl at her home, but she was as vague then as the day we discharged her.

This was when we instituted our no-drug policy. In addition to the hospital drug testing we also began unscheduled drug searches by the National K-9 Security Company. All employees were aware that a handler with a trained drug-detecting dog would check all rooms and lockers on our premises. Anyone found with an illegal drug would be discharged immediately.

Another of our well-meaning policies actually got us into

a lot of trouble. Because cats are the main carriers of toxoplasmosis, a disease that is readily transmitted to the fetuses of pregnant women and then often causes terrible birth defects, our policy requires any female employee who handles cats to take a leave of absence if she becomes pregnant.

When we hire female employees, we explain the policy and the reason for it to them and make sure they understand this condition of employment.

As luck would have it, one of our best receptionists announced that she was pregnant. Receptionists frequently have to handle incoming and outgoing cats. However, when we reminded her of our policy she countered that Illinois law forbade the discharge of a female employee because of pregnancy. She advised us that although her pediatrician had advised her to quit, she intended to work for as long as she was able.

I called the Illinois Department of Labor and they confirmed that despite the health risk involved, if we discharged the woman we would have to continue to pay her full salary until she was able to return to work. They had no provision for the consequences of toxoplasmosis or a deformed baby.

The idea of drafting a release and having her sign it occurred to me but both my own attorneys and the state's advised me that any agreement the mother signed would be useless because the state would bring an action on behalf of the baby.

It was a Catch-22. If we discharged her, we would have to replace her and still pay her a full salary while she sat at home. If we permitted her to continue working and she contracted toxoplasmosis, we would be sued for millions of dollars if the baby was born with any birth defects.

A few weeks had passed when the employee advised me that her pediatrician had insisted that she quit so this was to be her last day. I was relieved. My relief was short-lived. Sometime later, this same employee visited the pet motel to advise us that she had tested positive for toxoplasmosis and wanted us to know about it. Fortunately, the baby was born in perfect health.

Overall, employees who have not measured up have been

exceptions. In the vast majority of cases over the years, I have had a great deal of admiration and respect for the men and women who work for us. Most people who like to work with animals are special. There are always those to whom it is just another job, but there are many more to whom it is a dedicated obligation. These are the ones who take their lunch into the room of some new dog who is not adjusting well and sit there sharing their sandwich with the animal.

I never cease to be amazed that after only a few days on the job, these employees can identify any one of the dogs in their kennel by sight or by their room number. They can tell you how much the pet ate the previous day and even the condition of its stool. These are the people who make a pet-care facility outstanding.

On a number of occasions, I have walked into a kennel and found balloons hanging from an animal's mailbox, a cupcake complete with a candle, and maybe even a chew bone or other treat, all provided by one of the employees who wanted to give "her" animal a birthday party. It's a pure joy to have this type of worker.

Although we have had some excellent male employees, the majority of our animal attendants have been women. I often jest that we employ not only the best workers of any kennel, but also the best-looking ones. I would like to believe that our supervisors do not let looks influence their decisions, but for some reason, we have had some terrifically endowed employees whose figures were only slightly enhanced by our red, white and blue hot pants uniforms.

One of these was our grooming manager. Karen was about five feet tall with blond hair and a well-proportioned body. The lobby's glass wall permitted people to sit on a bench and look on while Karen and the other groomers bathed and groomed their dogs.

One of her regular customers was a local resident who was probably in his seventies or eighties. At first, every eight weeks, and then every six weeks, the man would walk his old, shaggy dog over to the pet motel to be groomed by Karen.

He would always make the appointment for ten o'clock and then come in one or two hours early. He was fully content just to sit in the lobby and watch Karen work for hours at a time, perhaps reflecting on other times, on days long past. Sometimes he would come in without his dog and explain that he was out getting his exercise and stopped by to rest. He would rest while watching Karen work.

We also watched and couldn't help but smile as the old man quickly adjusted his trifocals when Karen had to reach for something and the hem on her hot pants rode up, exposing a portion of her thigh.

I remember on one occasion when his wife accompanied him, she remarked that she couldn't understand why he insisted on having their dog groomed so frequently. I just had to smile.

Except for dog groomers, we preferred to hire inexperienced personnel and train them ourselves. There are too many bad practices in the industry that become ingrained, and many experienced kennel workers fail to share our concerns for the little things that we consider important.

As time passed, I learned that an employer can have years of experience and all kinds of college degrees, but still can learn from his employees.

I remember vividly the day an employee came to me and told me that Mary Ann, one of our attendants, was in the lunchroom crying uncontrollably. I immediately went in and asked if there was anything I could do for her. She shook her head no and continued to cry.

I learned that one of our clients had boarded her elderly dog with us and then had made arrangements with a veterinarian to have it euthanized. Instead of taking the dog to his clinic, the veterinarian put the dog to sleep in its room at the pet motel. The dog was in Mary Ann's kennel, and she had insisted on sitting next to it and holding its head while the veterinarian put it to sleep.

I was outraged that this veterinarian had carried out the procedure on our premises, and without thinking, I directed my anger toward Mary Ann.

"Why in the hell did you stay in the room if it affects you that way?" I demanded.

Without removing the crumpled handkerchief from her eyes, she began to explain. "Mr. Leeds, a few years ago I had an elderly aunt who was very ill. She had actually raised me and loved me more than anyone else in the world. The only thing she looked forward to each day was my visit with her when I got home from school. She had this terrible fear that I wouldn't visit her and that she would die without having anyone who loved her near her.

"One weekend I planned to attend a dog show in a nearby town and my aunt begged me not to go. She was so scared that she would die while I was gone. I was young and I wanted so much to go to that dog show. I kept assuring my aunt that nothing was going to happen, and when the weekend came, I went to the dog show with my girl friends.

"When I returned Sunday evening, I learned that my aunt had died. She died alone, calling my name."

The tears began to well up again in her already reddened eyes. "It wasn't right, Mr. Leeds. Nothing is so important as a living thing. No one should have to die alone, not even a dog."

Before this incident, whenever we were instructed to take someone's pet to a clinic to be euthanized, I always delegated it to one of the attendants. It was something I had difficulty dealing with. It affected me and I couldn't hide my emotions.

I changed after my talk with Mary Ann. From then on, regardless of the demands on my time, if the occasion arose, I insisted on taking the pet to its veterinarian. I would always remain with the pet, and, so that the animal knew it was not alone or friendless, I would hold its paw and stroke its head affectionately. I was no longer embarrassed to be seen talking to the animal or of the tears that coursed down my face.

Over the years, I never learned not to cry. I don't think I ever will. I am only grateful that this service was required so seldom.

I believe Mary Ann is the kind of person a good pet care facility has to have. I don't think a company can ever be more that what its employees make it. You can advertise gimmicks and spend money on public relations efforts, but your product and your success ultimately depend on your employees.

Prologue Chapter 11

BUM

Author Unknown

He's a little dog, with a stubby tail
And a moth-eaten coat of tan,
And his legs are short of the wobbly sort;
I doubt if they ever ran.

And he howls at night, while in broad daylight
He sleeps like a blooming log;
And he likes the feed of the gutter breed.
He's a most irregular dog.

I call him Bum, and in total sum
He's all that his name implies,
For he's just a tramp with a highway stamp
That culture cannot disguise.

And his friends, I've found, in the streets abound,
Be they urchins or dogs or men;
Yet he sticks to me with a fiendish glee,
It is truly beyond my ken.

I talk to him when I'm lonesome like,
And I'm sure that he understands
When he looks at me so attentively
And gently licks my hand.

Then he rubs his nose on my tailored clothes,
But I never say aught thereat
For the Good Lord knows I can buy more clothes,
But never a friend like that!

So my good old pal, my irregular dog,
My flea-bitten stub-tailed friend,
Has become a part of my very heart
To be cherished till lifetimes end.

And on Judgement day, if I take the way
That leads where the righteous meet,
If my dog is barred by the Heavenly guard
—We'll both of us brave the heat!

11

ROOM SERVICE, PLEASE

It takes a lot of customers to make even a small business a success. Ours came in every color, shape, size, and species, and while their own stories are of interest, the antics of their owners challenge description.

I have always maintained that anyone who owns a pet acts a little deranged at times. But, anyone who stays in the pet-boarding business has to have crossed the line. Happily, it's a degree of insanity we readily embrace and freely choose, and it is salubrious in its effect.

Perhaps our biggest problem in the beginning was the public's failure to perceive the pet motel business as a real business. Some people could not conceive of a pet-boarding establishment having regular hours or not being open twenty-four hours a day.

People frequently came at all hours of the day or night to collect their pets. On one occasion, an irate pet owner called the state police, and I had to explain in front of the officers why our offices were closed at 11:00 on a Sunday evening. It's a problem every kennel experiences.

Another time the president of one of Chicago's largest banks woke up our manager at 1:30 in the morning to retrieve his dog. He and his wife had just flown back from a two-week vacation, and she couldn't bear to be without her dog for a few more hours. It amazes me how people can manage to separate themselves from their pets so they can go off on a vacation, yet they can't live another moment without the pet when they return home.

Afterward, I wished I had thought to ask this executive if he would come down and open his bank for me at 1:30 a.m. if my wife got lonely for our money some morning.

When the kennel is closed and the lights turned down, the animals finally relax, stop their barking, and settle down for the night. The moment you re-enter the kennel to put a dog in or to take one out, you wake every dog in the place. It's a trip from perfect silence to total bedlam. Dogs are yelping, jumping up and down, urinating, defecating, tipping over their water dishes and expecting to be let out. By the time you've gotten someone's dog for him, the entire kennel is a total stinking disaster. It's another needless hour of labor for which you are not compensated. Running a kennel is a twenty-four hour job, and those who shoulder the responsibility cherish their few moments of freedom.

Many kennel owners are resolving this problem by charging twenty-five dollars to pick up a pet when the facility is closed. For some mysterious reason, most pet owners suddenly find they can endure the separation for a few more hours when the alternative involves a charge. Still, there were many who said they would gladly pay the twenty-five dollars. Thinking it might be a fair way to reconcile the dilemma, we decided to try it.

As luck would have it, my first client was a judge who wanted to pick her dog up on a Sunday. She explained to me that she had no alternative but to pay the assessment since she lived forty miles away and she had to be in court all day Monday. I was about to ring up the money when it occurred to me that this woman had driven forty miles just to board her dog with us. That is what I considered a complement and deserved consideration. I rang up the boarding charges and then handed her back her twenty-five dollars. However, the moratorium was short-lived. The demand for Sunday pickups was substantial and it involved a customer satisfaction consideration. There was always a manager or assistant manager plus a full staff of animal attendants on duty every Sunday. It was decided that we would open from 3 p.m. to 6 p.m. every Sunday without any additional charge.

It may not sound like a major problem, but except for the manager, weekend employees are usually part-time employees and are unfamiliar with all procedures.

Checking a pet in or out required someone trained to bring up our computer system and to make the correct entries. Medication and dietary requirements had to be properly documented. The pet's physical condition had to be checked for specific details and vaccination records carefully verified. A cash drawer had to be made available and balanced at the end of the day. The correct room had to be assigned and a host of other details taken care of. Trained people had to be available and that often meant overtime or the presence of the manager.

The desire of pet owners to be reunited with their pets as soon as possible tells us something of the romance between Americans and their pets. Whether it's a reflection of the family of today or not, I don't know, but many couples will rush from the airport to pick up the family pet but will leave the children at Grandma's for one more night.

The relationship between some people and their pets taxes the imagination. My psychic colleague, Beatrice Lydecker, isn't the only one who holds conversations with animals. In my experience, I found that most pet owners talk to their pets, although in a recent study, only 80 percent admitted to it. Certainly, almost all of our customers talked to their pets, and a few held extended conversations. They even asked their pets' opinions on certain matters, and, what is even stranger; they took their pets' advice.

We always encouraged people to come in and tour the facilities prior to boarding their pets, but we tried to discourage them from bringing their pets with them. Sometimes that was impossible. Every once in a while, a dog owner would insist on touring the kennels with his or her dog, and if there was no other way, we would permit it.

After the tour, most pet owners would make their reservation, but I was taking care of a lady one time who told me her dog said she wouldn't be happy there.

It was a real blow to my ego. I thought we had the world's finest pet care facility and this pampered poodle told its owner that we were not good enough for her. I have always had a nagging suspicion that this poodle went home and bad-mouthed us to other dogs in its neighborhood.

As we were becoming established, we had a disproportionate share of first-time boarders. For years, their owners had brought Grandma in from the coast to baby-sit the dog or else they packed Bowser into a crate and took him along. Now, although apprehensive, they came to the pet motel.

Pets were brought in accompanied by an unbelievable array of luggage. Three or four pages of typed instructions told exactly how owners expected their pets to be cared for: special medications, special diets, special treats, special grooming, exercising, teeth brushing after every meal, and on and on the lists went. Visitors stood in the lobby and were awed by what they saw and heard. There was the German shepherd who was checked in with a six-pack of beer. He was to get a half a glass every night at bedtime. And the cat with two six-packs of chocolate milk, one can for each day of its stay. The television show, "Real People," was filming in our lobby that day, and the crew interrupted their taping to include the "chocolate milk cat" in the program.

Then there was the lady who instructed me to have her dog's behind wiped with toilet paper after each elimination. The first few times requests like these made you wonder about pet owners. After a while you didn't even blink. It's a mad, mad, mad, wonderful world.

One of our frequent guests was a huge St. Bernard whose owner, a doctor, was greatly concerned for her health. Brandy began each day in our Regency Suite at 8:00 with a breakfast fit for a queen. She got three strips of lean bacon, fried crisp, and three scrambled eggs. "Don't mix the bacon with the eggs," we were told, or Brandy won't eat them. At 9:00 Brandy got a pound of roast beef (medium), and at 10:00, she got our regular serving of beef-protein dog food.

Now, I doubted that Brandy would decline to eat just because her bacon was mixed with her eggs, but our Director of Animal Welfare assured me that a new employee had indeed mixed the bacon with the eggs and Brandy, indeed, refused to eat. We had to prepare an entirely new breakfast and the bacon was kept separate from the eggs.

Brandy's visits were always rather a hardship for me. I seldom eat breakfast, and when the aroma of bacon and eggs came wafting through the building, my stomach begged to be appeased. Apparently, I was not the only one; on more than one occasion I caught the attendant munching on a piece of bacon while preparing Brandy's breakfast. The attendant assured me that Brandy's owner encouraged her to have breakfast with Brandy.

On one occasion, the doctor brought in a little three-legged stool for Brandy to eat her meals from because she had a sore neck. I don't know how the doctor could tell Brandy had a sore neck, but if he was correct about the bacon and eggs, I wasn't going to doubt him on the sore neck.

One of my favorite clients was an elderly lady who visited relatives in Germany every other year. When she brought her dachshund in for boarding, she always brought an ample supply of beer sausages as well. They were the spicy, garlic-laden salami sticks that are available in most taverns. "At home, Schnappsy always gets a piece of beer salami before going to bed." So, at the pet motel, Schnappsy always got a piece of beer salami before going to bed! (I can assure you that it really tasted good.)

One dog got an ice cream soda each night and another got a Hostess Ding Dong on Sundays. A dish of ice cream on Sunday was a common request and led us to eventually install a soft ice cream machine where we manufactured our own yogurt.

I am not belittling or making fun of these pet owners or their pets. I firmly believe there is a sound logic behind it. We develop certain routines with our pets that are mutually rewarding. Pets love the extra attention we give them, and in return, we receive the satisfaction of watching our pets enjoying themselves. I know that I would never dream of arriving home without a couple of dog cookies for my dogs. Like the majority of pet owners, I know my pets expect it.

One of the apprehensions a pet owner experiences when he boards his pet is the fear that the animal will feel it was being abandoned or loved less. By including the little amenities of special treats, a familiar toy, and sometimes a familiar piece of clothing, the owner believes the pet will remember him and not feel deserted. I don't know that it works this way, but I do know that the animals look forward to treat time and seem to enjoy it to the fullest measure.

I remember one occasion when I suggested to a young lady that she bring in a worn piece of clothing on her dog's next boarding, she went out to her car and returned with a rolled up piece of cloth. As I placed the cloth on the dog's bed, I realized that it was her brassiere. She went home a little lighter than when she came in.

Many pet owners needlessly suffer deep feelings of guilt over leaving their pets. I have witnessed many emotion-packed partings, and I have seen grown men, as well as women, break down and cry as they left their pets. One occasion will always stand out in my mind. It was the most poignant parting I ever saw. It was the time a young priest was boarding his newly acquired dog. He had adopted the Doberman pinscher puppy from the dog pound only a few weeks before.

I doubt he could really afford it, but he splurged and selected an Imperial Suite for the puppy, complete with a brass bed, mattress, and Snoopy sheets.

After closing the gate to the dog's room, the priest and the dog stood facing each other from opposite sides of the gate.

The priest asked over and over again if the dog might forget him since they had been together such a short time. Each time I assured him that he needn't worry, that dog's have a very long memory. Finally, the priest turned to me and said, "He really should have something of mine so he won't forget me."

He paused for a few minutes, and then reaching down, he removed his pair of highly polished shoes, set them at the edge of the dog's bed, and walked to his car in his stocking feet.

When I made the last bed check that night, I found the puppy sound asleep with his head nestled between the two shoes.

Actually, I think most pet owners would be terribly disappointed if they knew how short a time their pets missed them. It is true a dog or cat may spend one or two days adjusting to its new environment. But by the second or third day, if the boarding facility is any good, the pet will be completely fascinated with all the different smells and sounds. It's the attendant bringing the bowl of food, the terrier in the next room, or the cute poodle across the way that totally absorbs their attention.

However, there are exceptions, and that is why the selection of a good boarding facility is so important.

Our employees knew that their first obligation was to return a healthy pet to its owner. If they saw a dog curled up in a corner of its run, shaking like a leaf, they were expected to go into the dog's room, sit down, and begin socializing with the animal. It is surprising what a comforting hand and a reassuring voice can do.

We have dogs that repeated this behavior every time they came in. Each time we would go through the same process of socialization to get the pet adjusted to kennel routine. The results over the years proved it worked.

Take Duchess Denton, for example, a timid and nervous little Chihuahua. Duchess was a tiny little thing and I always teased the owner by asking what she had there; "A mouse on steroids?" It might have relaxed Mrs. Dunton a little but it didn't affect Duchess one little bit. She just nestled her tiny, quivering, one-and-a-half-pound frame into the corner of her run, totally intimidated by the barking of the other dogs. After one of us spent a little time with her, she was suddenly ready to take on the world. She was the first one to yell for breakfast and the last one to stop barking at a newly arrived guest. I guess she figured if others could do it to her, she could do it to them. It was funny to be walking a large dog to its run and see Duchess charge her gate and bark furiously at the strange dog. In response, there was no response. The large dog would just stand there and stare at Duchess as if it couldn't figure out what Dutchess was.

The first couple of times Duchess boarded with us, we had to hand-feed her boneless chicken to get her to start eating. After several visits she ate anything and everything set in front of her.

Another way of acclimating our dogs was by piping soft "elevator" music into their rooms and play areas twenty-four hours a day. Of course, the volume was reduced at night. About nine o'clock each night, we made the rounds and passed out Mother Hubbard Dog Cookies to all our canine guests. The size of the dog determined how many cookies a dog received.

The dogs really looked forward to their "cookie-breaks." At the appointed time, they lined up at their gates, almost as if they were soldiers on parade. Some of them would roll over or stand on their hind legs and beg, tricks they probably enjoyed performing at home for their owners. Even the most reluctant guest soon joined the parade and was on its way to a comfortable and trouble-free stay.

Special diets and medications were an important part of our responsibilities. All the details were spelled out on special forms so the attendant knew exactly what had to be done and when. Next to each date was a place where the person administering the medication or diet had to sign. In addition, the Director of Animal Welfare had a number of ways to check if things were done properly. If we told a pet owner we would do something, we did it!

There have been only two exceptions over a twenty-five year period that I am aware of. The first occurred when an elderly lady brought in her pregnant miniature schnauzer for boarding. The dog was up in years and probably should not have been bred. Out of her shopping bag the lady produced dozens of plastic containers in which she had frozen a special meal for each day of the dog's boarding.

"She's an old dog, so she needs a lot of vitamins," she explained. "I fixed all these health vegetables which will be good for her, so you won't have to feed her your regular dog food."

The first day we sat the concoction of something that looked like Brussels sprouts, spinach, and some other vegetables down in front of the poor dog, I swear it took on a look of total disbelief. Several times it looked down at the food and then up at us and then just stood there, probably in shock.

By the end of the day, the food remained untouched, and I decided an expectant mother deserved something better than greens for dinner. I went into the food preparation area and found the special dog food formulated for expecting bitches. I put a measured amount into a bowl and added a small amount of canned dog food just to enhance the taste. I placed this bowl in the room next to her dish of vegetables but the dog ignored both dishes. In the morning, the dog food was completely gone, but the dish of vegetables remained untouched. We went through the same sequence on the following day, but after that we served our own diet and the dog ate every bit of it.

When the owner returned, she was delighted to find her dog in such good condition. I explained the dog's reluctance to her food, but only mentioned that we had added some of our special food to get the dog to eat. I was a little reluctant to tell her that her dog would rather starve than eat her vegetable diet.

The other exception took place when a lady boarded a beautiful teacup Yorkshire terrier. The dog weighed only about one pound and would have fit inside your coat pocket. After registering, the owner set a loaf of white bread on the counter and ordered that the dog only be fed one slice of bread daily. All attempts to reason with her were futile. The dog was not ill, nor was there any other reason to feed it only bread. We contacted the lady's veterinarian and he could not offer a reason for such an irresponsible diet.

When the dog was placed in its room, I went back and made sure that its diet was supplemented with wholesome dog food.

Raising a dog solely on white bread is condemning the dog to a short lifetime of physical problems caused by a lack of proper nutrition.

I have often wondered if it wouldn't be more beneficial to license the pet owner instead of the pet.

American Pet Motels, Prairie View, Illinois

Partners in the grand opening of a grand adventure in pet care.
(From left, Robert X. Leeds, Joana Kroc, Ray Kroc, Peggy Leeds)

Socrates enjoying one of his
rough-housing sessions with Peggy.

"Take me to your Larder"

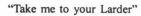

Marc taking Socrates out
for a romp in the woods.

Every pet was unique and went through a special check-in process. Because it was so small always wished we could build a much larger lobby to ease the congestion. On holidays, custo actually had to wait outside in order to be served.

The new $1 Million Dollar Lobby included six computerized reception areas, video wall, retail shop, and a 5 foot high interactive dog and cat, Cecil & Boo.

Two 5 foot tall animated animals (*Cecil* and *Boo*) stop visitors and asked
them questions. Customers can communicate their answers by pushing a
yes or *no* button and the animals reply with a humorous answer.
(From left to right: Robert X. Leeds, Boo, Cecil, Marc B. Leeds)

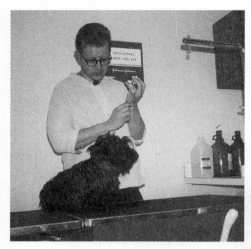

Veterinary care was always available for guests requiring it.

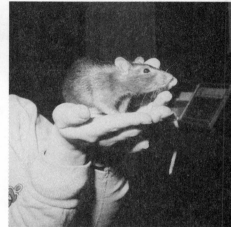

"Rocky the rat" was found as a little mouse and raised as a family pet.

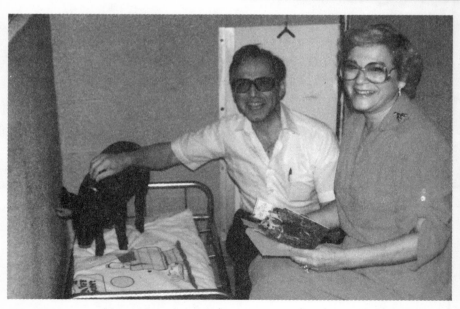

What can you give people who have everything? Chrisy was a Christmas gift from our employees. We found her in a dog run with a huge red ribbon wrapped around her neck.

Peggy and Gail feeding a few of our neighbors.

Our manager, Kim, showing her Australian Shepherd how to herd some of our guest sheep.

Any kind of cat was welcome . . .

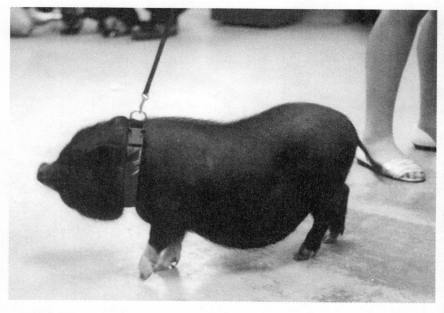

Our frequent guest, Boaris, should have spent more time in our exercise spa.

Guests arrive and depart in style afforded by a 60 inch stretch Cadillac Limousine.

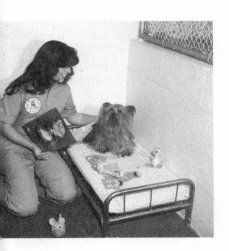

A pampered guest is read
a greeting card from its owner.

Our daughter Gail and her
incorrigible horse, Image.

Some employees enjoy getting wrapped up in their work.

An Iguana on its way to its room.

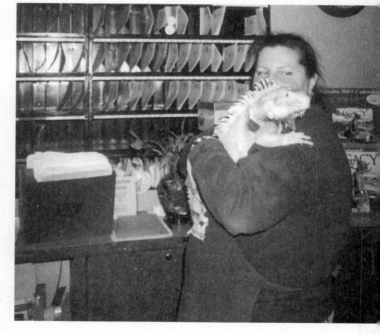

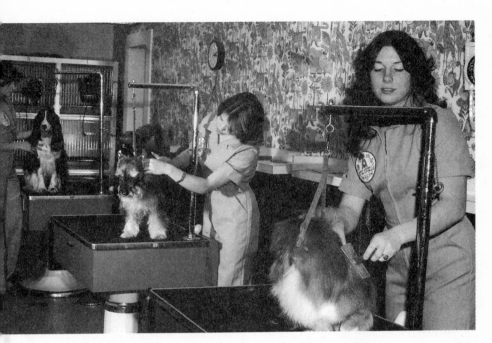

The original Grooming Parlor accommodated three groomers.

Our new Grooming Parlor (O'Hair Port), with hydraulic tables and a built-in vacuum system at each station, could accommodate twelve groomers. Four animal bathers worked in an adjacent bathing area.

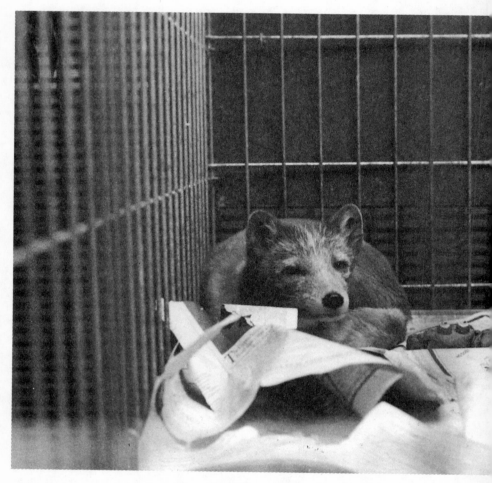

Rescued from the window of a Furrier's store, Reinecki,
an Artic fox, enjoyed numerous stays at the Pet Motel.

This Peruvian wooly monkey was among the largest simians we ever boarded.

In the jungle the Gibbon monkey can leap 50 feet and travel up to 35 miles per hour. Fortuately, this one was quite content to stick around.

A client introducing her Olingo to our Yorkshire Terrier, Casanova.

Our beautiful Aviary became a temporary home for almost every kind of bird imaginable.

Time for a catnap.

Nikki, a ten-year old malamute, was abandoned at the Pet Motel. He was adopted by the employees and lived the balance of his life at the Motel. Although he was free to roam, he would never approach an open gate or leave the premises.

"I enjoyed the cookies and ice cream,
but couldn't I stay up and watch the Lassie movie one more time?"

Prologue Chapter 12

TURN-ABOUT

W. Williams

Maybe I am quixotic,
Or, shall we say? Neurotic?
Well, here's a conundrum:
Why have men gift of tongue
When noble dogs are dumb?
Aye, that's the conundrum!
And if I could dispose it,
' Tis thus I would transpose it;
Our dogs should have the gift of tongue,
And every silly man be dumb!

12

McDOLLAR'S, THEY'LL HAVE IT THEIR WAY. . . OR ELSE

Despite the added cost of special care and the high cost of maintenance, we ended our first year with only a $12,000 loss. We made a profit our second year, and the most conservative projections told us that we would never lose money again.

We had actually done better than I had anticipated. We had started with a brand-new, untested concept, without any previous experience and without even one prior customer, and had boarding revenues of almost $300,000 the first year.

Our biggest problem and expense was our heating system. Conditioned air was pouring out through the openings in the ceiling ductwork and not reaching the floor. An investigation revealed two major ducts that had not even been connected to anything and were releasing all of their air into the ceiling area. During the coldest weather we could not maintain a comfortable temperature in any of the buildings. An analysis by an outside engineering firm revealed that our ventilating system was inadequate. In order to remedy the problem we would have to double our heating and cooling capacity. The expense was staggering.

Then our exhaust fans began burning out prematurely, and we found that they were non-standard units that had been manufactured prior to World War II. No existing replacements were available to fit the openings in our metal roofs. More thousands of dollars were spent to have these archaic fans rebuilt.

Use of the wrong primer resulted in the special epoxy paint peeling off the walls in huge sheets. All the paint had to be removed by sandblasting and then replaced.

When we found ourselves without water one morning, we called in a contractor who had to dig down through a kennel floor to find the cause. Instead of a broken pipe, he found no pipe at all, just traces of rust. Apparently, a black iron gas pipe had been used for the underground water line and, not being galvanized, it had just rusted completely away. The whole length of the kennel floor had to be opened up to run a new line so we had fresh water in the kennels.

Next, our high-pressure sanitizing system began malfunctioning. It had cost almost $43,000 to install and was supposed to utilize a special high-pressure pipe. Although the plumbers had used high-pressure pipe, they had used standard elbows and other fittings. When the heating systems couldn't provide enough heat, these water lines would freeze and the elbows and other fittings would explode like grenades and send pieces of shrapnel in all directions with the noise of a mortar shell. In order to correct the condition, the entire system had to be disassembled and then reassembled with the correct fittings.

When these water lines ruptured, water shot throughout the ceiling area, soaking the ceiling tile. When we opened in the morning we would come in and find huge quantities of soaked and broken ceiling tile on the floors.

These deficiencies meant that extra personnel, equipment, and supplies always had to be kept on hand to meet the contingencies we knew would arise. Heating and air-conditioning bills ran 500 percent higher than anticipated and approached $50,000 a year.

Of a more ominous nature was the movement of our building walls during the winter months. After only a few winters, entire walls were shifting several inches, opening huge cracks through which the granular insulation poured out. Steel doorjambs were actually twisted out of shape and it became impossible to open or close exterior doors. Furnaces had to be kept running continuously to provide the minimum heat needed for the animals.

Our exterior structures did not fare any better. Sidewalks crumbled, concrete slabs sank more than nine inches, and some of the run walls collapsed into piles of rubble. Several years later, the original masonry contractor confided to me that he had obtained a total waiver of liability from the architect because he knew the foundations had not been poured to the proper depths. In some places, he admitted, they had poured only a slab and no foundation at all.

It was disheartening, but there was nothing I could do, and as long as I could pay for the repairs and show Ray Kroc a profit, I did not intend to complain. Every indication and extrapolation indicated we would become more and more successful as time went on. Unfortunately, I could not foresee what my partner had in mind.

Toward the end of our second year, the prospect of the pet motel becoming extremely profitable was suddenly shattered. Without any prior notice, I received a letter from Kroc's attorneys that included a series of predated demand notes totaling $150,000 with back interest at 9 percent. In addition, the letter advised me that I would immediately have to begin paying Kroc an extra $8,000 a month for rent.

If we had filled every room in the motel, we still could not have paid the $150,000 plus another $96,000 rent and all the back interest. To me it was a cold and deliberate breach of everything the Krocs and I had agreed to. Ray had agreed to provide the building money in exchange for 85 percent of the company's stock. I had urged them to let me bring in outside investors and to borrow the construction money from banks while the interest rate was only 5 percent. It was his attorneys who had insisted on using only Kroc's money. Now he was demanding an exorbitant rent and interest in addition to 85 percent of the profits. Ever so slowly I was watching my brilliant future slip away and I was powerless to stop it.

One thing I could do, I could refuse to sign any of the notes. His lawyers kept writing and calling me. Over and over again, they assured me that the notes were totally meaningless to our company, and were necessary only for Ray's income tax. "It's just a paper transaction to provide him more tax shelter," they kept insisting. I refused to be swayed.

Even if the notes were meaningless, the idea of initiating a rental agreement of $96,000 a year was not. Not to me. I was projecting profits but with real estate taxes on a million dollar building, exorbitant maintenance and utility costs, there was no way I could see us adding an extra $8,000. expense each month.

As I thought about it, it was difficult for me even to conceive of Kroc having initiated these demands. Our relationship had been cordial and open, and in view of his and Joan's past assurances, I very much doubted that he would do anything to jeopardize the success of the company and the future welfare of Peggy and me.

I finally told his lawyers that I would absolutely not sign the notes nor would I pay any rent. I demanded a meeting with Ray. I would trust him to set the matter straight.

It took a few months, but the meeting finally took place in Ray's office at the McDonald's Oakbrook building. Present were his two attorneys, Don Lubin and Ed Lembitz, his accountant, Al Doty, Ray and me.

Ray was as cordial and friendly as always and it appeared as if he wasn't sure what the meeting was all about. His demeanor, however, reassured me that he would acknowledge the terms of our agreement. I didn't believe the man was capable of lying.

Don Lubin began by suggesting that I tell everyone what

was bothering me. In a way, it was a smart way to begin because it shifted the whole blame for any disagreement onto me. I could have recited a litany of complaints, but bringing up the building problems would only have exacerbated feelings. Instead, I merely reminded Ray of our original agreement. He was to furnish the construction money in exchange for 85 percent of the stock and 85 percent of the profits. Not at that time, nor at any time since, had there ever been any mention of loans, rental charges, or interest. I reminded Ray that one of my conditions was that I would never go into any arrangement that called for 100 percent debt financing. "Our arrangement was for equity financing—investment capital, not borrowed capital," I insisted.

"Our written contract stated that *if* the company had to borrow any money, you would lend it to the company at 7 percent. I've got five fictitious notes from your accountant and their rate is demanding nine percent!" I said bitterly. "And to top it off, now you are asking $8,000 a month for rent."

When I paused, Ray looked almost like he was bewildered.

He looked up at his accountant. "Hey, when I buy stock in a company, they don't pay me rent for the buildings or interest on my investment."

Before he could finish, his lawyers and accountant cut him off. "You don't understand," they told him. "Money has to earn money. Money begets money. Why, you could have put your money into tax-exempt bonds and gotten a better return." On and on they went, and Ray sat in his chair without uttering another word.

During the balance of the meeting, he sat there looking down at his desktop while his lawyers and accountant tried to legitimize this act of fiscal piracy. Still he said nothing.

Without his support I felt lost. Overwhelmed. This whole charade was apparently not his doing, but he would not speak out to stop it. Finally, as if making a magnanimous gesture, Don Lubin asked me to suggest a rent figure that would be fair.

"None at all would be fair," I replied.

Lubin smiled, but he was not going to leave empty-handed.

In my mind I ran our profit and loss statements and the results of our projections. After some length of time the figure of $5,000 was thrust upon me. Ed Lembitz tried to make me believe that Kroc was making a horrendous financial concession and suggested that I should really feel lucky.

With that concession I saw the company's profitability disappear and along with it our dream of financial independence.

I didn't expect anything better from his attorneys and accountant, but I did really expect Ray to speak up and come to my defense. He knew what was happening and I was sure he knew it was wrong. Instead he just sat there with his eyes staring at the top of his desk.

When I finally got up to leave, I took one last look at Ray. He refused even to glance up. He reminded me of a marionette waiting for some unseen hand to posture him, unable and unwilling to act on his own.

Within a few days, I received a formal notice that we would henceforth pay a rental of $5,000 a month. Also included was a new set of predated notes, payable on demand for $150,000. There was one other item. A new note for another $25,000 "to cover back rent" for the months of August through December, and an additional $6,700 for interest on the back rent!

Each month I would receive a request to please sign the notes and return them and each month I put the request in a drawer with the notes and the other requests.

There were telephone calls also to convince me that the notes were for Ray's income tax purposes only. I wasn't convinced. Finally, Don Lubin spelled it out to me in terms I could understand. Either I signed the notes or Kroc would not build the other two pet motels nor would he support the present one.

Although I tried, I was never able to meet with or talk to Ray Kroc again. He was never in when I called and he never returned my calls. It was as if an invisible shroud had suddenly enveloped him. I had seen my mentor for the last time.

We needed that second pet motel desperately. A second motel would be built without all the mistakes of the first one and, based on our growing experience, would prove how profitable good pet care could be. I told myself that I had no option. I signed the notes. With the stroke of a pen, American Pet Motels went from a very promising enterprise to one burdened by debt and only marginal profitability.

Fortunately, this would only be temporary. As our services expanded and our reputation spread, our occupancy rate grew to the point where we would sometimes have more than 500 people on a waiting list for rooms.

Prologue Chapter 13

DOGS FOR DISPOSAL

Margaret Mackprang Mackay

My dog is a nuisance, an absolute pest;
With him in the house there is truly no rest.
He leaves dirty tracks on the mirror-bright floor,
And scratches the paint from the tidy front door.

He slobbers his water and spills half his food;
The rugs are all gnawed and slippers are chewed.
He sheds tufts of hair and he scatters his fleas;
He buries his bones under bushes and trees.

He keeps us awake every night with his yaps;
The neighbors all curse him for spoiling their naps.
I'll stand it no longer. I'm getting fed up.
I won't be a slave to that bothersome pup!

Er - - pardon - - excuse me, but what did you say?
You ask if I'm giving the puppy away?
You've the nerve to suggest that you'll take him with pleasure!
Well, certainly not! He's an absolute treasure!

13

SPECIAL GUESTS— SPECIAL PROBLEMS

Our plans never anticipated any significant revenues from the boarding of animals other than dogs and cats. Even though there were millions of these animals being kept as pets, I did not know if there really was a boarding market for them. That we did attract such pets in quantities sufficient to make a good profit was an added blessing both for us and for the people who needed a place to board them.

Of the many different types of animals we boarded, none added more color and beauty to the surroundings than did the birds. From tiny finches to huge crested cockatoos and macaws, we had them all. If they were impressive to look at, the price some of the owners attached to them was overwhelming.

I accepted that the affection shown to dogs and cats by their owners often bordered on the bizarre, but I was soon to learn that such concern and affection was not limited to any particular species. Bird owners were no exception.

Although small, our first aviary turned out to be a spectacular sight. One of our summer employees was a very talented artist, and for a modest commission he decorated the aviary walls with a mural of a rain forest complete with a waterfall.

While smaller birds were generally confined to cages, with

a few exceptions, larger birds were permitted to stay on their specially built perches, free of any restraints. It was not unusual to have as many as twenty-five birds boarding at one time, and when they began chirping and singing, it was easy to imagine you were witnessing a real wildlife scenario.

The design and beauty of some of the cages and perches often rivaled the birds they held. Many bird owners take exceptional pride in designing something more distinctive and more impressive than what another bird owner could buy, regardless of cost, and many bird owners insisted on bringing these in with their birds.

Vitamins, special imported seeds, and a variety of special diets and tonics are all part of the bird owners' concerns, and they were never reluctant to leave long lists of meticulous instructions for their care.

Certain birds have an uncanny ability to mimic different sounds, especially the human voice. On one occasion, this talent scared the daylights out of us. It was about eleven o'clock at night, and I was working in the conference room with the bookkeeper. The rest of the building was dark and totally silent. All of a sudden, we heard a little girl's haunting voice calling, "Mommy. Mommy." The voice rose and fell in an eerie manner.

The bookkeeper and I looked at each other. "Good Lord," I remarked, "Some child is locked in one of our rooms." We jumped up and, turning on building lights as we ran from door to door, pleaded with the child to tell us where she was. Tracing the direction from where the voice was coming, we were soon at the aviary. We stood at the glass door trying to discern an area where the child could be hiding. All of a sudden I looked at a newly boarded mynah bird and realized where the voice was coming from. We had found the culprit.

The aviary was a favorite stop for the many group tours that visited the pet motel. I took special delight in showing the young Girl Scouts and Boy Scouts around the motel. I could always count on a loud response when I warned them not to step on any tails when we walked through the alligator pond.

On one occasion, I wanted to show a group of Brownies how well one of our guest mynah birds spoke. This particular bird was an incessant talker and had an exceptionally large vocabulary. I knew the little girls would get a big kick out of him.

I slid open the glass door and greeted the bird. There was no response. He just cocked his head to one side and stared back at the group. For ten minutes, while the girls looked on, I went through all kinds of verbal antics to evoke a response. It was useless. He absolutely refused. Embarrassed, I apologized to the scoutmaster and girls and suggested we continue the tour. Just as I turned to leave, the mynah bird in the next cage, whom I had never heard talk, suddenly shrieked, "That bird doesn't talk, stupid!"

The little girls exploded with laughter, but their chaperones probably don't believe to this day that the whole thing wasn't planned.

Some owners are extremely reluctant to leave their birds with anyone, and that they selected us was a mark of considerable merit. We even had a case where a man living in Texas contacted his mother in Chicago and asked her to check out our facilities. The man had a rare South American macaw that he had trained to speak three different languages. He was considering bringing the bird to our motel while he was away on a three-month trip to Mexico. Apparently we passed inspection because he made the reservation and flew with the bird to Chicago.

Because he was leaving Chicago on a Sunday, when we were closed, he chose to leave his bird with his mother for one day rather than bring the bird in on the preceding Saturday.

On Monday, the mother telephoned and advised us that she wanted to keep the bird for another week before bringing it in. The following day she called back with tears in her voice. She had placed the bird on the floor to acquaint it with her two little dogs. She said they were getting along just great until the telephone rang and she left the room to answer it. When she returned she found that her dogs had eaten the bird.

Whenever I think of that incident, I recall the story about a man who sent his mother a rare bird worth $50,000. When he called his mother to find out if the bird had arrived, she advised him that it had and that she had made a delicious soup from it. The son was shocked and admonished his mother.

"How could you cook that bird? He was the smartest bird in the world. He could speak fifteen different languages fluently!" her son yelled.

"So?" the mother replied, "If he was so smart why didn't he say something before it was too late?"

Pickles was a Red Lord Amazon parrot that was raised in a household where the owner enjoyed watching daytime television. The bird really shared her fascination with soap operas. When the owner boarded the parrot the first time, we were told that Pickles would be lost without his game shows, especially "Jeopardy." Although there were several other birds boarding during the same period, Pickles just sat forlornly on his perch. On the third day, one of our groomers brought in her portable television set and installed it in the aviary so Pickles could watch TV. The change in Pickles was dramatic. He knew the names of different soap opera characters and you could hear him join in a dialogue from twenty feet away. But his interest was greatest when "Jeopardy" came on. He bobbed and shrieked with more enthusiasm than any of the show's audience or contestants. The bird was a TV addict.

Dog-training classes became another popular activity that drew a lot of spectator attention. Folding chairs had to be replaced by permanent bleachers to accommodate the crowds who came to witness the transformation of unruly dogs into obedient household pets.

It was always a rewarding experience to watch the undisciplined mayhem that characterized the first night of class turn into an orderly and obedient collection of owners and dogs by the eighth week. Graduation was always a special event. In order to graduate, each owner had to train his or her dog to wear a four-cornered graduation cap complete with a dangling red, white, and blue tassel, the colors of the "Canine University".

It was also interesting to see old myths destroyed as dogs of all ages and breeds lost their undesirable traits and were transformed into pets that could co-exist with society.

It is a tragedy that more dogs are abandoned or euthanized because of their behavior than from any other reason. With very few exceptions, a professional dog trainer could correct behavioral problems permitting the family to enjoy the dog for many years.

One of the myths that I saw put to rest is the adage, "You can't teach an old dog new tricks."

At the conclusion of each training class, trophies were awarded for the three best-trained students. In the largest class ever graduated, a six-year-old cairn terrier, who was handled by its sixty-two-year-old owner, won the first prize. As the TV crews ground away, the lady only lamented that she didn't know who trained the hardest, she or the dog.

It was another owner who answered the question of who trained whom in her household when she described her personal training program.

To teach her dog to "speak for its dinner," she said she would get down on her hands and knees, hold the food out of the dog's reach, and bark until the dog barked. Then she would give the dog its food. Now, a year later, her dog refused to touch its food unless she first got down on her knees and barked.

Stories such as these caused our training director to wince in dismay. Bernie was one of the country's foremost dog trainers, and his success had conditioned him to be less than amused at such stories. His own dog had accrued more points in competition than any other dog in America to win the Ken-L-Ration Obedience Of The Year award for three consecutive years. Together with his dog he traveled more than 40,000 miles and defeated more than 50,000 dogs in ninety-four obedience trials in order to attain this record. But, at least one little boy was able to trump Bernie's remarkable talent.

At one of the country's largest dog shows, Bernie handled a huge German shepherd and put the dog through the trial with seemingly flawless execution. At the conclusion the dog was declared the winner with a total of 199½ points out of a possible 200.

Bernie took the dog out to the winner's circle to await the photographer; while he was waiting, a small boy approached him.

"Is that the dog that won the big show today?" the boy asked.

"It sure is," Bernie replied proudly.

The boy studied the dog for a while and then exclaimed, "He sure is a big dog."

"He sure is," Bernie replied.

Then the little boy turned his gaze up to Bernie. "Tell me, mister, if you tell your dog to give you his paw, will he do it?"

Bernie paused and smiled. "Um. Uh. Well, no. He doesn't shake hands." Bernie flushed a little. He had brought this dog through months of intensive training but had never bothered to teach the dog such mundane responses as shaking hands. He stood there, chagrined and sputtering, feeling more than a little foolish in front of his youthful inquisitor.

"Huh!" the boy responded with a note of contempt, "My dog's only half his size and he can shake hands."

A smile of satisfaction spread over the small boy's face as he turned and marched off into the crowd. Bernie stood there with the sudden feeling that the mighty had just been humbled.

I think it's safe to say that any dog would be a better pet if it were obedience-trained. Like a well-behaved child, a well-behaved pet is always a joy to have. But it was a friend of mine who proved there were advantages most of us would never entertain.

I ran into Patricia Widmark at the Cincinnati airport, following our appearance on a local television program about pet care. Pat is another of the country's foremost authorities on dog training and had been on the program with one of Robert Redford's golden retrievers. When Pat's flight was announced for boarding, I watched as she attached a seeing-eye harness to the retriever. After adjusting a pair of dark sunglasses over her eyes, she smiled sheepishly as she prepared to lead the dog onto the plane. "I like to fly with my dog near me and this way they never question it."

I smiled at the thought of attempting this with my two-pound Yorkshire terrier.

Recently there was a joke circulating that touched on this deception. It seems two neighbors were out walking their dogs when they decided it would be nice to quench their thirst with a glass of beer. Approaching the local tavern, they found a large notice on the door, "No Animals Allowed."

One of the men said, "Hey, that's no problem. Just do like I do." Having said that, he proceeded to put on a pair of sunglasses and entered the bar pretending to be blind. The bar tender, seeing the dog, told the man that they didn't allow dogs in the bar and he would have to leave or be thrown out. Immediately the man explained that he was blind and that his Doberman was a seeing-eye dog.

The bar tender apologized and gave the man his beer. Observing this from outside, the other man put on his sunglasses and joined his friend at the bar. Immediately the bartender came up to him and told him that dogs were not allowed in the bar and that he'd have to leave or be thrown out. The man responded that he was blind and that his dog was a seeing-eye dog.

The bartender challenged the man, "Are you going to try and tell me that that little Chihuahua is a seeing-eye dog?"

At a loss for words, the man blurted out, "Oh, my Lord! Do you mean those people sold me a Chihuahua?"

A very popular area of the motel was the stable. For some reason, children–especially girls–have an inexplicable fondness for horses. This fascination does not always extend to those who work around horses. Ask anyone who works in a stable, and he or she will tell you that horses are the dumbest of all animals, and equestrians will cite you dozens of reasons why this is so. But after having boarded a horse by the name of Image, I am not convinced.

Image was my daughter Gail's horse, and while it was one of many we boarded, it was the only one that stayed with us for a long period of years. It was one of those concessions parents agree to against their better judgment.

Our problems began when Image started forgetting he was a horse and began thinking he was a dog. Image loved dogs. Every evening, when the dog-training class assembled, Image would trot over and join the class. Except for exchanging sniffs, the dogs didn't bother Image and Image didn't bother the dogs. When the dogs were led to the right, Image would walk to the right. When the dogs were led to the left, Image would walk to the left. When they reversed their direction, Image would do an about face and go right with them. He absolutely refused to keep away from the dogs. In some respects, he was an outstanding student of canine novice obedience.

As if interfering with our training classes wasn't enough, Image decided that he would rather spend his time in the kennels than in the stable. On one of our busiest afternoons, I had to interrupt my schedule to respond to a frantic alarm that all of the Imperial Kennel dogs were running around loose in the courtyard. Sure enough, there was Image trotting around with a dozen dogs at his side. It was then that we discovered Image had learned how to open the kennel gate latches.

After that episode, with increasing regularity, I would be called by an animal attendant to remove Image from inside one of the kennels or from one of the courtyards.

The horse was uncanny. He would stand behind a building for hours, peering around the corner, watching each attendant's moves. As soon as someone failed to replace a latch promptly, Image would trot out, enter the courtyard, and begin letting the dogs out of their runs. He was the best friend they ever had. (Accomplice is perhaps a more appropriate term!) Surprisingly, not once did any dog attack, or otherwise provoke the horse. The dogs seemed to sense from the beginning that Image was their friend.

Each time we inaugurated a new device to thwart him, the horse responded with a new stratagem. He learned how to open the feed containers. By standing on his hind legs, he would reach hay that had supposedly been stored beyond his reach. If he became frustrated, he would dine on our pickup van's windshield wipers or maybe a nice section of the motel's bright red mansard roof. Eventually we had to equip every kennel gate with a latch and pin lock and the perimeter gates with spring-loaded snap locks to discourage his intrusions.

When I thought we finally had the horse isolated, Image struck back with a vengeance. His first act was to chew out all the screens from our barn's windows. Then he started on the plastic window frames. It soon looked as if we were either going to have to admit defeat and let him start staying in a dog kennel or ask Gail to board her horse somewhere else.

It was the owner of a nearby stable who told me Image was a very social animal whose only problem was a lack of companionship. "A goat," he said, "would solve all your problems."

With all the mischief that Image had caused, his boarding certainly had been an expensive experience. Now I was faced with the prospect of investing in a goat just to make a horse happy.

Marc located a goat for sale, and I authorized its purchase with the stipulation that he bring it back in the van and not the rear seat of my personal car. When he returned, I helped him unload the goat and lead it to the stable. To our surprise, we opened the stable door and found ourselves face to face with another goat. Unbeknown to us, Gail had gone out that same day and purchased a goat. We now had two freeloading goats to feed in addition to our equine freebooter.

To my surprise, and delight, this new arrangement appeared to be a match made in heaven. Image ceased his mischievous behavior, and he and the two goats became inseparable friends. But his odd antics did not stop entirely.

Shortly after the goats arrived, I was called outside to observe Image walking around the pasture with one of the goats standing on his back. Everyone denied having had anything to do with it, and as it happened again several times during the next few days, we came to accept this as something the two animals arranged between themselves.

Sure enough, one day we saw Image walk over to the bleachers in the dog-training area and stand next to the end of the structure. One of the goats went over to the bleachers, climbed the seats until he was level with Image's back and merely stepped across onto Image's back. For as long as we stood there, Image proceeded to walk around the pasture as if nothing unusual were happening.

Over the years, Gail found that her job, evening college courses, and social life were leaving her less and less time to spend with Image and she began entertaining thoughts of finding a new home for him. I did little to dissuade her and, in fact, might have even encouraged her a little. When she finally made the decision, I prevailed upon her to make the acceptance of the two goats a condition of the sale. I had nightmares of two goats chewing their way in the kennels and letting all the dogs out.

Unable to bring herself to sell Image to a stranger, Gail arranged with my old friend, Dr. Corbin, to pasture Image on his farm in southern Illinois. She also talked him into taking the two goats. I hope someday he will forgive us.

Prologue Chapter 14

JUST DOGS

Charlotte Becker

"Why's all that fuss?" the sergeant said,
    'To 'ear them scudding feet —
Just dogs a-comin' back again–
    Sancho an' Pat an' Pete."

Just dogs? Why, Sancho saved ten lives
    Half buried by a shell.
He dug them out with bleeding paws
    Where blinding shrapnel fell.

And little Pat bore under fire
    His Red Cross water can,
Quenching the cruel, burning thirst
    Of many a wounded man.

Pete tugged grenades at Loos,
    As brave as any soldier there;
The general knelt them all
    To give his Croix de Guerre.

Just dogs? Why, scarce a soldier gone
    Would find his heaven complete
Unless he heard beside his own
    That sound of scudding feet!

14

THE WANTED AND
THE WANTING

For obvious reasons, our policy of declining to board vicious or unmanageable pets was usually rigidly enforced. Not only had our attendants received serious bite wounds from seemingly nice pets but also, if a vicious animal required special attention, it was impossible for us to come to its assistance without exposing our employees to serious injury.

Sometimes a pet owner knew his or her pet would bite a stranger but they were reluctant to tell us for fear that we would not accept the animal. A classic example of minor proportions was the time I took a little Chihuahua from a customer's arms. The lady just looked on as the little dog suddenly clamped its jaws on my index finger. The little monster looked me straight in the eye as it pressed its jaws tighter and tighter.

"Oh," the woman exclaimed. "I should have told you that Pepe doesn't like strangers–"

On more than one occasion I have seen one of our attendants with a little dog hanging by its teeth from her hand, while the owner reluctantly admitted that the dog "sometimes bites."

In the case of small dogs, our employees were big enough and trained enough to handle any situation that came up, but only if the owners let us know about their pet's disposition before we were bitten.

With large dogs, it was another story. A 100-pound shepherd or a pit bull can do a lot of serious damage, and the size of the attendant was superfluous. These are the types of dogs we have to turn away.

Still, there were times when the circumstances persuaded us to waive this policy. Occasionally, we have regretted it, but in one particular case, I have always felt good about making the exception. At least for the dog, there was a happy ending, if not for us.

It began when I received a telephone call from a distraught woman. She was married to a career soldier who had served with a guard dog contingent in Viet Nam during the Viet Nam War. Upon his retirement, her husband had somehow managed to bring the dog back to Chicago with him. Now her husband lay dying in the veterans' hospital and she was unable to find anyone who would board the dog until she could get her present situation under control.

Due to the circumstances, I agreed to let her bring the dog into our kennel and I gave her my assurance that we would make special arrangements for the dog's care. Since we had special isolation runs, I felt the additional risk was warranted in this one case.

Duke turned out to be an enormous black, thick-coated German shepherd. He had strange ominous eyes, set deep in his head, and they seemed to almost glare a warning to be aware. Everything about him warned us to stay clear, and it alarmed me that only the owner could secure the dog in his private room. When she was ready to leave, she knelt and embraced the dog and the tears coursed down her face as she hugged the dog and squeezed the awesome beast to her face.

Although his actions were restrained while his owner was present, once she left the area, the huge animal became enraged and began attacking its enclosure. Though he stretched the chain links to their limit, they continued to hold, and after finally exhausting himself, he quieted down for the evening.

Each day I made it a point to walk back to his kennel to check that he was eating and to observe him from a distance. After first charging the gate, he would just stand there motionless, his cold, steely eyes staring directly into mine.

I wondered about the patrols he had gone out on while in Viet Nam. How many times was his life put in harms way as an "expendable" military subject? Most of all, I wondered what Duke was thinking about as he stared back from his concrete and wire enclosure. What stories could he tell of the Hell he endured?

I wanted so much to open the gate and pat his head, to try to help him understand that although he was once again in a foreign and alien environment, he was among friends. Over the years I had been able to make up with hundreds of seemingly hostile dogs. I could not make up with Duke.

With one exception, Duke would never let anyone approach him during the many months he was with us. That exception was a young male animal attendant named Dave Splett. Dave was another one of those sentimental animal lovers who worked with animals because he loved them, not because it was the most financially rewarding job he could have found.

I learned about Dave's conquest in a most disconcerting way. I entered the door to the food preparation room one day and found myself standing only a few feet from where a huge German shepherd was lying. Dave was kneeling next to the dog brushing its thick coat with a slicker brush. The dog raised its head and turned his eyes in my direction, emitting a low, rumbling growl from his throat. It was Duke.

"Down!" Dave commanded. "Dooown," he repeated in a soft, modulated tone. The beast turned his head toward Dave, studied him for a few seconds, and then laid his head flat on the floor. As Dave continued his brushing, Duke rolled onto his back and stared at me from his upside-down position. Slowly, I backed out the door and returned to the lobby. I knew I didn't have to check on Duke anymore. He was at home with his surrogate master.

During the first few months, although the owner checked frequently on Duke's progress, she neglected to send in her boarding payment. I knew the government wasn't the most efficient paymaster, but I had serious doubts that it could take that many months for her to receive some kind of benefit. When several months had passed without hearing from her, an inquiry revealed that her husband had passed away and she had just picked up in her mobile home and left town.

Duke was not the first, or the last, dog abandoned at the pet motel. Legally, we followed a procedure of sending a registered letter to the owner's last known address and if we do not receive a reply within ten days, we were legally free to dispose of the pet. In Duke's case, finding a home for him was out of the question. The only alternative was putting him to sleep. It was an option I could not bring myself to take.

While our business was good, our financial obligation to the Krocs was still a major consideration. When Duke's boarding bill reached $1,000, I pulled his folio and stopped ringing in the daily charges.

Several inquiries failed to furnish any information about the owner's whereabouts. I knew we could not afford to continue keeping a non-paying guest, but neither could I bring myself to put Duke to sleep. Each week I would postpone the final action for another week, and then another. I began again to make my daily pilgrimages to visit Duke. He was not as hostile as he once was and I would sit down on the concrete floor just outside his gate and talk to him for long periods of time.

"It wouldn't be right," I kept telling myself. Here was a dog that had served our country while my family and I were home enjoying the benefits of freedom. He required so little, after having given so much. It didn't seem right that he should be condemned to death because he couldn't pay for a warm room and a few handfuls of dog food. After each visit, I would walk back to my office and postpone again the decision I knew had to come.

More than a year later I was summoned to the telephone

by a call from a priest at the nearby Glenview Naval Air Station. He told me that he had received a letter from a lady who had left a dog in our care. She wanted the priest to find out if the dog was still alive. She told the priest about her problems and how she was trying to put her life back together. Torn apart by her husband's death, she had just picked up and moved to Florida. But, one part of her life was missing, her husband's dog, Duke. She wanted to get the dog back but she had no money.

At this time the dog's bill was almost $6,000.

"Father," I replied, "if you can find the means of shipping Duke to Florida, I'll write off the boarding bill."

A week later, Dave took Duke from his run for the last time. He was bathed and groomed and looked like a million dollars. We loaded him into a nice new shipping crate, which also contained several of our largest rawhide, chew bones, and bade him farewell. With the help of three sailors from the Glenview Naval Air Station, we lifted the crate into a naval station wagon. At the airbase, Duke's crate was placed into a waiting Navy transport plane flown by naval reservists on a training mission. Coincidently, their destination was Florida.

Whether the commandant of the base or any other authorized personnel participated in this action, I will probably never know. From what I was able to learn, it was the combined effort of a few fine people who wanted to help one of our four-legged warriors go home.

A few weeks later I received another telephone call from the priest to let me know that Duke had arrived safely and was basking in the Florida sunshine with his owner. He also wanted me to know that the lady had said that if she could ever afford it, she would send us the money she owed.

I smiled at the hopelessness of ever collecting this debt. "Father," I said, "Tell her the exact amount is $5,840 and not to worry about it. I won't need the money until 1986." (At the time, I had parted with the Krocs and had a balloon payment of $650,000 coming due in 1986.)

165

Most of the time it was my own employees, though, who resolved the dilemma of an abandoned pet. Neither their friends nor families were excluded from among the possible sources of a new home. "Just one more" pet was a familiar plea, and Peggy and I were not exceptions. Our first waif was a little West Highland terrier named Maggie, whose owner abandoned her at the pet motel. Maggie was about two years old and as sweet a dog as ever there was. Our second dog was named Scampy and was also a West Highland terrier. Scampy was a male, well advanced in age and the owner just couldn't keep him any longer. Teddy Bear, our third adopted "child" was a tiny Yorkshire terrier, also well advanced in age. His owners' story was that he didn't get along with their grandchildren, so they were going to put him to sleep if they couldn't find a home for him. The three of them were an odd assortment. Maggie always wanted to be in our laps. She loved human companionship. Scampy was more aloof and preferred to be left alone unless he sought out your company. In the evenings when Peggy settled down and Maggie had found a comfortable arrangement in her lap, then Scampy would come to her and, being unable to jump the distance, would stand on his hind legs asking to be lifted up to share her lap. Teddy Bear, being so much smaller, always stayed away from Maggie and Scampy. In fact, he also stayed away from us. We were shelter, room and board, and while we could pick him up and hold him, he was always eager to be freed to seek his solitude.

There are a number of reasons people give up their pets, but, to me, abandonment is the cruelest answer of all. Over the years we have heard many excuses, but few justify the act. For many animals, abandonment does not end happily.

Occasionally, someone would bring a dog to the pet motel in the middle of the night and leave it tied to our entrance gate. Sometimes there was a note asking us to take good care of it, but more often there was just a poor, cowering, bewildered animal.

I recall driving in one bitter, cold morning to find an old Great Dane tied to our driveway gate. The gray hair around his eyes and muzzle confirmed his advanced age. He was terribly thin, and callused folds of skin on his elbows indicated the dog had been sleeping on a hard wooden or concrete surface for a long time. I untied the dog and led him into the nearest Extra-Large Imperial room. It was a Tuesday and I knew the room probably wouldn't be needed until Friday. For a few days at least, the old dog would know the comforts of carpeting and a foam-rubber mattress.

I made out a diet card calling for ample mixed canned meat and our regular dry dog food. The old dog ate as if it were his first meal in weeks. I ordered him three meals a day and he finished every one. He didn't move any faster when the animal warden called for him on Friday morning, but he did appear several pounds heavier and a little more content.

Ironically, the following morning I received a telephone call from a man who was inquiring about the dog. He claimed he had given his dog to a couple of boys who had agreed to give the dog a home. He didn't explain how he knew the dog was at the pet motel, nor did I ask him. All I did was tell him that the dog had been turned over to the dog pound, and if he hurried he might just be able to retrieve it before it was euthanized.

There were other pet owners who checked their pets into the pet motel without any intention of ever picking them up. For some reason, these were almost always dog owners, very rarely cat owners. Over the years, we learned to recognize the profile this type of person usually fit. Invariably, he or she was either moving or in the process of getting divorced. Young women seemed to abandon pets more frequently than men, perhaps because of poorer economic situations. Sometimes it was because of a landlord's restrictions, and often because a parent had ordered the son or daughter to get the pet out of their house.

When a problem is apparent, we ask for a sizeable deposit. However, this does not always discourage some people. Some are natural con artists who aren't the least inhibited from going the limit. They will not only give you the information you seek, they will offer their minister's name as a reference. Of course, the information will all be erroneous. They'll put their dog in the most expensive suite, order special diets, exercising, and grooming, all with no intention of paying. Perhaps they feel that as long as they are abandoning the pet, they shouldn't scrimp on their parting gesture.

What they fail to consider, or perhaps don't care about, is that everyone else–the groomer, the dog walker, all of us–lose. And, in the end, the pet loses too. Recently, many communities have begun passing ordinances to deal with people who abandon their pets. In some communities, the local authorities will vigorously prosecute any individual who abandons an animal. It is a good ordinance and long past due.

But not all abandonments can be so harshly judged.

Over the years, there has been an increasing tendency for older people to move from private dwellings to apartments and condominiums, some of which have restrictions prohibiting pets.

Occasionally we received a call relative to perpetual boarding, and while many deemed the cost too high, we had several permanent guests who would live out the balance of their lives with us.

While we try to make life for these animals as pleasant as possible, I am sure the transition from a home environment to a kennel has some effect on them. In the home, a pet will seek out its master when it desires attention or just the simplest affection. In a kennel, this is not always possible.

To ease the transition, we encouraged our employees to spend extra time with these pets. They were taken from their rooms and played with, given extra food and extra treats, and were regularly groomed or bathed at our expense. On occasion, one of us would take a pet home for a few days to let it share again the daily experience of home life. With all the extra services, we sometimes questioned whether we were making any money on these pets. I never checked and, to the consternation of my partner, I didn't care.

Two of our permanent boarders were not really abandoned. They were picked up from a veterinary hospital in accord with some telephone instructions from a lady who said she was elderly and could not care for them in her own home.

Since that time, I learned that this lady had at least a dozen dogs boarded around the Chicago area. All of the dogs were strays that she found, and rather than turn them over to the dog pound and possible death, she had them checked by a veterinarian, treated if necessary, and then boarded in a kennel to live out their natural lives.

Although I corresponded with her, I never met or spoke with her after our initial contact. I have no conception of her financial means, but assume that the bills for keeping all these strays must have been considerable. Each month her check would arrive promptly and, occasionally, she included a short scribbled note about Daisy, Snoopy, or one of her other four-legged orphans. I often think about this lovely lady and pray that her fellow human beings provide as well for her, if circumstances require it, as she provided for those strays.

Sometimes, something would happen that gave me reason to wonder how some people can behave as they do. Among our more affluent clients was a couple that boarded their miniature schnauzer quite often because of their frequent traveling. They appeared very well off, and then one day they told me that a distant relative had died and had left them several million dollars. They had decided to leave Chicago and retire to Arizona.

One day I commented on how long their dog, Patches, had been boarded with us. It was then I learned that the people had purchased a condo in Arizona that did not permit pets. The dog that had been their companion for several years was to be boarded for the rest of its life. In this case it was not because of any hardship. It was just the opposite.

Patches boarded well for the first several months, but then we noticed a gradual deterioration in her appearance. Her appetite kept decreasing, and on some days she refused to eat at all.

Her movements became more labored and she began acting more and more as if she had lost interest in living. Nothing we did seemed to stem the process.

I began having Patches brought up to my office each morning, where she would spend the entire day with me. She was extremely well behaved and, surprisingly for a schnauzer, rarely barked. Except to go to her water or food bowls, she seemed content just to lie at my feet and get some occasional petting, until the time came to return to her room.

At home, I began talking about Patches with increasing regularity, until at last I prevailed upon Peggy's sentimental nature to such an extent that she suggested I bring Patches home for the weekends. Our own dogs, Maggie and Scampi, were both accustomed to my bringing stray dogs into the house, so they offered no resistance to the newcomer.

At first, Patches was a little frightened and shy, but over the next few months her appetite and spunky behavior began returning. She soon learned how to jump up on the furniture, and we started awaking with three dogs in our bed instead of two. Gradually too, her coat returned to its former lustrous condition and her behavior matched that of our own two dogs. In fact, when I opened the patio door, there was general mayhem as the three dogs vied with each other to be the first through the opening.

One day, her owners returned to Chicago and called for Patches. They took her to a veterinarian and had her put to sleep. For the people with millions of dollars, the meager boarding cost was too expensive. They never even gave us the chance to adopt the dog. I shall never understand people like this. I am sure that, had the circumstances been reversed, the most wretched cur would have turned down any amount of money before it would have given up its friends.

There were other occasions when the decision to arrange for lifetime boarding was an act of compassion. Sometimes sick or elderly persons will want to make a provision for the continued well being of their pet, in contemplation of their own death. Regrettably, where there are heirs, greed and avarice are frequently sufficient motivation for having this provision set aside by legal maneuvering. Then it is only a matter of time before we received a court order directing us to have the animal(s) put to sleep. In only one case did the attorneys permit us additional time to find the dog a home.

One particular case was so tragic that it will haunt me the rest of my life.

Late one April, I received a telephone call from an elderly lady who was entering a hospital for major surgery. Arrangements were made for us to pick up her two German shorthair pointers and board them until she recovered. The dogs had been her husband's most cherished possessions, and since his death had become this lady's constant solace.

When she talked with me, her concern was not about herself or the pending surgery; it was only for the two dogs. Aware that her situation was tenuous, she explained that in the event anything happened to her, she had appointed her sole nephew as the administrator of her estate and that she had made adequate arrangements for the continued welfare of the two dogs at the pet motel.

She left no doubt in my mind that, more than anything else in the world, her preoccupation was with the welfare of her husband's dogs.

Apparently, the operation was successful, but the general health of the lady declined to the point where she was unable to return home. Eventually she was transferred to a nursing home, and although her condition continued to deteriorate, she never failed to telephone each week to inquire about the welfare of Victoria and Hannibal.

During the last few months, her telephone calls became less frequent and her voice more distant and rambling. She would keep me on the telephone for long periods of time, recounting memories of her husband and the two dogs and the happy times they shared.

171

Regardless of how busy I was, I accepted, as a personal obligation, the duty to take her calls. As we grew more familiar, I began chiding her for her needless concerns and sternly lectured her to follow her doctor's advice so she could hurry home to Hannibal and Victoria.

Then, one day, I received a telephone call from a lawyer that represented the lady's nephew. The nephew had had his aunt declared incompetent, and in exercising his power as administrator, had obtained a court order to have the two dogs destroyed.

It was not a question of there not being enough money for both the nephew and the dogs' maintenance; it was the specter of greed.

There was no alternative to the court's order. Both dogs were surrendered to a veterinarian and I held each one as the lethal dose of liquid was injected.

It was not the end of the incident. Although the lady was supposedly incompetent, from time to time she still telephoned me to inquire about the dogs and just to talk. I hadn't the heart to tell her of her nephew's perfidy, so instead I lied to her. I told her that I had placed the two dogs with a friend of mine who had a large farm in Wisconsin. I told her how the dogs loved to romp through the wide-open fields and how much better they seemed since regaining this measure of freedom. It seemed like such an insignificant sin and one not altogether unworthy. Finally, after a few more weeks, the telephone calls ceased completely. I thought the nightmare was finally ended.

I was wrong.

About three months had gone by when I suddenly got a call from a voice that was vaguely familiar. My heart almost stopped when the caller vigorously identified herself as the owner of Hannibal and Victoria.

"Mr. Leeds," the voice said joyously. "I beat him. I beat my nephew!"

She then told me that she had made up her mind to get better and she had done so, to the extent that she was able to have the court declare her sane and competent. She was now coming home and she asked me to deliver her two dogs the following day.

I was stunned by the turn of events. No one had yet told her that her two dogs had been put to sleep. I didn't know how much of what I had told her she remembered, but I could not continue the charade. The only thing I could do was tell her the truth. It was one of the hardest things I have ever had to do.

There was silence at the other end of the line. Then her voice choked up and I heard her crying uncontrollably.

"He tried to steal everything from me," she cried. "Do you know what my nephew did, Mr. Leeds? He bought himself automobiles with my money and went on trips to Europe. But you shouldn't have let him kill my dogs, Mr. Leeds. You shouldn't have let him kill them. Why did you lie to me? Why did you let him do it?"

Her voice trailed off and I heard the line disconnect.

She called again later in the day and then the next day and the next week. For months after she would call me. Like a voice coming out of a fog, she would interrupt her crying to ask me, "Why did you let him do it? Why did you let him kill Hannibal and Victoria, Mr. Leeds? Why?"

The calls finally stopped coming, but within my own mind the telephone continues to ring and I hear her distant voice crying and asking me, "Why? Why, Mr. Leeds? How could you let him do it?"

Prologue Chapter 15

THE LITTLE DOG ANGEL

Bur McIntosh

High up in the courts of heaven today
A little dog angel waits;
With the other angels he will not play,
But sits alone at the gates.
"For I know that my master will come," says he,
"And when he comes he'll call for me."

And his master, far down on the earth below,
As he sits in his easy chair,
Forgets sometimes, and he whistles low
For the dog that is not there.
And the little dog angel cocks his ears
And dreams that his master's call he hears.

And I know that at length when his master waits
Outside in the dark and cold,
For the hand of death to open the gates
That lead to these courts of gold,
The little dog angel's eager bark
Will comfort his soul while he's still in the dark.

15

LESS THAN PERFECT

Within a few years of our opening, we were boarding 10,000 dogs and cats a year plus hundreds of exotic pets, and although we encountered problems, the catastrophe the experts predicted never materialized. We were confident in our claims. We were perfect.

As time went on, experience confirmed that the number-one hazard of boarding was stress. Illness, injury, and death were more the product of inadequate care, rather than normal circumstance.

One such hazard that we refuted was what the trade referred to as "the collie syndrome."

"You cannot board collies," we were warned. "They get lonely, won't eat, and they'll just pine away and die on you."

It was pure nonsense. Over the years, we boarded every kind of dog and cat, including thousands of shelties and collies, and we never had one "pine away" and die. The idea that you can't keep dogs from dying of so-called "grievance disease" is absurd. Actually, there is no such thing as grievance disease, except in the minds of those too incompetent to recognize and treat the problem of stress.

Stress may account for as much as 90 percent of boarding problems, but it can be dealt with by kennel operators who will take the time and effort to minimize it.

There are many kennel operators and veterinarians who never visit their facilities on Sundays and holidays. Animals, sick and healthy, are cooped up in cages, where they are forced to eat, sleep, and eliminate, without any human attention, sometimes for more than two days. They are neither fed nor given their required medications. Their cages are not cleaned and they are forced to wallow in their own waste until the next regular work day.

This is the real reason many boarding facilities will not permit you to enter the area where your pet is housed and it is often the real reason they require that your pet be bathed before you pick it up. They do not dare to let you see the animal, so encrusted with urine and feces, until it is cleaned up.

We have heard the specious argument many times that it is good for an animal to go without eating one or two days a week. I have heard people recommend this same practice to other pet owners. "It is healthy to purge your body by fasting one day a week."

We have yet to see one piece of scientific data to support this claim. In the wild, an animal will gorge itself, and then may not eat again for several days, but usually because it is not hungry or because no food is readily available. No one has ever shown us a dog or cat that regularly declines to eat every seventh day of its own choice. It is the opinion of most that such a practice is the result of economic considerations for the kennel owner, rather than concern for the pets' welfare.

There is another widespread misconception rampant in the boarding industry that accounts for the illness and death of many pets. This is the mistaken belief that if a pet doesn't eat, it will eventually get hungry enough to eat anything you offer it. Too often this can lead to tragic consequences. Because of stress, an animal can, and often will, continue to refuse food and/or water until it becomes dehydrated, sometimes causing irreversible organ damage. It literally will starve itself to death even though food is available.

One of our most valuable tools was our Report Card. This record, kept for every pet, recorded how much food the animal ate each day as well as the condition of its urine and stool. Space was provided for notes to detail any change in the animal's disposition or appearance. Experience taught us the importance of eating regularly if a pet were to stay healthy.

To assure that proper care was maintained, we adopted a strict policy regarding our pets' eating regimen. Young dogs and cats must eat a full meal by the third day of boarding and pets eight years of age or older must eat a full meal by their second day.

The task of enforcing such a policy is a little more arduous than it sounds. Being suddenly plucked from the security of its own familiar surroundings and placed in a strange confinement, amidst strange people and animals, some pets will refuse to eat even the same food they ate every day at home. This situation called for a variety of ploys and subterfuges.

Starting them out on a can of cat food can successfully motivate most problem dogs. I suspect the strong fishy aroma has a lot to do with it. If that fails, Mighty Dog, a dog food manufactured by the Carnation Company, and a very close approximation of human food, usually succeeds. If that fails, our next recourse is cooking hamburgers or bringing in leftovers from our own dinner table. There are few canines who can refuse Peggy's quiche or one of her other culinary achievements.

For those rare pets that decline the Leeds' gastronomical enticements, substantial doses of vitamin-laced NutriCal are given, and as a last resort, an injection of Vitamin B_1 by a veterinarian has never failed to achieve the desired results.

Another misconception in the industry, but believed by pet owners, is that because their pets lost weight while boarded, they were deliberately deprived of food. I doubt that was often the case. Loss of weight while being boarded is frequently not an indication that the animal didn't eat well. On the contrary, it may have eaten twice as much as it ate at home.

In fairness to boarding facilities, pet owners should be aware that there are some dogs who will eat like pigs while boarding and still lose weight. Some breeds, particularly German shepherds, Irish setters, and Great Danes may become so stressed that their metabolism speeds up and their systems start pumping out adrenaline, causing them to burn up most of their caloric intake.

The worst case we ever had was a huge German shepherd that was boarded with us for several months while its owners were in Europe. He was a very nervous dog and would rarely lie down or relax. All day long he would just walk around his run in circles without stopping or lying down. Although he ate all of our regular diet, after only one week, we could see a noticeable weight loss.

Our first suspicion was that the dog had worms but a fecal exam confirmed the dog did not have any internal parasites. We immediately began increasing his food portions.

Eventually we got up to feeding the dog six pounds of food a day and he ate it all. We fed him two pounds of dry dog food, two pounds of canned dog food, and two pounds of cottage cheese. He ate every bit and still did not put on weight. We even tried every old remedy that anyone suggested. Honey, molasses, garlic, and dozens of health-food supplements, all failed.

Since our local veterinarians couldn't resolve the dilemma, we contacted the veterinary college at the University of Illinois.

"Give up," they counseled. It was impossible for the dog's system even to process the quantity of food we were feeding. Most of the food was going right through the dog without benefiting him at all.

In the end, we cut his ration down to three pounds of food a day, but over the next several months, despite continued efforts, we were unable to restore the dog to its former weight.

When the owners called for their dog, they were outraged. Despite our explanation of all the efforts we had made, they threatened to sue us for having mistreated their dog. A few weeks later, one of the owners telephoned to advise us that the dog had made a miraculous recovery and had completely regained all of the lost weight and that they were dropping the whole matter.

We have seen this kind of problem several times. Some pets will always lose weight in a kennel, but when they return to their home environment, they regain it in a surprisingly short time. We can only attribute this to the stress this particular pet suffers when it is away from its natural environment.

Problems like this would rarely occur if people socialized their pets more during their formative years. Exposure to other people and dogs helps develop a good personality in a pet. There are many in the industry that believe a neurotic pet is often a reflection of the environment it was brought up in. Pets that are boarded while they are very young learn to enjoy the experience and they fare much better when their owners leave them alone.

With the report card, we were able to catch minor problems early and, as they were treated immediately, more serious problems virtually disappeared.

Unfortunately, the cost of having veterinarians treat even minor problems added another financial burden, and there were some who argued that since these problems were not within our control, the costs should be passed on to the owners. I disagreed. Even though it was fair, I knew it would upset most customers to return from a trip and find a veterinary bill in addition to their boarding bill.

Except where there was a veterinary record of previous treatment available to us, it was virtually impossible to determine if some conditions existed prior to boarding. Arguing each case risked offending our clients and damaging our reputation. I didn't want to do what some of the other kennels were doing. I wanted to do better!

Our Pet-I-Care Warranty was revised to include reimbursement for any illness, injury or death of a pet, regardless of cause. Although certain limits and exceptions were kept, a preexisting illness was the only exclusion. Even fleas and ticks were covered, and because a condition sometimes showed up after a pet had left the motel, we even extended the coverage to include a reasonable period of time after the pet had gone home.

We were aware that offering to pay for any kind of a problem could become a Pandora's box. Ninety-nine percent of the complaints were about problems over which we had no control. A dog would injure its feet by trying to dig through the concrete floor of its room or damage its tail by swinging it back and forth against a wall. Sometimes a dog would get diarrhea or begin vomiting because its owner fed it or gave it too much water immediately upon bringing it home from boarding. But, regardless of the cause of the problem, we wanted to give pet owners financial protection for the first time.

With very few exceptions, the Pet-I-Care Warranty worked far better than anticipated. The nice thing about it was that the pet owner did not have to prove any liability. If any kind of a problem developed, we paid for the veterinary care.

Of course there were always some people who would abuse an offer like ours. On more than one occasion, a sick pet was deliberately boarded with us in order to get us to pay for the required treatment. It also happened that an owner would pick up his or her pet and immediately begin a fine inspection of the animal's body and point out a sore or wound in some obscure place. Even though we were highly suspicious, if the pet's veterinarian stated that he had never treated the animal for this problem, we ended up paying for the medical care.

In a few cases, the problem was leukemia, infectious peritonitis, cancer, or some other disease with a long incubation period. In most cases the people's veterinarians would confirm that it would have been impossible for the pet to contract the disease during its short boarding period. I always recall the time one family caused an ugly scene in our lobby by pointing out that their dog had a huge tick on its nose. After a close inspection I was able to console the family by proving that the "tick" was actually a mole.

It is likely the mole had been on the dog's nose for years but it went unnoticed because it was hidden by a tuft of hair.

Problems were the exception. The vast majority of pets went home in as good or better condition than when they came in to be boarded, and most returned many times. It was one of our receptionists who suggested that we celebrate a guest's one-hundredth visit by boarding it in a Regency suite and giving it all the available amenities free of charge. It became a common occurrence.

When a Chicago resident set a record with United Airlines by flying to all fifty states within a thirty-day period, the public was unaware that during each trip this lawyer's dog was boarded at our pet motel. Over a ten-year period, Louki, his large white Samoyed boarded with us more than 200 times without suffering so much as a broken toenail. It can be done.

Completing our second year, we thought we were perfect but nature has a way of humbling the overconfident. We were to find out that we were not immune to the ravages of those rare animal diseases that can strike regardless of the precautions taken. One of these, feline rhinotracheitis, would teach us a bitter lesson. The disease broke out in one cattery and soon spread to all sixty cats in our two catteries. A virus that affects the nasal membranes of cats and also brings on ulcerations of the tongue and mouth causes the disease. A cat first begins sneezing, then a discharge begins from its nose and eyes, and finally its mouth fills with small ulcerated sores. Once a cat's nasal passages become obstructed, it can no longer smell and will refuse to eat or drink.

With many illnesses, if you can keep an animal eating, it can usually recover. It may take time, but the animals own body will generate the antibodies necessary to overcome the disease. But with rhinotracheitis, cats refuse to take nourishment, and the chance of dehydration and subsequent death is a very real threat.

When the disease first broke out, each cat was taken to its own veterinarian for treatment, even though there were six veterinary clinics within a few miles of us. In some cases that meant traveling more than sixty miles. Rhinotracheitis was diagnosed and the antibiotic Tylocine and Sulfa, 200mg, and URD, an upper respiratory decongestant, were prescribed. In addition, the need to get food into the cats to sustain them was stressed as vital.

Recognizing that we were going to have a problem getting them to eat on their own, several veterinarians recommended forced feeding. This meant putting a tube down the cat's throat into its stomach and forcing a solution of baby food into the stomach by use of a large syringe.

If the experience was distasteful to us, it was no less unpleasant for most of the animals. We first had to wrap the cat in a towel so it couldn't rip us apart with its claws, and then one person would hold it while another person inserted the tube and injected the food. Some of the cats accepted the procedure stoically, but the majority fought it with vengeance.

On a couple of our first attempts, a relaxed grip on the cat's muzzle resulted in the mouth closing and the subsequent severing of the rubber tube. Let me assure you, it was a terrifying experience to find yourself staring at the end of an apparatus that suddenly is missing a foot or more of rubber hose of which only a small portion was sticking out of the cat's mouth.

Fortunately, on both occasions that this happened, the missing tubing was retrieved without any untoward effects, and a call to one of the nearby veterinary clinics produced a novel solution, a wooden yoke that fit in between a cat's jaws. A small hole in the center of the yoke permitted the stomach tube to be inserted and the problem of severed tubes was eliminated.

Despite our best efforts, the disease spread until every cat being boarded was sick. With sixty sick cats, it became logistically impossible to continue to take each one to its own veterinarian for treatment. Instead, we called upon one of the local veterinarians to come into the pet motel and direct the treatment process. There was really nothing he could do other than to furnish us with the medicine and advise us to continue with the treatment we were already administering.

It was an exasperating period. Each day, we would begin the treatment early in the morning and not finish until late that night. Within only a few days we began to see some improvement. Some of the cats began eating on their own and the visible symptoms slowly began disappearing.

When the owners began returning from their vacations and were advised about the illness, only a few were upset, but as might be expected, all were anxious to take their cats home with them right away. Rather than incur the risk of inadequate home treatment, we tried to persuade them to leave their cats with us until they were completely well. We were well aware of how difficult it was to give a cat its pills and also how important it was to monitor how much the cat was eating and drinking. The majority of cat owners agreed but some insisted on taking their cats home to have their own veterinarians treat them. In a few cases this was a terrible mistake, but we were powerless to prevent it.

Cage boarding of cats is an important source of profit for many veterinary clinics and in some clinics, sick cats are kept in the same room as the healthy boarded cats. Because rhinotracheitis was such a virulent disease, some of the veterinarians refused to hospitalize their clients' cats for fear of spreading the disease to their patients and boarders. Instead, they gave out bottles of pills and sent the cats home. For some, it was a useless gesture. Pilling a sick cat required a skill few owners could master. The end result was the needless deaths of several of these cats.

Of the cats that remained with us for treatment, every single one recovered.

We concluded that the virus must have been introduced into the motel by one of our feline guests. There was no way we could have prevented the epidemic. Regardless, we paid everyone's veterinary bills plus an additional $250 to owners whose cats did not survive. This was in accord with our Pet-I-Care Warranty. What hurt me the most was the evidence that if all the cats had been left with us for care, they all probably would have survived.

It was a traumatic experience, both emotionally and financially. No cat-boarding facility in the country had as many safeguards as we did, and still we were vulnerable. It was hard for us to rebut a suggestion that we discontinue boarding felines but we remained adamant. All-pet boarding was a concept that we refused to give up on.

The problem was resolved within weeks of the incident when Pitman Moore Laboratories announced a new vaccine effective against rhinotracheitis. For the boarding industry, the introduction of this vaccine was a milestone in feline health care. For us it offered salvation. Henceforth, along with rabies and distemper vaccinations, all boarding cats would be required to have the rhinotracheitis vaccination.

As an additional safeguard, we required that all vaccinations must be given at least ten days prior to boarding because pets vaccinated with live-virus vaccines may actually shed the virus and infect other animals of the same species. We would not take any unnecessary risks. Because this policy was strictly enforced, we occasionally lost the business of a cat owner who preferred to board his cat elsewhere rather than bother with vaccinations. For a long time most of the boarding facilities that did not require the vaccination were operated by veterinarians. Today, almost every cat is vaccinated for rhinotracheitis when it receives its other vaccinations.

Prologue Chapter 16

RAGS

Edmund Vance Cooke

We called him "Rags". He was just a cur,
But twice, on the Western Line,
That little old bunch of faithful fur
Had offered his life for mine.
And all that he got was bones and bread,
Or the leavings of soldier-grub,
But he'd give his heart for a pat on the head,
Or a friendly tickle and rub.

And Rags got home with the regiment,
And then, in the breaking away –
Well, whether they stole him, or whether he went,
I am not prepared to say.
But we mustered out, some to beer and gruel,
And some to sherry and shad,
And I went back to the Sawbones School,
Where I still was an undergrad.

One day they took us budding M.D.'s
To one of those institutes
Where they demonstrate every new disease
By means of bisected brutes.
They had one animal tacked and tied
And slit like a full-dressed fish,
With his vitals pumping away inside .
As pleasant as one might wish.

I stopped to look like the rest, of course,
And the beast's eyes leveled mine
His short tail thumped with a feeble force,
And he uttered a tender whine.
It was Rags, yes, Rags! Who was martyred there,
Who was quartered and crucified,
And he whined that whine which is doggish prayer
And he licked my hand — and died.

And I was no better in part nor whole
Then the gang I was found among,
And his innocent blood was on the soul
Which he blessed with his dying tongue.
Well! I've seen men go to courageous death
In the air, on sea, on land!
But only a dog would spend his last breath
In a kiss for his murderer's hand.

And if there's no Heaven for love like that
For such four-legged fealty-- well!
If I have any choice, I tell you flat,
I'll take my chance in Hell.

16

DOGGED BY VETERINARY INTRANSIGENCE

With all the faults and deceptive practices prevalent among boarding kennels, we reasoned that the veterinary community would welcome us and support the concept of good, professional pet boarding.

That was a naïve assumption. The shocking conditions I found in some veterinary boarding facilities (in some cases even worse than those of kennels, since healthy animals were being boarded among sick animals with contagious diseases) should have forewarned me that there would be some veterinarians who would not welcome our kind of competition.

Time would prove that this group would never support our objectives or us. Indeed, they would devote a disproportionate share of their time and ability to opposing any effort to improve the quality of pet care in their area, using the various veterinary associations to do so.

Fortunately, there were many other veterinarians who welcomed our arrival. Some were skeptical at first because we promised so much, but after a short time, we began receiving the referrals we had been seeking. The real bonus was in the friendships and relationships we established.

The majority of veterinarians, though, parochial in their interests, hardly noticed the arrival in their midst of a revolutionary concept for boarding pets.

From the very beginning, however, the uniqueness of our concept became a media fascination. Not only in America, but also in Europe and Asia, our pet-care program was written about in the leading newspapers and magazines and talked about on radio and television.

With our national exposure, the face of the boarding industry began to change. It was more than just a facelift; it was a major overhaul. Many kennel operators finally began to realize that the boarding of an animal extended beyond just storing the pet until its owner returned. They began dressing up their facilities, installing music, heat, and air conditioning. They started keeping health records and began accepting responsibility for the pets boarded. It seemed as if half the kennels in America became pet motels or pet spas overnight. Unfortunately, in many cases, nothing changed except the name.

Once again things had settled down to a routine when, in April 1979, we received a telephone call from Dr. Robert Mahr, a veterinarian who operated several kennels northwest of Chicago. Although we were competitors in the boarding business, when questions or problems arose, neither of us was reluctant to solicit the advice of the other.

On this occasion, Dr. Mahr offered some information that sent a cold chill through me.

A new and mysterious virus had broken out among dogs in Illinois. A dog that was in apparent excellent health one minute could be dead in a matter of a few hours and no one knew the cause or how to treat the dog. To make matters worse, no one was even sure how the disease was being spread, though veterinarians suspected it was a virus spread in canine fecal matter.

In addition, the disease was extremely contagious, and once it broke out in a community, it spread rapidly among the dog population. Not only had several local kennels already closed down due to the outbreak, but even one of the local veterinary hospitals also had to close because dogs coming into the hospital for routine vaccinations were becoming infected.

The cost of an outbreak at the pet motel immediately ran through our minds. We were boarding more than 260 dogs every day and because of our Pet-I-Care warranty, we could be facing thousands of dollars in veterinary bills and more than $75,000 in death benefits. While an outbreak would surely bankrupt us I was thinking beyond that. It would mean the end of this great experiment.

We could imagine the newspaper stories and the public's reaction if we had an outbreak. All of the time, effort, and money we had invested to prove the merits of our concept would fade forever in the face of such a calamity. We knew that we could not afford to sit around and wait.

We began contacting other veterinarians and research laboratories to gather as much information about the virus as possible, hoping someone would know of a preventative measure. Unfortunately, most of the veterinarians were not even familiar with the disease, and some even challenged the validity of the report.

After days of frantically searching, we were finally able to obtain the information we needed from the James A. Baker Institute for Animal Health at Cornell University. Two of their researchers, Doctors Leland Carmichael and Roy V. H. Pollock, had been successful in isolating the virus. They were calling it parvovirus.

The virus caused lesions in a dog's intestines identical to those found in a cat's intestines from the feline distemper virus. With that clue, the viruses were compared and found to be serologically identical. This was the breakthrough the researchers needed.

The reasoning was this: If the feline distemper virus was identical to the virus that was causing parvovirus in dogs, it was conceivable that the feline distemper vaccine, given to dogs, could prevent parvovirus.

The theory was tested at the Baker Institute by giving a limited population of dogs two doses of killed virus feline distemper vaccine several days apart and then exposing the dogs to the parvovirus. Another group of dogs were not given the vaccine but were also exposed to the same batch of the parvovirus.

Every unvaccinated dog became ill, but not one of the vaccinated dogs contracted the disease or became ill from the vaccine. The researchers felt certain they had at least a short-term solution.

Still, there were a lot of questions to answer about the virus before anyone could feel safe. Other viruses usually died in a matter of minutes when shed from their host. Not the canine parvovirus. This one was a new and frighteningly different virus. It defied temperature extremes, surviving for months, and maybe even years away from its host, in freezing temperatures as well as in torrid heat. Not one of the known bactericidals or virucidals used for cleaning in animal facilities was found to kill the virus. Oddly enough, the one cleaning agent that did prove lethal was common household bleach. The formula was one part bleach to thirty parts water making it the least expensive sanitizing agent available. We were extremely fortunate that our automatic metering devices could be used to feed this bleach solution into our high-pressure sanitizing system. We considered the cost insignificant when compared to what might result from an outbreak of the disease.

Theories on how this new virus might have developed began to proliferate. The most fascinating one was that some researcher, while cultivating a feline distemper vaccine, used a dog's blood instead of a cat's, and through a quirk of fate, the new mutant virus was formed. Fortunately, the virus affected only dogs and was harmless to cats, other animals, and humans.

The solution for combating this threatening disease seemed easy and logical, but there is nothing simple and logical about the human mind and its propensity for creating problems. The Food and Drug Administration approved feline distemper vaccine only for use on cats. Even though millions of doses had been administered to cats, it had never been clinically tested on dogs. The limited testing by the Baker Institute for Animal Health was not adequate to accurately predict any long-term results. Only time could do this and we didn't think we had the time.

In less than six months from the day it was discovered, outbreaks of parvovirus had spread all over the world. Reports of outbreaks came in from England, Europe, Australia, and from every one of the United States, including Alaska. Over the next few weeks, I received calls from kennel operators all over the country reporting massive outbreaks of canine parvovirus, with horrible loss of animal life. One facility lost over 100 dogs, while another one reported eighty-five dead. The stories kept coming in from every region of the country. No place was safe. Researchers began referring to the disease as the Legionnaire's Disease of dogs.

Dr. Mahr and I continued exchanging information, and after due consideration decided we would both require every dog coming in for boarding to be vaccinated with two injections of killed feline distemper vaccine given ten days apart. If the owners refused, we would not board their dogs. We advised other kennel owners of our decision, but only a few were willing to go along with us. The others felt they would wait until they experienced an outbreak before taking action. Unfortunately, the boarding kennel trade association advised their members that the problem was not serious enough to worry about.

The task of persuading our customers that they should have their dogs vaccinated with a vaccine approved only for cats was not going to be easy. We decided the best way to do it was to print a pamphlet and mail it to every dog owner.

To eliminate any conflict with the local veterinary association, I employed Dr. David Epstein, a local veterinarian, to contact the Baker Institute and obtain all the necessary information from doctors Carmichael and Pollack, the two veterinarians responsible for most of the parvovirus research. Dr. Epstein had good credentials, and in addition to operating his own veterinary hospital, had a weekly radio program that dealt with animal health matters.

Over 15,000 pamphlets, titled "*A Killer Is Stalking Your Dog*", were printed and mailed to our clients. In addition, a copy with a cover letter was sent to every veterinarian in the greater Chicago area.

Although some of the veterinarians discarded the literature without reading it, many more began calling and requesting additional information. Customers asked for additional copies to mail to relatives who owned dogs in other states. Pet shops and kennels from all over the country requested, and were granted, permission to reproduce the brochure. There is no way of telling how many dog owners read this pamphlet, but we received mail from as far away as Thailand. This particular letter, written in broken English, thanked us for helping them stem the outbreak in Thailand.

As news of increased outbreaks was received, we decided to send a copy of our pamphlet together with a press release to the major wire services. Public awareness of the disease was still lacking and neither the newspapers nor public broadcasting services had issued any warnings.

All three major wire services indicated interest in the story. If true, it was a spectacular news item, a mutant killer virus that appeared mysteriously and could result in the death of a dog in less than twenty-four hours. Naturally, its authenticity had to be verified before the story could be released. Regrettably, the news media did not check with the Baker Institute. Instead they called the Chicago Veterinary Medical Association.

Despite all of the evidence at their disposal, the Chicago Veterinary Medical Association assured the news services that there was no imminent threat, and that parvovirus was just a minor inconvenience that would soon pass.

Only one Chicago newspaper mentioned the disease.

Under the heading, "Scare Tactic or Epidemic?" the *Chicago Sun Times* printed the responses of several veterinarians to our pamphlet.

The president of the CVMA ridiculed our assertions and was quoted as saying that "No one will stand by the vaccine." This same veterinarian went on to state that he was, however, administering the feline distemper vaccine to valuable show dogs! Another veterinarian who operated a large boarding kennel in Des Plaines, Illinois, also advised the public against using the feline distemper vaccine, although he conceded to the reporter that he was vaccinating every dog that boarded at his kennel!

The reaction of our adversaries in the Chicago Veterinary Medical Association was to urge their fellow members to begin a boycott of American Pet Motels.

A boycott wasn't enough for some of the members and they embarked on an organized letter-writing campaign. State veterinary associations, national veterinary associations, the Department of Agriculture, and various national veterinary journals all received letters protesting the distribution of our pamphlet. If these other organizations thought we were out of line, not one contacted us to say so. We did hear from some of them, but not for the purpose our antagonists intended.

DVM, The Newsletter of Veterinary Medicine, conducted a telephone interview with the CVMA and with us. In the July 1979 edition of the magazine, they published a very fair and unbiased review of the interviews. Again the CVMA again went on record stating that American Pet Motels was using scare tactics and trying to tell veterinarians what vaccines to use. "We think the danger is being overemphasized," the Association's spokesman proclaimed.

Ironically, on the front page of this very same publication, the main headline stated in bold black print, **"Canine Parvovirus Diagnosed in All 50 States; Linked to FPL."**

An article in *TIME* magazine reported an estimated 1,500 dogs dead of parvovirus in the Minneapolis-St. Paul area alone;

124 deaths in south Florida; 1,000 deaths in Corpus Christi. In Seattle, Washington, an epidemic forced the city to close its animal shelter. Serological studies in New York and Washington showed 25 percent of household dogs tested had evidence of previous infection. In Washington, D.C., New Jersey, and Georgia, the figure was 50 percent. If the Chicago Veterinary Medical Association was correct, American Pet Motels and the rest of the world was wrong.

The veterinarian who wrote us from Thailand reported that almost 100 dogs had died with symptoms of parvovirus. Due to our pamphlet, veterinarians began a general inoculation of the dog population with feline distemper vaccine and the outbreak was immediately brought under control.

More and more major newspapers, including the *WALL STREET JOURNAL*, printed daily reports of growing outbreaks and deaths from parvovirus, but still the Chicago Veterinary Medical Association assured Chicago's dog owners and its own members that the virus was nothing to be concerned about.

The disease did not bypass Chicago and its suburbs. Almost four hundred beagles at the Argonne National Laboratory, on the outskirts of Chicago, became infected. The mortality rate was never made public. Willy Neckers, a kennel that had operated since World War I, had to close due to an outbreak. It never re-opened. From Hinsdale to the shores of Lake Michigan, outbreaks of parvovirus were reported. Dogs living in high-rises along Chicago's swank million—dollar mile were not spared, although some had never been out of their apartments. Unfortunately, the disease also struck the Society for the Prevention of Cruelty to Animals, in the heart of Chicago, and resulted in an unspecified number of deaths and the closing of the shelter.

One veterinarian member of the letter-writing campaign who operated a veterinary hospital and kennel in Glencoe, felt so strongly about the issue that he took the time to write and assure us that we would not have to be concerned with parvovirus if we kept our kennel clean. Obviously this was another professional who had never visited our kennels or read the newspaper reports. The Argonne National Laboratory was anything but a pigsty and they had four hundred cases of parvovirus.

While responsible veterinarians all over the country were advising their clients to have their dogs vaccinated with the killed virus feline distemper vaccine, in Illinois, many dog owners were told that the vaccine was worthless and in some cases, that it could kill their dog.

At the height of the problem, spokesmen for the CVMA distorted the statements of the Baker Research Institute to convince their membership that the vaccine was ineffective and possibly dangerous. Their persuasive argument was that ". . . even Dr. Carmichael, the head researcher at the Baker Institute, would not recommend the use of feline distemper vaccine for dogs. . ."

It was a cleverly contrived distortion of the facts.

What Dr. Carmichael said was that ". . . as a research scientist, it would be a violation of federal law to recommend, across state lines, the use of a drug for dogs that the FDA had approved only for cats."

They did not report that he also said, "Experiments in our laboratory have shown, however, that two doses of commercial inactivated Feline Panleukopenia vaccine given two weeks apart, provided protection against the canine parvovirus." There was another statement Dr. Carmichael made that was not included. *"My own dogs have been vaccinated with it and all of my friends' dogs have been vaccinated with it."*

More and more we felt this was a disagreement that needed to be resolved without any delay. Failure to recognize the truth, and to warn every dog owner, would result in the needless deaths of thousands of dogs in Illinois. We felt the continuing argument over whether there was a serious threat could be, and should be, resolved without any further bantering.

In a sincere effort to resolve our difference of opinion, we telephoned the CVMA and suggested that they conduct a survey of the area's veterinarians to find out how many dogs with symptoms of parvovirus they were treating each month. We were told that such a survey would be much too expensive to conduct.

We then made an offer in genuine good faith. We offered to pay for the printing, mailing, and tabulation of the survey, and let the CVMA could have total control of the survey and its results. We even agreed never to acknowledge that our company paid for the survey.

"It would still be too expensive." we were abruptly told. "We just can't do it!" The discussion was ended. The parochial mind could never admit that it might have made a mistake. It didn't matter that one hundred or one thousand dogs would die due to their position. They didn't want to be deceived by the facts. They could not tolerate a layman giving advice. What mattered was that a few "professional" men in a "professional" association be correct regardless of the facts.

The CVMA boycott of American Pet Motels did hurt our business, but the real damage was the needless suffering and widespread loss of animal life among the dog population in Illinois. Our requirement of feline distemper vaccinations, the use of bleach in our sanitizing system, and the prompt treatment of any suspicious symptoms permitted us to get through the epidemic with just a single incident, and fortunately, it had a happy conclusion.

Several days after she had picked up her dog, the owner of Oliver, an often boarded, Old English sheepdog, telephoned and reported that Oliver was in a hospital with parvovirus.

I knew Oliver well. He was one of those huge, shaggy bundles of energy that constantly demonstrated an adolescent disdain for obedience and an insatiable appetite for love and affection.

Now, he lay on a table with IV needles stuck in his veins, disgorging huge quantities of blood. There was no doubt about the symptoms and less doubt about the eventual outcome.

Although the disease may have been contracted after the dog left our motel, I still told the owner that we would cover all her veterinary treatment up to our $250 limit.

Several days later, Oliver's owner called to tell me that Oliver was still ill, but that the bill was now more than $300 and she could not afford to continue treatment. She was going to let the veterinarian euthanize Oliver.

One of the benefits of being the president of a company is the power to over-ride a policy. It is a virtue for those rare occasions when the book says one thing and your heart tells you something else.

I could not let Oliver's life be terminated as long as there was the slightest chance he could recover. I told the woman not to do it. We would pick up the charges.

Oliver remained in a comatose condition for several more weeks, receiving huge quantities of intravenous fluids and being pumped full of antibiotics. Still, he clung to life with a tenacious grip.

Finally, his veterinarian called us. Oliver was on his way back. In a few days he would be going home.

We paid the entire bill. Bad business judgment, perhaps, but it was the right decision for me. I have learned to argue the justification of such actions by insisting that the welfare of the pet must at least equal any other priority of our business!

Prologue Chapter 17

THE DOG THAT WENT TO CHURCH

Hilda Van Stockum

Outside the church the dogs were waiting.
    Outside the magic door they knew
They could not enter. They were waiting
    For their masters to come through.

They discussed among each other
    How it was that only here
In this place, their owners left them,
    Would not tolerate them near.

Suddenly their chatter halted
    As with popping eyes they saw
How a great big grey police dog
    Calmly walked in as though HE was called.

"He'll be kicked out," they predicted.
    "Watch and see him howl with pain."
But though eagerly they waited,
    They didn't see the dog again.

He was sitting near the altar
    With a dignity unmatched,
While his little master, kneeling,
    Received Communion as he watched.

Then the dog with gentle movements
      Led the child back to his seat,
And later, when the Mass was over
      Out again into the street.

The other dogs there watched in silence,
      Moved aside to let them pass.
They understood. To aid the sightless,
      Even dogs may go to Mass.

17

GROOMING FOR
HEALTH

After telling people how we lost our ocelot, we began to
hear more and more stories of other people whose pets had been
injured or almost strangled by being snared by their collars. As a
result, we made it a fast and firm rule that no boarding animal
would be allowed to wear a collar, choker, or harness while staying with us.

The wisdom of this policy was demonstrated again when
I took in a year-old Eskimo spitz with long, bushy white hair. As
the owner removed the leather collar, from habit, I ran my fingers
over the neck area for a choker. I could only feel two ridges of
skin, but when I probed deeper, I found a tight leather choke
collar buried in the folds of the flesh.

The owner was surprised and embarrassed. This collar
had been placed on the dog when it was still a puppy and had
been completely forgotten. Now, as the dog approached full size,
the collar was almost completely hidden within the fleshy folds of
its neck. We were able to remove it by cutting it with a special
pair of clippers we kept available for just such occasions, as this
was not the first time something like this occurred.

Before entering this business, we were as ignorant about
the subject of dog grooming as the majority of dog owners still

are. We had always presumed grooming was something that was done more for the satisfaction of the owner than for the health of the dog. For show dogs, it was a process of cutting and brushing the hair into weird and grotesque styles.

But dog and cat grooming is far more than a cosmetic exercise, and in some cases it turns out to be a matter of life or death. Proper bathing and grooming of certain breeds involves much more than most pet owners realize. In fact, the lack of grooming can sometimes mean a life of pain and torment for a dog or cat, and I suspect more than one poor pet has been put to sleep because the owners thought it was vicious when in fact it was merely a victim of its owners benign neglect.

Over the years our groomers removed fish hooks, needles, pieces of barbed wire, and a host of other foreign objects that they found embedded in the bodies of the dogs they were grooming. Infections, tumors, growths, and numerous skin problems, not even suspected by the owners, were found frequently during the grooming process. Few owners really give their pets' bodies the thorough going- over that a qualified groomer will. Most often, the owners' inspections are limited to pats on the head or a few strokes on the back.

On one occasion, a groomer found a metal choke collar embedded underneath the skin of a dog's neck. The choker had been placed on the dog while it was a puppy. As the dog grew, the chain cut into the dog's neck and its flesh actually grew around it. This case required veterinary surgery.

Almost weekly we found dewclaws that had grown completely around and into the fleshy part of a dog's feet. A dog that runs on concrete will wear its nails down. But today, most dogs are raised in a carpeted house, and their nails will continue to grow until someone cuts them or they finally curve around and grow into the flesh. I have seen dogs whose legs were actually misshapen because the length of their toenails interfered with their gait. When their nails reach such proportions it is virtually impossible for a groomer to clip them. The dog must be taken to a veterinarian and anesthetized in order to surgically remove the ingrown nails.

Shorthaired dogs may need only an occasional bath and brushing, but longhaired dogs require frequent brushings. Dogs shed their hair and grow a new coat each season. I've heard owners threaten to have their dogs put to sleep because their hair was getting all over the carpets and furniture. The truth of the matter is that some of the fault lay with the owners. If they would take the proper type of brush and comb and use it frequently, they and their pets would be a lot happier and healthier. There are some dogs whose nature seems to just manufacture loose hair. Pet owners should know the particular traits of a breed before they buy it, not after. In this case, the easiest resolution is to resign yourself to a hair-raising experience.

There were a number of times a dog would be brought into the pet motel with such a fetid odor that you wondered how the owner tolerated it in the home. The worst cases were those in which the dog could barely move because its hair was knotted together in one massive tangle. Even the eyes are sometimes stuck closed due to the accumulation of dirt and discharge around them. Every grooming parlor in the country has experienced cases so bad that they had to refer the owners to a veterinary clinic where the pets could be shaved while anesthetized.

All too often, the removal of this matted hair will reveal large sections of raw flesh, the result of air being unable to dry the skin, which actually rots away. Except for the odor, the owners are usually unaware of the real problem because they never groom the pet or have it groomed by a professional dog groomer.

The wisdom of grooming was never more emphatically impressed on me than by an incident that occurred in our own pet motel.

The lesson for one family began when they brought in two Lhasa Apsos for boarding. Jason was neatly brushed, with the hair over his eyes tied out of the way by a small child's plastic barrette. The other dog, Molly, was a basket case. Her hair was long and badly matted, and the odor that emanated from her was noticeable from across the room. The owners were quite conscious of Molly's condition and kept apologizing that there was nothing they could do because she had such a terrible disposition. They could not hold her or even touch her without her snapping at them. The dog not only bit strangers but also had bit them on several occasions. Because of her behavior the family had been afraid to have her groomed for fear she would bite the groomer. As they stood in our lobby, the owners debated the wisdom of putting the dog to sleep.

I shuddered when I heard the receptionist automatically ask the owners if they would like to have both dogs bathed and groomed and the owners agreed. Knowing the attitude of our groomers, developed over several years of being snapped at and bitten, I doubted if any one of them would touch Molly.

The dogs were boarding together in an Imperial Suite, which I passed several times each day. One of my pleasures was to visit each room and spend a little time playing with the occupants. Heartbreak was when a dog wouldn't let me. Molly was one such dog.

She and Jason would be lying on the bed together, and when I approached, Jason would jump up and squeal with excitement. He loved to have me brush him and he'd climb into my lap and run his tongue all over my face in an enthusiastic display of affection.

Molly was not so inclined. She would crouch in a far corner of the bed and growl continuously. The slightest move toward her resulted in her snapping and trying to bite me.

Usually we bathed and groomed dogs on the day they were going home so they were clean and neat for the occasion. If a dog was badly matted, the groomer would spread the dematting and grooming over several days so the dog was not put under too much stress or pain. Perhaps because she felt she would have a lot of trouble with Molly, Karen, the manager of our grooming shop, decided to shave her soon after she arrived.

Knowing Karen's reluctance to even handle problem

dogs, I can only presume that it was another act of divine providence that she even attempted the feat. In the several years that Karen had been grooming, she had never been bitten, a claim few groomers can make. Of course, as manager, she could choose which dogs she would groom, but the minute a dog proved uncooperative, she simply put it back in its room and refused any further attempt to groom it. More than one recalcitrant dog went home only partially groomed. Although our receptionist had meant well, I was confident that none of our groomers, least of all Karen, would groom Molly.

Then, one morning when I was ringing in the previous day's grooming charges, I was surprised to find a charge for Molly. I couldn't believe it. I opened the sliding glass door to the grooming parlor and asked Karen if she had the correct dog's name on the charge slip. She laughed as she nodded. She knew exactly what I meant.

Apparently, with the help of another groomer and a leather muzzle, Karen had managed to shave the dog and remove the matted entanglements. I found it hard to believe her when she told me that once she had Molly half shaved, the dog had ceased its struggling and biting, and had actually let Karen finish her with only minor objections.

After work that day, I went to Molly's room and looked in. There was Jason; just as presentable as the day he came in. Next to him lay Molly, looking like a plucked chicken. Bright pink blotches and small sores, caused by her previous condition, covered her skin. A coating of skin lotion reflected the light.

As soon as I entered the room, Jason jumped off the bed and began begging me to pick him up. I had just knelt down so he could climb into my lap when Molly jumped off the bed and also came to me. I reached down cautiously and began patting her head. Her long naked tail, with a little pompom at the end, began swinging back and forth wildly, and her little legs began pawing at the air in an attempt to climb into my lap. I helped her up, and the two dogs reached for my face with their pink tongues darting in and out of their mouths. Apprehension gave way to laughter, as the three of us rejoiced like old friends.

Molly was not a vicious dog. She was merely a victim of benign neglect. Probably at some time she had been permitted to get dirty and, as her hair became matted, her movements became painful. Each time she moved or someone picked her up, it was like someone pulling her hair. In pain, the dog responded in the only way she knew how. She tried to protect herself by biting. The longer the condition continued, the more dirt and discharge her hair collected, until finally, the hair in front of her eyes no longer reflected the light necessary for her to distinguish friend from foe. All she saw was shadows and each shadow was a threat of pain.

The matting problem is not unique only to dogs. Longhaired cats, such as Persians and Himalayans, also require frequent brushing, or they can suffer the same painful experiences.

For those who think grooming is unpleasant for the dogs and cats, I wish you had been in the lobby when Fred Chase, a large standard poodle, was brought in for his six-week grooming. His owner had only to drop his leash and Fred would bound into the grooming parlor and jump on Karen's table. If he found all the tables occupied, he would gallop into the bathing room and jump into one of the unoccupied bathtubs. This dog enjoyed grooming so much that he had memorized the entire grooming procedure. He would even hold up his paws in their accustomed sequence without being told. The standing joke at the pet motel was the owner's insistence that Fred had a crush on Karen.

While many health problems can be avoided by regular grooming, I can think of at least one time when it created a health hazard—for an owner, not for the dog.

A neatly dressed man entered the pet motel one Saturday morning and asked to have his dog completely shaved. He wanted every hair stripped from the dog's body. The dog was a beautiful, black standard poodle with a long, handsome coat meticulously trimmed in a show cut.

When I heard the man request the dog stripped, I was

certain he was making a mistake and questioned him. "No," the man assured us. He knew exactly what the term implied, and he wanted the dog shaved completely bare.

I still thought it was a bad decision and suggested that maybe it would be better just to trim the dog or maybe put it into a puppy cut so it would still have some hair covering its body.

The man was adamant. He wanted the dog shaved as smooth as a billiard ball.

I sensed something was wrong, but you soon learn that when dealing with pet owners, nothing is bizarre. I watched Karen lead the dog into the grooming parlor and instruct one of the groomers to strip it.

Just before noon, a very smartly dressed lady called for the dog. She was wearing an expensively tailored suit, and her fingers sported several large diamond rings.

As Karen led the dog from the grooming parlor, the lady quietly remarked, "You've got the wrong dog. That's not my dog."

We assured her it was.

Her face turned ashen. "Oh, my God!" she shrieked. "What have you done? That's a champion show dog. How could you? I'm supposed to fly her to New York in two hours for the International Dog Show. How could you? How could you?"

Karen and I looked at each other and then at the dog. It really looked like an oversized plucked goose. I would have given her a written guarantee her dog certainly wasn't going to win any prizes with that haircut. I didn't think they would have even allowed the dog on the beach looking the way it did.

I pulled the grooming card and read her the exact instructions her husband had given us. I had written down every word, fearing that some problem might arise.

When I finished, the lady just stood there. Then, quietly, she apologized for her outburst and explained the strange situation. She was heavily involved in showing her prized dog all over the country and as her traveling increased, so did her husband's objections. When this particular dog show came up, his resentment precipitated an intense disagreement between the two.

That fateful morning, she made the mistake of asking her husband to take the dog to our grooming parlor to be bathed and brushed out. When he stalked out of the house, she never dreamed what he had in mind to resolve the problem. It would be many months before she would need to travel again.

Another kennel problem, more common in the South, is that of fleas.

In our Florida pet motel I saw the water in bathing tubs turn red with blood from dogs whose skins had been perforated by hundreds of fleas. So completely had they been infested that the groomer had to remove huge nests from the dog's ears and even from under the eyelids. In some cases, the dogs had been bled to the extent that their gums were almost white, indicating a severe anemic condition. There are recorded cases of pets dying of anemia caused by fleas.

When we were interested in acquiring a small kennel in Florida, everyone told us that flea infestation was a fact of life. Some boarding facilities even required every boarding pet to first be dipped in a bath of chemical flea killer. Even so, there was no guarantee that your pet still wouldn't go home with fleas. Kennel owners in the South are not joking when they state that animals receiving flea and tick baths are guaranteed to be free of fleas and ticks only up to their front door. All guarantees end there.

Not knowing any better, we refused to accept that this was how it had to be. We felt that checking pets when they came in and bathing those with fleas and ticks, daily sterilization of the animal quarters with a high-pressure sanitizing system, and regular treatment of the grounds and facilities would make it possible to guarantee that every pet would leave our facility without any fleas or ticks. We gave that guarantee in Chicago and we became the only pet boarding facility in the South to offer that same guarantee.

When we took over the Sarasota facility we had no idea of what we were getting into. When I turned on the lights the first morning I was paralyzed at the sight. Every wall was alive with cockroaches, palmetto bugs and a variety of ants. Carpets in the dog runs were shredded and turned upside down. Water bowls fared no better. It looked like a hurricane had gone through the place. Apparently, when the lights were turned out on the preceding evening, all these bugs started coming out and the dogs had been almost driven crazy in trying to dispatch them.

In surveying the kennels and storage rooms it was apparent that every hole and every piece of hollow tubing used in our gates and dividers was a breeding area for these pests.

Still convinced that we could have a vermin-free facility, we embarked on an ambitious program. First, expanding foam was introduced into every gate and fence post, leaving no room for the insects. Every wall hole and open mortar joint was filled in with a concrete patch. Twice a day the walls, floors, and outside runs were liberally sprayed with a solution lethal to these insects but harmless to animals. Only one area presented a problem; the ceiling. It was Peggy that came up with the solution. As a gourmet cook she had read hundreds of homemaker magazines and in one of them was a recipe for sure-fire roach killer cookies. As we recall, the ingredients called for a batter of oatmeal cookies to which was added a healthy portion of baking soda. Whatever it was, the results surpassed our expectations. When we reopened, we reopened as a bug- free facility.

Prologue Chapter 19

HE'S JUST A DOG

Joseph M. Anderson

Here is a friend who proves his worth
Without conceit or pride of birth;
Let want or plenty play the host,
He gets the least and gives the most —
He's just a dog.

He's ever faithful, kind and true,
He never questions what I do;
And whether I may go or stay,
He's always ready to obey —
'Cause he's a dog.

He watches me all through the day,
And nothing coaxes him away,
And through that night-long slumber deep,
He guards the home wherein I sleep —
And he's a dog.

As mortals go, how few possess
Of courage, trust and faithfulness,
Enough for which to undertake,
Without some borrowed traits, to make
A decent dog!

18

THE GERIATRIC
TRADE

A surprising part of our growth came from an unexpected source–old and ill dogs and cats. The illnesses were not contagious diseases, but were associated with advanced aging.

Along with this business came additional responsibilities. Our canine and feline senior citizens were the most likely to suffer kidney failure due to stress. Once uremic poisoning began in their system, it was virtually irreversible.

Because of our reputation, more and more veterinarians began referring these clients to us. Blind animals, deaf animals, cardiac cases, epileptics, and diabetics began coming to us with increasing regularity. Most veterinarians referred them because they knew we would furnish the extra care required and they could use their own space for hospital cases. Others had a different motive.

Admittedly, some of the animals should never have been admitted, but the seriousness of some problems was not apparent to us. We were so accustomed to seeing owners coddling their pets that we did not think it unusual when they insisted on carrying their dogs to their rooms. Only after the pet owners left would we realize that their dogs could not walk or even stand up.

Each day, these dogs had to be lifted into a bathtub and

bathed because they could not control their body functions and soiled themselves continuously. Others had to be hand- fed or required frequent veterinary attention. In one case, an old St. Bernard was actually restored to life by our Kennel Director's application of mouth-to-nose resuscitation.

All of our "senior citizens" received a disproportionate share of the staff's attention, but sick and injured pets also added new emotional demands on all of us that were unfair. More than once I found an attendant sitting with one of them, crying, because of the animal's plight. These pets belonged in a hospital, not in a boarding facility.

To resolve the problem, we finally initiated a new policy: All dogs had to be able to walk to their rooms.

You would have been surprised at the ingenious ploys some owners devised to get their dogs past the reception desk. Some openly exhorted their dogs to make a valiant effort to walk the distance. One of the saddest scenes was watching an owner urging on his dysplastic German shepherd. The poor animal would pull itself up and with the first step, as his hips gave way to the weight of his body, he would again collapse on the floor.

Because so many of these older guests required special care and unanticipated veterinary attention, we were constantly being pressured not to accept older pets. Once again I refused to give in. Again, the reason was strictly personal. I knew the kind of care these pets would receive in some boarding facilities and I knew the kind of care they would receive from us. I always felt they had a better chance of surviving with us and they deserved at least this.

Unfortunately, this policy was sometimes unrewarding. In one case a diabetic dog had to receive insulin injections every evening at eight o'clock. When injections were required, we permitted only the Director of Animal Welfare, Marc, or me to administer them. In this particular case, I was the one administering the insulin.

Everything went well until the day the owner picked up

her dog. For some reason the dog did not eat all its food that morning and the owner was so advised because the effect of insulin often depends on the type and quantity of food the animal eats.

The next day, the owner telephoned and told me that her dog was in the hospital and might not survive. She was irate because her veterinarian had told her that his test indicated the dog had not received its scheduled insulin injection the previous evening. Her veterinarian was wrong. I was sure the dog had received its insulin because I was the one who administered it.

For some reason this veterinarian neglected to tell the lady that there could have been a number of reasons for the dog's condition. The stress of seeing its owner, the body temperature, how much food it ate and the type of food, were all factors that could have caused this condition. Even though we felt the dog went home in good condition, we paid the veterinarian's charges for treating the dog until it was stabilized again. Unfortunately, the owner remained displeased, certain that we had not administered the medication the dog required.

A common condition among elderly dogs is blindness. Most dogs develop cataracts in their advanced years, and while these can be removed in many cases, the cost of surgery prevents some owners from having the problem treated.

Surprisingly, blindness did not become the problem we anticipated. Apparently dogs adapt to the hardship by using other sensory organs to a higher degree. Given only a few minutes in their room, most blind dogs were able to find the way to their outside runs and to return at will. They found their water bowls and food without help and maneuvered on and off their beds without assistance. I never ceased to be amazed that I could leave a cookie anyplace in the room and the dog would be able to go to that spot and retrieve it. Instead of being a burden, most of these dogs were better boarders than their healthier counterparts because their appetites appeared to have improved. I do not recall a single instance when we had a problem getting a blind dog to eat our standard diet.

There were some remarkable occasions, but the one I remember best was the time a huge Great Dane was boarded together with a twenty-two-year-old blind and deaf miniature poodle.

It was literally impossible for the poodle to move without the Great Dane following it. The enormous Dane would hover over the poodle, permitting it to move freely until it approached some obstacle. Then, the Dane would intercede with its head and deflect the poodle in a safe direction.

When you entered the room and approached the poodle, the Dane would step forward, between you and the poodle, and stare directly into your eyes. There was a message there, "Don't hurt my friend!" When you held the poodle's head to administer eye drops, the Dane would not interfere, but just stood there, as if poised to strike should you make one harmful gesture toward his friend. He would guide the poodle to its food and water, but never drink or eat himself until his friend had had its fill. I have witnessed hundreds of similar examples of unusual devotion by one animal to another. People hearing these stories tell similar stories of their own, yet still many people ask if I believe animals can think or reason. It makes me wonder if people can think or reason. If animals cannot think or reason, I defy anyone to explain the things we experienced at the pet motel.

Call your travel agent for reservations or take out a suitcase, and observe the change in your dog or cat. I've heard of cats hiding till their owners missed their planes. One veterinarian told me of a case where a German shepherd walked into its masters' bedroom where they were packing their suitcases for a trip. The dog took one look at the suitcases and leapt out the second-story window. It didn't help. The owners still went on their vacation while the dog recovered from a broken leg in the veterinarian's hospital. The veterinarian was quite serious when he told me he was sure the dog was attempting to commit suicide.

Most dogs and cats actually seem to enjoy the boarding experience. Some apparently do not. Some owners have told us that when their pets went home, they behaved in very strange ways. Some would totally ignore the owner, while others would hide under a couch or bed, making the owner feel guilty. I have heard of several instances where the pet went home and deliberately eliminated on its master's bed. I can only concede that pets have a variety of ways to convey their feelings.

One of the more humorous cases involved a small Jack Russell Terrier that was shipped to us from Japan. The dog boarded excellently while the owner got relocated in the Chicago area. When the owner finally came in to pick up the dog, we called for an animal attendant to bring it to the lobby. When coming down the corridor from the kennel, the dog saw its master; it immediately raised its left paw and limped to where the owner was standing.

The owner showered the dog with affection and concern, but none of us could find the cause of the limping. The attendant insisted the dog displayed no problem while walking to the lobby. In accord with our policy, I suggested the owner take the dog to a veterinarian to find out why the dog was limping, and, if there was any problem, to have it corrected and send us the bill.

X-rays and a thorough examination failed to reveal any problem, and the following day the dog was bounding all over his new home as if nothing had ever been wrong. It cost us almost sixty dollars in veterinary bills to learn that.

Within a few weeks we were called upon to board the little dog for another two weeks. When the owner called for the dog this time, his pet came down the corridor limping again, but holding his right foot in the air this time.

The owner took one look at the dog and publicly admonished him. "Scooter, you ol' faker. Put that paw down and behave yourself." Acting like a child caught with his hand in the proverbial cookie jar, the dog lowered his paw and looked around at all of us. Then, he followed his owner outside with his head bowed but his feet firmly touching the ground. This particular dog was one of many canine con artists who knew exactly how to extract the last measure of sympathy and attention from their masters.

Because of the growing number of pets that were being put on vitamins and questionable herbal treatments, we finally initiated a modest charge for the administration of any kind of medication. Most pet owners were happy to pay this fifty-cent charge in exchange for the knowledge their pet would receive the medication. The additional charge helped reduce the number of frivolous requests for unnecessary supplements. Unfortunately, there were a few instances where the pet owner did not tell us a pet was on a specific medication. Apparently the fifty-cent charge was more a consideration than their pet's health. In at least one case there was no doubt that it cost the pet's life. In other cases, symptoms developed that led us to contact the pet's veterinarian and the pet's life was saved. If the veterinarian felt it was important, we would have our driver pick up the medication, and we administered it for the balance of the pet's stay. Surprisingly, it was not uncommon for some of these pet owners to deny the veterinarian's advice and refuse to reimburse us for the medication or the service.

It is very important for pet owners to advise a kennel about any illnesses or problems their pets have incurred. If they don't, it is easy for the kennel to not notice certain symptoms until there is blood or some other obvious sign. A pet owner is wagering his pet's life against the few pennies it would cost to have the proper medications administered as prescribed.

Some owners would conceal an illness out of fear that we would not accept their pet. In the vast majority of cases, this did not happen. When it did, it was because the pet had a contagious illness or its condition was so poor that it belonged in a veterinary hospital.

Heart trouble, epilepsy, kidney stones, and dozens of other problems were sometimes left for us to find out about on our own, and this meant the loss of valuable time during which a needless examination was made to discover the problem. When the problem was finally established, additional time was lost in obtaining treatment from the owner's veterinarian. On a few occasions the wasted time proved critical for the pet.

Regardless of what we did or didn't do, some pet owners were always suspicious of wrongdoing. No matter what you told them, they preferred to believe something else.

I recall getting a telephone call from one such customer who complained that his dog barked incessantly. He demanded to know what he could do to silence him. The only thing I could recommend to the man was to have the dog obedience trained.

The man was not satisfied with that answer. He wanted to know what drugs or tranquilizers he could use. I assured him that drugs were not the answer. Besides being expensive and dangerous, they would only have a short-term effect. The dog would probably return to barking as soon as the drugs wore off.

"Well, what drugs do you use in your pet motel?" he finally asked. "You must get a lot of barkers in there."

"Very rarely," I replied. "The dogs do bark when it's feeding time or when we're taking dogs in or out of the kennel, but as a rule, even the worst barker will settle down after a short time."

Nothing I said seemed to satisfy the caller. Finally, I suggested he contact his veterinarian. There is one method, a surgical procedure that involves severing the vocal cords of the dog. I had never recommended this to any one. It is not a common procedure and I was reluctant to even bring it up to the man. I've not met more than one or two dogs that had been "debarked." It is only used when the dog's barking has become such a nuisance that the only other option was having the dog euthanized.

Finally, convinced that I held no magical solution, the man confessed the real reason for his questions. His dog had boarded with us and after it returned home, it merely lay around the house and didn't bark at anything. Prior to boarding, his dog barked incessantly. Now that he was home he was a completely different dog. Nothing seemed to bother him and he had stopped his obnoxious barking. The owner was sure we had some secret method that we had used.

I wish we did know the secret of how to stop certain dogs from constantly barking. We would have bottled it and made millions.

Another owner had a different way of presenting her complaint. She had been waiting in the lobby for her dog to be brought from the kennels. Every few minutes she would interrupt one of the receptionists, seeking to be reassured that her dog had been receiving its special food and medication. No matter how many times she was told that it had, she still seemed to harbor some doubts.

When the attendant finally arrived with her dog, the lady scooped the dog up in her arms and hurried from the building. A few minutes later I turned around and saw the lady hurrying toward me, holding the dog backward under her right arm.

Lifting its tail up with her left hand, she thrust the dog's backside into my face.

"Look!" she yelled at me. "Look at that!"

I stood there speechless, gazing into this dog's posterior, for what purpose I didn't know, while dozens of onlookers also looked on in bewilderment.

When I had sufficiently recovered, my first urge was to reply, "Yep, there's another one!" but diplomacy forbade such a response. Before I could think of something else to say, the lady withdrew the dog without another word and left the building. To this day I am not sure of what she was talking about, but I suspect it may have had something to do with an anal gland problem. However, to achieve an amicable resolution of any kind of complaint, I urge pet owners to approach the kennel owner face to face.

We were always aware that all pet owners worried about boarding their pets, but we failed to realize how some were almost paranoid. You can satisfy most, but you will never satisfy all. The surprising thing was that the ones who complained the most continued to come back over and over again, finding something to complain about each time.

They would moan about the hours, groan about the service, complain about the charges, but they kept coming back. Some customers were so unreasonable and unpleasant that our receptionists told us they would refuse to wait on them if they returned. I fully understood how they felt, but I had to remind them of what the alternatives were. We did not exist solely to serve the pet owner; our primary obligation was to the pet. Our employees had to understand that no pet would find as good care anywhere else, as they would at American Pet Motels. We were there for the pets, not for the owners. With rare exceptions, we would continue to board pets even though the owners were obnoxious.

A few owners had to learn the hard way. One was a mature lady who brought her Old English sheepdog in for boarding. This was before there was a vaccine for tracheobronchitis (kennel cough), a very common benign viral infection that causes dogs to cough and sound like they're almost strangling. As luck would have it, shortly after going home her dog showed all the symptoms. The lady called and claimed that the virus was due to our lack of proper care and insisted that we should refund all of her boarding and grooming charges in addition to paying her veterinary bill. In accord with our Warranty, we assured her that we would pay her veterinary charges but would not refund her grooming and boarding charges.

Unhappy with our offer, the lady contacted the Better Business Bureau, sent in a complaint to the Department of Agriculture, and wrote in to the consumer action column of the Chicago Tribune, claiming that we were "disreputable and irresponsible" and should be forced out of business. We responded to inquiries from all these sources with ample industry statistics and veterinary documents to dispel all of her claims. The matter was dropped and we assumed we would never hear from this lady again.

About two years later, I received a personal telephone call from this same lady. She was extremely apologetic and obvi-

218

ously embarrassed. She didn't have to remind me, but she mentioned the occasion of her first boarding and its subsequent consequences.

"Mr. Leeds," she admitted, "I know now that what happened had nothing to do with the pet motel. Since boarding with you, I have boarded my dog with several kennels and even with my veterinarian. You can't imagine the problems I've had. I would like to come back if you'll have me. I am really sorry for what happened and I promise I won't cause you any trouble if you will just board my dog. Quite honestly, if I can't board him with you, I would not board him with anyone else and I really would like to go and visit my grandchildren."

I neither needed nor wanted any such assurances. I was delighted to have another chance to prove to this pet owner that we were every bit as good as we claimed. She remained a good client for many years and she never failed to ask for me when she came in. She made it a point of telling me how much her dog enjoyed boarding with us and how wonderful the dog looked when it went home. The best part was that she always complimented us with a voice that could be heard by everyone in the lobby. We couldn't have bought advertising like that.

A similar case was Mr. Carson, the owner of a small cocker spaniel. We thought the man might be an attorney, but in any case, we were constantly on trial. He was rude, insolent, and down right contemptuous to the animal attendants and especially the women at the front desk. Although his dog never had any problems, this man had the worst personality we ever experienced. Although we tried to prepare for him and even rehearsed for his appearance, it was impossible to escape his scathing remarks. After a while, Marc would try to be present when he showed up, and on a few occasions asked Mr. Carson to lower his voice and act like a gentleman. For whatever reason, he failed to be influenced. Then, one day he showed up in a particularly vile mood. He used a variety of vulgar terms and was so mean that the receptionist fled her post in tears. At that time Kim, our Director of Animal Welfare, came and told us that we had a choice. Either the receptionists could leave or Mr. Carson could be refused boarding privileges. It was no longer any contest. Mr. Carson would no longer be welcome. When Mr. Carson returned to pick up his dog, Marc took him aside to inform him that he would no longer be welcome at American Pet Motels. The worst thing he could have asked was why. In a very frank exchange Mark told him he was the meanest, most inconsiderate and ungrateful S.O.B. with whom we ever had the displeasure of doing business with. Shocked by Marc's tirade, and without another word, Mr. Carson picked up his dog and stormed out of the building.

I was certain we had seen the last of Mr. Carson.

Then, a few months later, I heard Mr. Carson's name come up. I looked up at Kim and asked her if this was the same Mr. Carson we weren't going to serve anymore. With a sheepish look she said, "Yes, but have you seen his dog?"

"Not today, but I've seen his dog plenty of other times," I replied.

"His dog has cancer," she began. "He's spent a fortune on the dog, taking it down to the veterinary hospital at the University of Illinois. They've removed a whole portion of the dog's jaw and now he can't keep his tongue in his mouth and it just hangs down on the side where his jaw is missing. He'll do anything to save his dog so I thought we ought to give him another chance." This was the message from the same young lady who threatened to quit if we ever let Mr. Carson board his dog again.

I didn't have anything more to say. I did go out to the lobby the next time he came in and I heard him warn the receptionist not to let the dog's tongue touch the floor if he lay down.

Mr. Carson didn't become a model customer, but he did become tolerable. Despite the cost, he kept his dog alive as long as he could and when the inevitable time came and the dog was in pain, he went with her to his veterinarian and had her mercifully put to sleep.

Within a month I was a little surprised to see Mr. Carson standing in line at the reception desk. Then I noticed he was holding a little black cocker spaniel puppy. I smiled and turned away and suddenly I heard his booming voice, "Jesus Christ! Can I get a little service here?"

I couldn't help but laugh. Mr. Carson was back! He continued to board his new dog with us and although he wasn't the most gracious customer, he never again was as rude as his former self.

I have found one thing to be true: *People who care for their pets take care of their pets.*

While living in Nevada, Peggy and I always stopped at the same small restaurant for breakfast. Another diner was a frequent patron and one day we began talking and he told us that he was living in Nevada while his wife lived in Michigan. He probably noticed the sudden lull in the conversation so he proceeded to explain. They had four old dachshunds and two of them were diabetic. Each dog required insulin injections two times a day and had to be fed small portions of food four times a day.

"You see," he explained, "I couldn't ship them to Michigan. They'd never survive the trip, so we decided I would stay here until they passed away and then I'll join my wife in Michigan."

I assume the expense of maintaining two residences and the cost of his wife flying back and forth was considerable but it was not a consideration for two people who cared for their pets.

I saw it again one day when I visited my sister in California. She never cared for dogs or cats. I think she was conditioned as a child by one of our family dogs that, she claimed, constantly threatened her. I vaguely remember the family coming home one evening to find her standing on the dining room table while our Labrador was running around the table, barking. When I entered my sister's home I was surprised to see an old miniature white poodle walking aimlessly around the house. A little surprised, I asked her about the dog. It turned out that the poodle was 18 years old and blind. Noting my surprise, my sister just smiled and said, "I know. But, she's been a good dog and she isn't any bother."

Pets seem to find a way into our hearts and people who care for pets will care for them to the very end.

Taking care of someone else's pet is an awesome responsibility. It is unfortunate that no matter how good any boarding facility is, problems will always occur that are beyond its control. Heaven knows a kennel has enough problems; it shouldn't be blamed for those that can't be helped. A dog tries to dig through the concrete floor and goes home with the pads of its feet raw and bleeding or is missing one or more toenails. There's the other dog that tried to chew his way out of the chain link enclosure and broke off one or more of his teeth or lacerates its mouth. I have heard of cases where dogs have actually broken their jaws doing this. There are pets that were exposed to some contagious disease before they were brought in and the disease was still incubating and not apparent. Even the owners are not aware that a problem was incubating until several days later when their pets are sick and half a dozen other pets have been infected. These are the types of problems over which the kennel has no control.

We also found that it was virtually impossible to predetermine how a pet will behave when it is boarded. The results may even be entirely different from one time to another. The vast majority of pets boarded well and went home in as good or better condition than when they came to us. It is a very small number of pets and owners that causes 99 percent of the problems.

I have always thought of unusual problems as unusual opportunities. One of these appeared in a request to board a police department's canine dogs. Even though these dogs were highly stressed and wholly unapproachable when with their handlers, they boarded well, like most other dogs, when their handlers left. The success of this experience led to us regularly boarding the attack-trained dogs of several nearby cities' police departments. The only thing that was different was that certain dogs required either all male attendants or all female attendants. We arranged this and naturally we only assigned attendants who were comfortable and not afraid of these special guests.

I doubt that pets are much different from people, and I haven't met many people who didn't need a few days to recuperate after their vacations. I'd wager that most pets go home after the vacation period in better shape than their masters. But for the other one percent, boarding was a "trying" experience: trying to out-yodel every dog in the kennel; trying to jump on every pet and person passing by; trying to bark at every little noise, day and night, neglecting their sleep and keeping others from theirs; trying to do everything but rest.

The continuous mellow music in all of our animal facilities did have a pacifying effect, but there was always one troubadour beagle or basset hound that thought it was a sing-along and he'd try harder.

Yes, for some it was a very "trying" experience.

Many of the compensations and rewards of this business do not show up on the profit and loss statement. They are there every time some elderly pet owner steps up to the counter and says, "My name is Mr. (or Mrs.). Such and Such. I boarded my little dog Fido here. Is he still alive?"

It became such a familiar routine that we'd automatically break out into a smile.

"Why, certainly," we'd reply. "In fact, he was just asking about you this morning."

Then you would watch their faces as their dog came charging down the long corridor from the kennels and climbed into their outstretched arms for a tearful reunion. That moment is the highest reward a good kennel can earn.

Prologue Chapter 19

THE NEW DOG

I. B. Malleson

There's a new dog lies on the parlor rug
Where the old dog used to lie,
A dog with a short white curly coat
And a brown patch over his eye.
He takes his meals from the old dog's dish
And sleeps on the old dog's chair,
And the rest have forgotten the Spaniel dog
Who for ten long years slept there.

But at night when the house is fast asleep
Sounds a step I used to know,
And the dog that I loved comes stealing back
From the land where the Good Dogs go.
A dark shape opens the bedroom door;
I hear a familiar whine,
There are two brown paws on the counterpane,
And a dog's head close to mine.

There isn't a secret he keeps from me
Of life in the Great Beyond.
There are shining seraphs to take him on walks,
Real bones and a splendid pond;
And the Baby Angels throw balls for him,
In the fields where the grass is sweet,
And he hasn't forgotten the strange brown stone
That he used to lay at my feet.

He remembers the days in the grassy parks
And the cats he used to chase.
(And yet they can talk of another dog
Who shall take the old dog's place).
He tells me he looked for the old green chair
Where his basket used to be,
But he found an intruder sleeping there,
So he came to look for me.

Oh, the new dog is a faithful chap
And earns his daily bread
And the right to feed from the self-same dish
And sleep on the self-same bed.
And of course he must be on the parlor rug
Where the old chap used to lie,
But a brown dog visits me every night,
Pathetically asking why.

19

SOMEDAY YOUR "PRINCE" WILL COME

It was impossible for a dog owner to stand in our lobby for any length of time before another dog owner would engage him in a discussion of what kind of dog makes the best pet.

This rarely, if ever, happened to cat owners. Possibly, because every cat owner already was convinced that the breed of their own cat was the superior breed. Another cat owner disputed my theory. She said it doesn't happen because cat lovers love all cats!

But if there were a thousand different breeds of dogs and you asked a thousand different dog owners, you would receive a thousand different replies.

There is a special dog for each of us. However, of the many guests I had the opportunity of knowing, there were two breeds whose owners seldom reported a fault; the golden retriever, in the large dog class, and the West Highland Terrier, in the small dog class. Having been obedience-trained, each of these breeds is well-behaved and possesses a limitless reservoir of love, loyalty, and devotion. I have always found them to be the most social of all breeds. They get along excellently with children and they welcome attention from anyone and everyone.

It is wrong to categorize any particular breed as all bad. If

I had to name one breed that might be less desirable as a family pet, I would acknowledge that many pit bull terriers leave something to be desired. These dogs were bred as fighters for centuries, and this breeding comes out too often. I have seen vicious pit bull terriers and Dobermans, but I have also seen vicious Pekingese and Chihuahuas, but the ill-natured dog is an exception to most breeds. There are some bad dogs of every breed.

Like other people in this business, I find it reasonable to recommend a small dog for a small home and a large dog for a home with a lot of space. It is logical to assume that large dogs, like Irish setters and German shepherds, need more space to exercise in than a Chihuahua or a small terrier. It seems reasonable to assume this, but it is not the case.

Every breed of dog has been raised in the confines of research kennels, and they have lived full and normal life expectancies. Experience with many thousands of pet owners showed me that a St. Bernard can grow up in a two-room apartment and attain all the health and happiness that loving care could provide, just as well as any toy breed. And, of course, I have not found small breeds deficient just because they were raised in huge open spaces.

We boarded numerous large dogs, even the giant Irish wolfhounds and Great Danes, who lived with their owners in small apartment units and were always healthy and appeared normal. Experience made me a strong believer that it isn't the quantity of space that counts; it's the quality of space.

I have a theory about pets. I don't believe most people actually choose their pets; I believe the opposite. I believe that by some almost divine intervention, most pets choose their owners. It's a confirming act of mystic intercession that often the person who swears he would never own a cat ultimately ends up with one, and the person who hasn't the slightest desire to be the owner of a dog ends up with two or three. It is as if some dimension of life is not complete without them.

Pets come to most of us in a variety of unexpected ways.

The kids come home from college with a four-legged roommate. Junior is transferred out of town and can't take his pet with him. You open a newspaper and there the picture of your next four-legged family member staring right at you from the Humane Society's "Pet of the Week" column. A particular stray follows you home and you haven't the heart to turn it away. You are not about to lose that sausage-colored dog.

Cold, calculated, rational reasoning selects thousands of pets, but millions more have joined our households by their own design. In the past thirty years, I think I have heard most of the stories. Judging by the results, I'd admit that these millions of dogs, cats, and assorted other animals have done very well for themselves and as well for their masters.

Considering the ability of some dogs and cats to travel thousands of miles to find their old masters, I can't imagine why so many animals appear at a stranger's doorstep, unless they were deliberately seeking a particular home. It's the most commonly told story I have heard. A family member got the urge to go to the all-night food store for bread and there was this poor little ol' dog just sitting there waiting for him. Or some feline just followed one of the kids into the house when she returned from playing. That was eight years ago. After all, what are you going to do with a lonely dog you found at the 7-Eleven or a cat that just walked in? Sometimes these guests are destined to spend the rest of their lives with their chosen family, but sometimes their brief visits only serve a purpose.

For instance, take a couple of ducks we met in Florida. During the four years that Peggy and I operated a small pet motel in Sarasota, we had a huge ceramic flowerpot containing aloe plants on each side of the entrance door. One day we came in to find one of the plants shredded on the ground. In its place was a nesting wild mallard hen. With thousands of acres of marshland nearby, this one duck decided to camp at the front entrance of the pet motel. Each day, for thirteen days, the duck added one egg to her nest, and twenty-eight days later, they began to hatch. Of course, being the host, we provided her with ground corn and water, which she accepted as if due her. Each day her male companion would fly in and she would get off her nest and take a walk with him. Apparently, an internal time clock told her when it was necessary to return. When the ducklings matured, the two of them led the little ducklings to our nearby lake each day to teach them to swim. Finally, the whole family took the walk to the lake and didn't return. They had returned to the wild.

We figured we had seen the last of them, but the following year they reappeared. There was our beautiful new aloe vera plant shredded on the ground and in its place was our annual guest. This happened for four consecutive years. The odd thing about it was that hundreds of hunting dogs went in and out our front door and passed only inches from our nesting duck. The dogs would stop and stare at the duck and she would just stare back. It was as if they had some mutual agreement to respect each other while the expectant mother occupied the pet motel's grounds.

Another pair of visitors who chose us was a hen and a rooster, but at least the hen paid for their corn by providing us with a nice fresh egg each day.

And let's not forget the pets that arrive as gifts. There appears to be no limit to these, as Peggy and I found out when we went into the kennel one Christmas morning and found a cute baby pig all decked out in bright red, white and blue ribbons. Chrisy was a gift from Kim and Cindy, two of our thoughtful employees. Chrisy enjoyed kennel life and provided a ready solution to the problem of leftover dog and cat food. She ate everything we gave her and a lot of things we didn't. One of her favorite pastimes was getting a weekly medicated bath from Peggy, after which she would go directly outside and wallow in the dirt. Chrisy may have thought she was a dog, but her natural instincts could not be suppressed. Once in the courtyard, she would put her nose to the ground and begin routing. I swear she plowed up an acre of ground before she got to the external high-pressure hoses of our sanitizing system. It didn't take many repair bills before we came to the conclusion that Chrisy might be more at home on our neighbor's farm.

Fox Fehling seemed destined to meet one of her pets, a Norwegian blue shadow fox. Ms. Fehling was a violinist with the Chicago Symphony Orchestra and traveled frequently with the orchestra. On a trip to Idaho, Ms. Fehling passed a fur store and in its window was a live six-week old fox. The fox was being used temporarily for a fur coat sales promotion. When she got back to her hotel, she began thinking of the possible alternatives the little fox had. She put her coat back on and returned to the fur store where she negotiated the purchase of the fox. She took the fox back to Chicago and raised it with her four cats and her dog. None of the animals was caged, and they lived together without any acrimony.

Roseann and Bryce Lee were always fond of Great Danes, but they never envisioned what that fondness would result in when they moved to Las Vegas. Shortly after their Great Dane died from cancer, they purchased a Great Dane puppy from a local breeder. They decided to name the dog Rapscallion.

About a year later, Roseann and Bryce were driving around and "just happened" to pass the Humane Society. For lack of anything better to do, they turned the car around and returned to the shelter to look around. Looking revealed a huge, three-year old, black mixed shepherd in desperate need of a permanent home. When they left the shelter they put Myrtle in the back seat, and the three of them drove home.

Shortly thereafter they met a young couple that had just moved to Las Vegas and had rented a small house. The house was too small for them, their children, and their Great Dane. Ro and Bryce couldn't turn down an opportunity like that, so they just adopted this sixteen-week, fawn, Great Dane, Calli.

It wasn't too long after that when Bryce got an urgent call from his secretary. She was watching television and the animal shelter was showing pictures of their "Dog of the Week." It was an emaciated four-year old Great Dane that weighed only forty pounds.

Bryce and Roseann looked at each other and reasoned the obvious. How much more work is there to caring for four dogs than three? Roseanne jumped in her car and headed for the animal shelter. Unfortunately, when she arrived, she was told that they had received several telephone calls for the dog and the people were already on their way to claim it.

"Wait a minute!" Roseann said, "They're not here. I am!" She searched through her purse and counted out the bills and change to make up the sixty dollar fee necessary to adopt the dog.

Waiving the bills in front of the employee, Roseann insisted on claiming the dog. In the face of such determined insistence, the employee finally relented, and Roseann and Bess walked out of the shelter together.

While each of the dogs has its own peculiar behavior, none is as unique as Cali's. Shortly after bringing Cali into their home, Roseann bought a small, stuffed rabbit for her to play with. From the day she received it, Cali has carefully carried the rabbit around by one of its ears and whenever she sets it down, she will maneuver it with her nose so it is always sitting upright. The dog will never let her stuffed rabbit lie on its side. It has to be upright and looking at her.

Fortunately for the Lees (and the dogs), the Lees' residence has four bedrooms and a spacious yard that includes a huge swimming pool, and the dogs have acclimated themselves to it all. However, despite the abundance of bedrooms and other rooms, for some reason the dogs seem to gravitate to the master bedroom each night. When she finds her space too encumbered by limbs of assorted sizes and colors, Roseann will pick up her pillow and seek out a vacant couch on which to spend the balance of the night. The Lees often joke about life with these four huge mammals, but it's obvious they wouldn't change it if they could.

I recall the time one of our customers, who was boarding

her cat, told me how she hated cats while growing up. Then, one day, when she opened the front door to let in her miniature schnauzer, she saw that her dog was carrying a tiny bundle of fur in its mouth. Thinking it was a dead rat, she screamed for her husband.

What appeared to her as a rat turned out to be a kitten only a few days old. That was twenty-one years ago and she wouldn't take a million dollars for her precious cat.

They are very smart, these animals, and in most cases don't you believe they are not discriminating. They simply have a different value system! The odds that you will really choose your next pet are probably a million to one, so why worry about it. Make up your mind that at the right time and place, your four-legged prince or princess will find you.

There were many matches that I'm sure had to be inspired. I recall a very attractive lady who used to bring her boss' dog in for boarding. Contrary to the dress conventions of the time or the nature of the weather, this young lady always wore pantsuits or slacks.

One day I arrived in the parking lot at the same time she did, and I watched her walk to the lobby with a perceptible limp. It was obvious her clothing concealed a defective limb.

Several days later, she arrived at the pet motel to board her own dog, a small fox terrier that she had recently acquired from the Humane Society. The dog was normal in every respect except that one of its legs was atrophied. The dog walked, ran, and jumped as normally as any other dog, but with three legs instead of four.

When one of the animal attendants thoughtlessly mentioned the handicap, the lady responded sharply, "Hey, he doesn't know he's handicapped, so don't tell him he is." She picked the dog up, hugged it, and then set it back down on the floor. "He gets around just fine," she said. And he did. They both did.

Another of our clients, Renee Alper, admits her dog chose her. Renee, a victim of psoriatic arthritis, could only get around in a wheelchair maneuvered by her constant human companion,

Joanne. One day Renee thought that she might like to have a dog to help brighten her long hours of confinement. She and Joanne decided to visit the Save-A-Pet Animal Foundation's kennel and look for a companion dog. Renee was wheeled from one pen to another. With so many dogs to choose from, she couldn't make up her mind, until, in one of the rooms, a small mixed terrier forced his way to the foot of her wheelchair and began licking her toes. The decision was made for her. Dumpling, an abandoned nine-month-old mixed terrier, had licked two problems. He had found a home and Renee had found her companion.

About a year after adopting Dumpling, Renee heard about an organization called Support Dogs for the Handicapped. This organization, operating on the same principle as the Leader Dogs for the Blind Association, counseled Renee that only a special dog could be trained to perform the many tasks a Support Dog was required to do. Renee was not convinced and she certainly wasn't going to give up Dumpling. Instead, she had a friend make the required special harness and began teaching Dumpling to "heel" to her wheelchair. With a minimum expenditure of effort, Dumpling responded and for the first time since her confinement, Renee dared to begin taking trips out of doors without her human companion, Joanne.

Learning to fetch and retrieve necessary objects came easily to Dumpling and within a short time, the dog learned to answer Renee's special speaker telephone by using her mouth to lift the receiver off the cradle. The dog's ability to respond to each new challenge was uncanny. Before long, Joanne was able to move into her own bedroom, where the dog would summon her if Renee needed assistance. Both women gained a new measure of privacy and confidence. A short time later, this hitherto unwanted mutt became the fifth dog in Illinois to be certified as an Official Support Dog for the Handicapped.

To many, it seems that Dumpling was saved for a special purpose and that it was more than coincidence that brought Renee to Save-A-Pet that particular day. Can you blame them?

Another match that I suspect had to be preordained happened to two very close friends of mine, Harold and Birdie Diebert. Birdie is the kind of person who always has to have a dog in her home. Although Harold was now retired, Birdie probably spent more money now on donations to animal shelters than she did when Harold was working for General Motors. Birdie likes to joke that Harold's pension money buys the food for their table. Her Social Security check buys the food for the local animal shelters.

In addition, every year she fills a huge basket with pet food and treats and delivers it to the local animal shelter on the day before Christmas. It's a nice custom that more and more people are adopting.

Last Christmas was the only time Birdie ever missed her annual visit, and I think I know why. Having been told by her veterinarian that their old dog was dying, Birdie immediately began talking about acquiring another dog. However, since Harold and Birdie spent six months each year traveling around the country in their motor home, Harold was not enthusiastic about getting another pet. Finally, he laid down the law. "No more pets!"

About the same time, Birdie began to notice the German shepherd in the yard behind hers. Without any shade from the hot Florida sun, the dog was often tied to a tree in the yard for hours on end, without food or water, and seemed to receive minimal attention from its owners. When Birdie checked from her kitchen window, she usually found the dog lying as close to her property line as its tether would permit, with its sad eyes staring back at her. Feeling sorry for the dog, Birdie began taking it water and food whenever the neighbors weren't apparent. Birdie even gave the dog a nickname, Jo Jo.

When their old dog passed away, Birdie decided to spare herself the pain of visiting the animal shelter that Christmas, and, instead, mailed them a check as her donation. Harold didn't object to supporting another animal shelter, but he remained firm about not getting another dog. A few days after Christmas, while doing her shopping, Birdie found herself filling her grocery cart with pet foods and all the assorted cookies and treats that people lavish on their pets. The animal shelter was about to receive a belated Christmas gift. On this occasion, perhaps as a penance, Birdie cajoled Harold into driving her there.

As she went from cage to cage, she suddenly stopped in front of one that held a large German shepherd. She stared into the dog's eyes and began shouting for Harold to come and look at it.

"Isn't that Jo Jo?" Birdie asked.

"Harold laughed at the suggestion. Even the possibility seemed too remote.

"It is too Jo Jo," Birdie replied, continuing to study the animal.

A check with the manager confirmed that the dog was indeed the same one that had been living in the house behind theirs. Their neighbors did not want the dog.

"I want him!" Birdie snapped without even looking at Harold.

"He's not a good dog," the kennel manager warned. "He's due to be put to sleep tonight."

"I want him!" Birdie demanded with more conviction than before. Harold shook his head but never said a word. When they left the shelter, Birdie held the leash of their Christmas dog, Jo Jo.

If Birdie had visited the shelter on December 24, the day she usually made her Christmas visit, she would have missed Jo Jo because he hadn't been brought in yet. If she had visited the shelter one day later, she would have missed Jo Jo because he was due to be euthanized.

From the day they took him home, Jo Jo became Harold's dog. Don't ask me why it happens, but it does. You will not find one without the other. He is still shy of strangers, but he has never been anything but meek and unswervingly loyal to his new family.

One of the interesting things about the story is that even though Jo Jo is allowed out in their unfenced yard several times a day, he has never once left their yard or even approached his former home. As they've traveled around the country in their mobile home, not once has Jo Jo ever strayed more than a few feet from his new owners' sides. Personally, I think Jo Jo picked a couple of good owners; the Dieberts actually think they picked the dog.

Another dog found a nice home through his owner's default. The huge malamute was boarded by a law student who ran into some hard times and finally admitted he could no longer keep the dog. He offered to pay most of his bill if we would just get rid of the dog. Nikki had already been boarding with us for several weeks and was well known and liked by all the attendants. He had an exceptionally thick silver and black coat that suggested that he may have spent the majority of his life outdoors. Because he liked to be out of doors all the time, the door to his outside run was frequently left open so he could go outside and enjoy the brisk winter winds.

Weeks of searching for a new owner failed to turn one up. The dog was extremely large and already twelve years old. There would be few homes open to a dog like this.

At our weekly staff meetings, no one was in favor of getting rid of the dog. Instead, Marc said that he was adopting the dog and making it the pet motel mascot. Because the dog was so docile and friendly, he was given the run of the entire 8½-acre site. To provide him with shelter when the weather turned extremely cold, an extra large dog-door was installed in the rear door of Kim's apartment. Except to get his food and water, Nikki rarely used the indoor shelter. If there was a heavy snowfall, you would always find him outside, completely covered by a pile of snow. It was his kind of weather.

Although hundreds of different dogs passed by him on their way to the exercise yard, Nikki never approached any of them nor did he ever threaten one. He was completely at home socializing with the help and was not about to jeopardize his newly found position.

There were numerous times when attendants would open

the twelve-foot gate to let a van go in or out or to let an attendant take out a tractor load of garbage. Many times Nikki would walk up to the open area and look out. Sometimes he would step two or three paces past the gate and look around. Then he would always glance backwards at the gate attendant to make sure he wasn't going to be locked outside. I don't know what he was thinking for sure, but the fact that he would always turn around and re-enter the yard convinced me that he knew the difference and was satisfied with this choice.

He was a good and great dog that every employee loved and enjoyed, and after his brief time with us, at the ripe old age of seventeen, he lay down one night and his spirit fled his body.

On a wall in the pet motel is a beautiful plaque that the employees of the pet motel had made. It is inscribed:

"All things Bright and Beautiful,
All creatures Great and Small,
All things Wise and Wonderful,
The Lord GOD made them ALL."

In loving memory of Nikki
1970 – 1987

When it comes to four-legged princes and princesses, I've kissed my share of frogs. If I have been singularly blessed, it has been in having a wife who tolerates my impulsive commitments on behalf of the animal world. Since buying our first home, there has not been a time when we did not have some kind of dog or dogs running loose in our home. One was actually bought from a breeder. All the others came to us as they came to so many others. I think they planned it that way.

It was usually a stray that wandered into our yard, but after we opened the pet motel, we never lacked for a source again. The unfortunate part was that most of these dogs were advanced in age and so we only got to share their companionship for a relatively short time. Even so, it was a good life for them and for us. Among them were a mutt named Pogo; three Yorkshire terriers named Casanova, Teddy Bear, and Sebastian; three West Highland terriers named Koira, Maggie, and Scampi; one mixed Labrador retriever named Plato; and our present dog, a Jack Russell terrier named Bingo. However, these were only a few of the dogs that were entertained in the Leeds' home.

Whenever a dog was boarded for a long period of time or if there was a dog that was not boarding too well, I would try to ease its stay by taking the dog home for the weekend. Neither Peggy nor our dogs seemed to mind and the extra four feet around the house never presented a problem. In some cases the owners finally gave up on their dog and our adopting it resolved an un-pleasant alternative.

There was one problem that never really resolved itself. Most of the time Peggy and I chose to live in rural, secluded areas which were heavily forested and filled with all sorts of animals. One species was particularly bothersome: the raccoon. Every day they would find a new way to get into our garbage and dine, leaving the inedible refuse scattered all over the driveway. I couldn't put out poison as some of my neighbors suggested, so I came up with the bright idea of setting out a bowl of food just for them. "If you can't fight them, join them." Someone from a highly urbanized area must have come up with that solution.

In the morning the food was gone and our garbage was intact. On the second morning, however, the food was all gone, and our garbage was again strewn all over. That night I decided to sit on a yard swing and watch what happened. As soon as it got dark, a small figure emerged from the underbrush. It stood up on its hind legs and studied me. Cautiously it made its way to the food bowl and began eating. Soon a couple of more raccoons made their appearance and they too approached the food bowl. Then, within a fifteen-minute period several more raccoons made their appearance. I had definitely underestimated the food requirement. Going into the garage I took a bag of dog food and poured several piles out on the driveway. All of the raccoons re-appeared and ate while I looked on. It became a routine that the whole family joined in on. We even moved our swing onto the driveway and tempted the raccoons onto our laps with marshmallows. Neither the children nor Peggy and I were ever bit although we hand-fed the raccoons from our fingers.

One raccoon in particular was quite old and very fat. We affectionately referred to him as Grandpa. He would just sit at our feet and expect to be fed and when he had his fill, he would saunter off into the woods with his cumbersome body swaying from side to side. One evening in the fall, we failed to notice the acceleration of darkness and were sitting at the kitchen table when we heard someone rapping on the window. Looking up we found ourselves looking directly into the upside down face of "Grandpa." He was hanging from a giant black walnut tree just outside our kitchen window. Without a doubt he wanted to be fed, and there was no food on the driveway. We promptly remedied the situation.

There were always a couple of pregnant raccoons. When the bitter cold began, all of the raccoons disappeared. Then, with the first sign of spring they would start reappearing, and the new mothers would introduce us to their litters of three and four babies.

In Illinois we also had deer, and in addition to the visiting raccoons, we had skunks and possums. It was not unusual at all to have raccoons, possums and one or two skunks eating kibbled dog food from the same bowl.

Our dogs never got used to having fifteen or twenty small animals eating on our porch, but then, those animals never got used to our dogs.

This story would not be complete if I didn't tell you a little bit about our present waif, a Jack Russell Terrier named Bingo.

Bingo was another one of those candidates for a shelter. Apparently one of our young customers saw a television show named "Frasier" in which a cute Jack Russell terrier was a star. With nothing more to recommend it, this customer went out and paid several hundred dollars for a Jack Russell terrier to give to his aging mother for companionship. This was a big mistake. This feisty little terrier is not the kind you could call and cuddle with. It is the kind you could chase and never catch. I think it might have been bred to refute the admirable traits so generously ascribed to the canine species. It is extremely intelligent without a doubt, but it uses its God given talents to frustrate the best intentions of the human heart. It arrives as a cute package that rivals Pandora's Box. Once released, you will witness the most unruly, undisciplined, and incorrigible breed of dog ever seen.

Apparently the woman had tried everything from a rolled-up newspaper to a broom handle to subdue the dog but without success. Worn out and on the verge of a nervous breakdown, she brought the dog into the pet motel and asked the receptionists to find a home for it or have the dog put to sleep. Kim and Carol knew of just the right softhearted mark, me.

From the moment I set that fleet-footed, miniaturized, hair-enclosed, bundle of energy down on our living room carpet, she took off running. Peggy and I stood there scarcely believing what we saw. The dog did not believe in walking; she ran at an amazing speed without ever changing her direction simply because there was a piece of furniture or table in the way. She simply would levitate into the air and scarcely touch down on the furniture and tables as she sped through her rounds. The worst part was that she was not affectionate, which was Peggy's only demand. If you did manage to corner the dog, she would start trembling and shrieking like you were beating her. Possibly it was a reaction conditioned by her previous owner's punishment.

There was one thing in her favor. She was an asset for my exercise program. Every morning the two of us would run for several miles. Then, when I caught her I would take her outside on a leash where she would go one and two. Then I would release her in the house and she would go three, four, five, and six.

Obviously, this breed was misnamed. It should have been called a Jet Rocket Terrier. I have no doubt that an autopsy would reveal hundreds of Energizer batteries.

It took only two days for Peggy to give me an ultimatum. Either the dog had to be obedience trained or I had to get rid of her.

Having years of managerial experience, I knew exactly what to do. I passed the ultimatum on to our Director of Animal Welfare, Kim: "You got me into this. You get me out!" Now, Kim was a great dog trainer and I was confident that she could turn out any dog in one or two weeks of private lessons. I checked Bingo into the pet motel to begin her rehabilitation. After one week I summoned Kim to report her progress. "Another week," Kim replied.

The following week, Kim sort of smiled. "Another week," she repeated. Each week the report was the same. I was becoming afraid that if this continued I was going to become stuck with another old dog again.

Finally, after two months of intensive obedience training, Kim proudly announced that Bingo was ready to go home. I will never forget that evening I returned home and set Bingo down in front of Peggy's waiting arms. The moment I set that fleet-footed, miniaturized, hair enclosed, bundle of energy down she took off running. It was across the living room floor, up over the couch, through the passage into the family room, through the kitchen, around the bar, back into the living room, across the living room floor, up over the couch. . . Peggy and I just looked at each other. Finally, after several passes, Bingo stopped in front of us. I think she may have been expecting an Olympic Medal. She had just done the three-minute mile in less than two minutes.

Seizing the moment, I gave her one of the main commands she should have learned in obedience school. 'SIT!" She stood there and just looked at me. "SIT! SIT! SIT!" I commanded. Slowly, she took the sit position. "Down!" I commanded, pointing to the floor. She readily responded by lying down. She was home for good.

Bingo is now two years old and has gotten over some of her fears. She will still cower and shriek if someone thoughtlessly picks up a rolled-up newspaper or a broom in front of her, but now she readily seeks our company and companionship at all hours of the day and night without our coaxing. Peggy picks her up and hugs her like a rag doll and Bingo never objects. We still play tag each morning and then we are off to the tennis courts. Once we are inside, I remove her leash and throw tennis balls for her to retrieve. When she has finally exhausted her store of energy, she will take the last ball to the gate where she drops it and waits for me to put on her leash to take her home. She has another interest. Andre Agassi and his friends use these courts and apparently, when someone hits a ball into the bushes, they don't always find it. Bingo does. She has a super sniffer. In fact, Bingo now has a bushel basket half filled with Agassi's tennis balls. She's a strange dog, but we're awfully glad she found us.

Prologue Chapter 20

EPITAPH TO A DOG

Lord Byron

When some proud son of man returns to earth,
Unknown to glory, but upheld by birth,
The sculptur'd art exhausts the art of woe,
And stoned urns record who rest below;
When all is done, upon the tomb is seen,
Not what he was, but what he should have been;

But the poor Dog, in life the firmest friend,
The first to welcome, foremost to defend;
Whose honest heart is still his master's own,
Who labours, fights, lives, breathes, for him alone,
Unhonour'd falls, unnoticed all his worth,
Denied in Heaven the soul he held on earth;

While man, vain insect! Hopes to be forgiven,
And claims himself a sole exclusive Heaven!
Oh, man! Thou feeble tenant of an hour,
Debased by slavery, or corrupt by power,
Who knows thee well, must quit thee with disgust
Degraded mass of animated dust!

Thy love is lust, thy friendship all a cheat,
Thy smiles hypocrisy, thy words deceit!
By nature vile, ennobled but by name,
Each kindred brute might bid thee blush for shame.
Ye! Who, perchance, behold this single Urn
Pass on — it honours none you wish to mourn:

To mark a Friend's remains these stones arise,
I never knew but one, and here he lies.

20

THE CHRISTMAS GIFT

From the day we opened, our concept of pet care became the benchmark of pet boarding not only in America, but also throughout the world. Our uniqueness would be featured in almost every major American periodical including *Newsweek* and *U.S. News & World Report*, and we would even make the cover of *Time* magazine.

Our fame wasn't confined to America; it was parroted all over the world. In France, it was *Paris Match* and in Germany, *Stern*. The Japanese government sent a film crew to incorporate us into a documentary entitled *Animals and Man*. In many countries of the world, a new level of pet-boarding concern gave pet owners new hope.

From *Country Gentleman* and *National Geographic* to *Mad Magazine* and *Penthouse*, regardless of a person's choice of reading material, the story of a new dimension in pet care was brought to the public's attention. In the book *Amazing America*, American Pet Motels was singled out as one of the places a visitor must see when visiting the state of Illinois.

Many people learned about us from television. In addition to special news features shown on all of the major networks, our story would be included on such leading TV shows as *Real People, Sorting It Out, Hour Magazine, Good Morning,*

America, and *P.M. Magazine*, just to mention a few. Camera crews from *National Geographic* and *Ripley's Believe It or Not* also filmed our operations. All kinds of celebrities, including the lovely and personable Erma Bombeck, televised syndicated programs from the pet motel. Good pet care was now believable. The nicest thing was that all of this was accomplished through the word of satisfied customers, not by the efforts of an advertising agency or public relations firm.

During 1976, every room in the pet motel was booked, and at times we carried more than four hundred names on a waiting list. Soon we found ourselves turning down even steady clients unless they failed to make reservations one or two months in advance.

There was no question about our viability. There was no question about our need to build the other two pet motels.

During those early days, charging as little as five dollars a day gave us a projected annual gross of almost $400,000 and a healthy after-tax profit. A second pet motel in the Chicago area would add an additional $50,000 to our profit just by sharing the Yellow Pages advertising costs and our corporate overhead. Moreover, we had learned many lessons from our first effort. These mistakes would not be repeated, and we could expect additional profits from these economies.

At a directors meeting attended by Kroc's two lawyers and his accountant, I laid out our expansion plans and profit projections. In our figures, I identified 103 new pet motel locations. A five-year plan was also included calling for the addition of two more pet motels in the Chicago area and another seven in nearby metropolitan areas. Following economic trends I could predict our revenues would reach almost $2 million a year for each pet motel, $206 million a year and I had the data to prove it on the table in front of them.

They listened politely until Don Lubin glanced at his watch. "Hey," he said, "It's almost lunch time. Al, would you like to join Ed and me for lunch?" There was an awkward silence as Al Doty waited for Lubin to complete the invitation by also asking me to join them. It didn't happen. With a curt request that I leave all the papers on the conference table, Lubin and his two friends walked out of the room without another word and left me standing there while they went to lunch.

I wasn't sure what I was supposed to do, but the abrupt adjournment did away with any appetite I might have had. Instead of having lunch, I sat down and waited for the three directors to return. By two o'clock it seemed obvious they were not returning and I was not going to get any indication of when we might begin our expansion.

The actions of the board members bothered me, but in a few months the anticipation of the Christmas season eclipsed those concerns.

Christmas of 1976 was shaping up to be the most joyous occasion of our lives, and we planned it accordingly. Marc was still serving with the air force in Korea, but I notified Leslie and her husband, Michael, that I was sending them plane fare and expected them to join Gail, Peggy and me for a festive Christmas celebration.

One American trait that Peggy excelled in was shopping. I always told people that she learned to speak English by reading the price tags in Macy's department stores. Her love of shopping was never diminished by the fact that she was buying things for someone else. After the past few years of hardships and worrying, we were finally on our way.

Only days into December, fate, in the form of a telephone call, was to decree that such dreams were not to be. On December 5, while tending the reception counter, I received a personal call.

"Merry Christmas, American Pet Motels," I answered merrily.

There was a slight pause before the other party recovered. It was Ray's attorney, Don Lubin. "Bob, I wanted to let you know that Ray has decided to close the pet motel on December thirty-first. He wants you out of there not later than that date."

His words sent a cold, sobering chill through me. I couldn't speak. I stood there almost frozen, trying to understand what was happening.

Lubin's voice broke the silence. "We'd like you to wrap up all of your personal affairs and be off the premises as soon as possible, but in no event later than the thirty-first."

By this time I was able to catch my breath. "But, why? We're making more money than we even anticipated. We're completely booked all the way to January tenth. Every single thing points to this being a huge success. Why would Ray want to close the business? Besides, we're going to have four hundred animals in here until January tenth. What am I supposed to do with them, put them out on the street?"

Before he could answer, The other attorney's voice came shrieking across the line. "Don't you worry about that!" he shouted, "We're taking care of everything." His voice was as cold as a steel dagger and just as painful.

I couldn't comprehend what it all really meant. Except for my opposition to the imposition of the rent and interest, I could think of nothing that might have provoked this situation. I had given in on everything they demanded. I had signed their notes. I was paying the illegitimate rent. I could think of nothing that might have provoked this situation. Perhaps I had given in too much, I thought. Perhaps, too easily. I searched my mind for the answer to what was happening, but Lubin's voice brought me back to the present.

"Bob, don't worry about the business. Just be sure you have everything off the premises by the thirty-first. Someone else is coming in to run the business on that date."

Suddenly there was another dimension to the matter. I had a five-year management contract. Kroc couldn't bring in someone else unless I was guilty of some wrongdoing. There was no way they could prove something like that.

"I thought you said Ray was closing the business," I said.

"He is," Lubin replied. "He owns eight-five percent of the stock and he is dissolving the company and selling the assets to another party who intends to operate a pet motel there."

"Is the new owner going to change the name of the company?" I asked.

There was a slight pause. "No."

"Well, if the company is being dissolved, are we going to disconnect the telephone service?" I asked again.

Again Lubin replied, "No."

It became obvious to me that the business was not going to be closed. Something else was happening.

Finally, Lubin admitted part of the truth. "Actually, we have a buyer for the pet motel and he has some plans to make it more profitable."

My mind began spinning again. I or anyone else could have made the pet motel more profitable. All we had to do was become a kennel. I envisioned the rows of steel cages lining our kennel walls. Someone else could get two hundred more dogs in each of our kennels by using cages, double-dipping and by splitting runs. It wouldn't take much capital, just a contempt for the lives of the boarded animals. This was something the Kroc's had sworn they would never do. In my ignorance, I told myself that I wasn't going to allow them to do this.

"Wait a minute," I asked. "I've got a five-year contract with Ray. This is *my* business. It's *my* concept and *my* name. If you're going to dissolve the business, then let's dissolve it. We'll shut off the telephones and lock the doors!"

Apparently this was more than one of the attorneys could tolerate hearing. His words came screaming across the line, "It's not your concept or your business! It's Kroc's! It's all Kroc's! You just pick up your pencils and get out of there!" I lifted my head up and suddenly realized that everyone in the lobby could hear his voice.

Quickly, Lubin's modulated voice came back on the line. His voice was quiet and the tone of reason. "Bob, the company does not have enough assets to satisfy Ray's claims. He is calling his notes for the one-hundred-eighty-thousand dollars for back rent and interest. Ray holds eighty-five percent of the stock and that's enough to dissolve the corporation. If you will look at your employment contract and other agreements, you will find that they are all with American Pet Motels. When the company is dissolved, all your contracts are voided."

I couldn't recall my attorney mentioning this aspect of the agreement to me. It was a bad time for me to receive a lesson in contract law, but I had no reason to doubt what Lubin was telling me. They had probably structured our agreement for just such an occasion.

I had been giving Ray and Joan $60,000 a year plus 85 percent of the profits. Apparently, it still wasn't enough for the $685 million couple who controlled the McDonald's empire. I recalled the night we celebrated our future in the Kroc's penthouse and the afternoon luncheon where Joan told Peggy and I how they were going to make us rich. They were doing it all for us. Lie and lie after lie.

Lubin's voice came back on the line. "Bob, with the purchase of the San Diego Padres and his other investments, Ray has had an unusual amount of income this year that needs sheltering. We've no other choice but to sell American Pet Motels and use the loss to offset some of Ray's income."

The frivolousness and shallow logic offered stunned me. I could think of nothing that might have swayed their decision. I just muttered, "O.K." and hung up. Turning, I saw the receptionist at the front desk staring at me.

"Mr. Kroc is closing down the pet motel on December thirty-first," I said.

Suddenly, tears began to well up in my eyes. I held my head down against my chest and blindly made my way back to the seclusion of my office. For the first time, the full implications of what was going to happen struck me. I sat down at my desk and buried my head in my arms and began to cry. I could not restrain myself any longer.

"Oh, God," I cried. "What have I done to deserve this? What have I ever done to this man? To anyone? With all of his millions. With all of his wealth, why would he do this? How could a man like him do this?"

For the balance of the day, I remained there. I could not stem the flow of tears and my throat ached from trying. A sharp, tearing pain caused an almost unbearable cramp in my chest. I begged to understand why this was happening. In view of every promise Ray and Joan had made, how could they do this?

Intermittently, I recalled my conversations with them "Don't worry about a thing," they had assured us. "We're doing this all for you." "We don't care if the business never makes a dime, we have more wealth than we'll ever be able to use." "We just want to see you and Peggy become wealthy and enjoy some of the luxuries we do."

Over and over again, I kept recalling their glowing assurances of trust and confidence. The popular McDonald's jingle came into my mind. "We do it all for you."

"Yes, you certainly do," I thought. "You'll do it to anyone!"

Driving home that night, I began to realize what I was really up against. Except for a few thousand dollars in mutual funds and General Motors stock, I had completely exhausted our savings. Bolstered by the assurances I would never have anything to worry about again, I had not made any effort to rebuild our depleted finances.

To make the company look good and improve our cash position during the start-up period, I had personally absorbed as many trivial expenses as my salary permitted. When I took guests and business associates out for lunch or dinner, I paid the expenses from our personal checking account. I had even purchased the company's typewriter and calculators, as well as most of the office supplies. I had bought all these things in the naïve belief that all of this was an investment that I would recoup with our future success.

Not only had I not taken the minimum precautions to protect Peggy and the children against such a catastrophe, I had even encouraged them to believe that our mode of living was just the minimum of what they might expect.

As I drove home I began counting up the numerous monthly obligations we had acquired with our benign sense of security. They were overwhelming.

I was almost fifty years old. How long would it take before I would find employment? How would we live? How would we face our friends and neighbors? How many of them would believe me when I told them I was not at fault for what happened? But, above all these concerns rose the one that hurt me the most: What would they turn American Pet Motels into, once I was out of the way?

In one brief instant, I had plunged from the pinnacle of success to the very nadir of failure. I had gambled everything we had and lost. My pension program, our stock savings program, all was gone. Worse, I had talked Peggy into letting me sell her dream home and invest the money in my pet motel fantasy. My promise to replace it one day would not be kept.

It was all one gigantic deception. I had cheated her and the children not only out of what we already had, but also the likelihood of any future well being.

All my life I had lived a fairy tale, believing that honest endeavor and hard work would bring us security and success. I thought about my father. He had been shipped to America when only eight years old and was brought up in the backroom of an uncle's tavern. Without any education, he opened a small painting business and together with my mother had raised five children. There were times when there was little to eat, but he never found cause to be bitter. He loved this country for its promise, and throughout his life, he always taught us that honesty and hard work would bring its own rewards. He built no estate. He never even dreamed of having $10,000 let alone $685 million. But in the best of times and in the worst of times he never cheated anyone or took advantage of them. Before he died he joked that he was leaving me the greatest treasure a person could want: *America!* "Be honest and work hard," he would tell me. He was sincere, and I knew from his voice he believed it. Perhaps he just never had partners like mine.

It seemed ironic that Ray Kroc, who had traveled a similar path to mine, would be the one to destroy this myth. Yet, he could buy his respect in the marketplace of public opinion. Price was no object for a man who had $685 million. His $3 million donation to the local zoo for an ape house would buy him more public honors than any breach of integrity could ever tarnish.

The pain of insecurity sharpened as I opened the front door to our house. Casanova, our Yorkshire terrier, and Koira, our West Highland terrier, came bounding down the stairs to greet me, but I had no treats to offer them this time. It was a ritual I had never missed before, but this day I had no stomach for it. I pushed past the dogs and walked into the bedroom.

It is strange what irrational and seemingly insignificant thoughts a person thinks of under conditions like this. I was wondering where we would get money to buy them dog food and to get them groomed? How would we pay for their veterinary bills? What would happen to our dogs if we ended up where we began our married life, in a city- operated housing project that didn't permit pets?

These seemingly trivial matters became of paramount concern to me and served to reinforce the terrible burden that already weighed on my mind.

I closed the bedroom door behind me and locked it. My eyes were blurred with yet more tears as I considered the dimensions of my failure. I opened the bottom door of the nightstand and reached behind the heating pad for the .38 caliber service revolver I kept there. It lay among some old battle ribbons and two citations; one for *"Service Above and Beyond the Call of Duty"* and another for *"The Display of Heroism and Courage Without Hesitation."*

I no longer had the will within me to fight another battle. Life had become too full of disappointment and heartache to want to experience more. I wanted it to end. I wanted it to end now.

Prologue Chapter 21

THE ROAD TO VAGABONDIA

Dana Burnet

He was sitting on a doorstep
As I went strolling by,
A lonely little beggar
With a wistful, homesick eye.
And he wasn't what you'd borrow,
And he wasn't what you'd steal;
But I guessed his heart was breaking
So I whistled him to heel.

They had stoned him through the city streets,
And naught the city cared;
But I was heading outward
And the roads are sweeter shared.
So I took him for a comrade,
And I whistled him away
On the road to Vagabondia,
That lies across the way.

Yellow dog he was; but bless you,
He was just the chap for me!
For I'd rather have an inch of mutt
Than a mile of pedigree.
So we stole away together
On the road that has no end
With all the new born day to fling away
And all the stars to spend!

21

THE PATH
IS CHOSEN

There had been a time when I believed suicide was a worthless and futile gesture, meaningless and unsupportive. No longer.

I had known several persons, some very close friends, who had chosen suicide as the means of resolving personal problems. My very best friend deliberately drank himself to death, while another friend, with whom I had shared numerous harrowing wartime experiences, literally starved himself to death. The young and beautiful wife of a well-known radio personality went shopping with Peggy and took her life the next day with an overdose of sleeping pills.

Each time, I shook my head and lamented the useless and tragic waste of life. Now, for the first time, I could understand and share their compulsion to flee this life–a life where dreams and aspirations are suddenly snatched away, where a tranquil existence is suddenly replaced by hopeless despair, where one's absolute faith is betrayed by someone he most trusted.

Suicide was an act that I would never condone or even try to justify for another. But for me, this was the point beyond which continued existence became too bitter to sustain.

I consider myself an extremely religious person even though I attend no church on a regular basis and do not surround myself with religion's visible trappings. I had moved through these experiences in my youth. Over the years, I had formulated a dogma that I subscribe to with the reverence of the most venerable deist. I had come to accept that the magnitude of order in the universe makes it impossible to deny the existence of some supreme force. But, my conception of this deity differs from most traditionalists. My God was an understanding and forgiving God. He created me in His image, and to a lesser degree endowed me with all His powers. Even the greatest powers, to create life and to take it, were mine. Beyond that I must walk my own path and leave this earth better off than when I came upon it.

Having contemplated the prospect of death during some of my adventures, I had even decided on two different sayings that I would have liked for my epitaph: *"Diogenes, put down your lamp."* and *"When God made Robert X. Leeds, he didn't do anything else that day except sit around and feel good."* It was a code I had tried to live my entire life by.

I believe that it was not without purpose that He put me here on earth, but although this purpose may not be revealed to me, the least He expected was that I live my life so that, except in times of war, no man could claim an injury or harm because of my deliberate doing.

Beyond this, my God expected little more of me. Not being a pompous or vain God, I knew that He would understand this one last act of contrition.

I opened the chamber of the revolver and turned the cylinder slowly around until a filled chamber was opposite the barrel, and then I locked the cylinder in place.

No one had loved or appreciated life with a fervor greater than I. Now, lying across the bed with the cocked revolver in my hand, I suddenly began recalling how many times I had been at the brink of death, only to be led back to safety by some unseen hand of fate.

I thought about the time when, as a sixteen-year-old member of a flying circus, I had fallen 7,500 hundred feet with both of my parachutes fouled, and survived. During World War II, I had served in the South Pacific with the Merchant Marine until I was old enough to become an air cadet in the American Air Force. I was the only air cadet to go through basic training with more theater ribbons than most of my instructors.

After the war I volunteered to fight for the Chinese Nationalists and was arrested as a communist spy. Tried by a kangaroo court, I was stood up against a wall in front of a firing squad and was saved only seconds before being executed.

During the 1947-1948 Middle East War, when flying to a destination behind the Iron Curtain, my plane was struck by anti-aircraft fire over Albania and made it all the way to Czechoslovakia before crashing. I was one of ten people who walked away from the crash. At 21, I trained and commanded the first Israeli Airborne Brigade during the Middle East War. By my twenty-first birthday, I had made more than 160 parachute jumps and had been involved in three wars, suffering little more than a slight head injury.

There were so many times, so many close calls; I opened my eyes to the stark reality of the room around me. The handle of my revolver seemed like ice in my hand.

"Good God!" I cried. "Is this how it's going to end?"

Suddenly, the room around me seemed to fill with a dust-like cloud. I saw cattle, thousands of cattle being driven by hooping and hollering cowboys. I could actually smell the dust and hear their raucous voices. As in a version of an old John Wayne movie, I saw the stereotyped villain counting his money and telling his hired hands that the rangeland was his. All his! He would drive the homesteaders off the range and it would be all his.

I knew it couldn't happen this way. In every Western movie I had ever seen, the homesteaders finally stood up and fought back against the overwhelming odds, to win in the end.

"Is this any different?" I asked myself.

I had been so close to death so many times, and yet, each time, fate had snatched me back and returned me to continue living. The right to honest endeavor and to the fruits of that labor was my sacred heritage.

If my ancestors had the guts to stand up to the beef barons of yesterday, the least I could do was to stand up to the ground-beef barons of today.

There had to be a purpose to my life. Had I been saved to die like this?

In that instant, I knew I mustn't give up. I had no idea how, but I would fight Ray Kroc and his $685 million if it was the last thing I did. My hand was drawn to the night stand drawer and I slowly placed the revolver back in its holster before falling into a deep sleep.

I didn't awaken until early the next morning. I dressed as usual and drove into work. I was suddenly confident that a call to an attorney would bring salvation. I was emotionally exhausted, but the simple belief that Kroc's actions were contrary to every part of our agreement gave me the confidence necessary to try and save what I felt was really mine.

At eight o'clock I sat down and beginning with the A's, began calling law firms listed in the Yellow Pages. I selected those firms where a string of names appeared in their listing, hoping it might imply a higher degree of effectiveness by virtue of numbers.

My first problem was that many firms were closed on Saturday. My second problem was more serious. Most of the lawyers I did speak to were of a common mind. As soon as I mentioned the name of Ray Kroc and my limited financial resources, the discussion came to an abrupt end. One law firm after another confirmed that Kroc's 85 percent equity gave him the right to do anything he wanted with the corporation. The process of proving he had broken specific agreements could involve thousands and thousands of dollars and years of litigation. Without the financial resources to match Kroc's millions, one attorney after another counseled me to walk away and save the little I still had.

It was late afternoon before I reached the W's and the name Walsh, Case and Coale. Robert O. Case, a senior partner, patiently listened to my story. I could sense his reluctance, but I pleaded for his assistance. Finally, he agreed to meet with me on Sunday and study the merits of the case. Once again some force, stranger than coincidence, intervened. This law office was also due to be closed December 6, but a last minute decision was made for Case and the firm's senior trial lawyer, Ralph Brown, to meet at the office that afternoon and discuss a pending case.

The following day was Sunday, December 7, Pearl Harbor Day.

Case arrived on time and brought with him Ralph Brown. They listened as I told them the entire story. They conceded that all of the written documents appeared to favor Kroc's position. "However," they added, "his motion of dissolving the company and then immediately reopening it with the same name, telephone numbers, and mode of operation suggests his actions are just a ploy to deprive the minority stockholder of his equity."

While I hated to admit it, the possibility that the entire business arrangement was set up from the very beginning with this in mind became a very real consideration.

After lengthy consideration, the two lawyers came up with a proposal. Their firm would take my case on the basis that, if we lost, I would only pay them their actual labor costs and out-of-pocket expenses. If we won, I would pay them their regular fee, which could amount to many thousands of dollars. Without any consideration, I accepted.

There was one other requirement. An $8,500 retainer had to be paid before they would begin their efforts. With only a fraction of that available, I nonetheless shook hands on the agreement.

The prospect of winning was dampened considerably when the attorneys advised me that even if we won, there could be no punitive damage award. The most I could expect out of a lawsuit was to force Kroc into continuing the company's existence. There would remain a variety of options for him to exercise his wrath once my employment agreement expired in 1977. I recalled Ray's smile when he told me he never got mad. He just got even!

That evening, I finally explained to Peggy what had happened. If it had been difficult for me to believe, I could understand it being impossible for her. She recounted all the nice promises Joan and Ray had made, but there was nothing I could say to explain or justify this tragic turn of events.

For a person who feared the unknown and was almost paranoid about our financial security, her prompt response surprised me.

"Let's fight them no matter what it costs!" The last of our life's savings was going to be pledged to a dubious outcome.

A check for $4,000 was put in the mail that evening. The balance of the retainer was paid over the next few weeks as the money from the sale of our stocks and mutual funds dribbled in. The mortgage company approved a second mortgage on our house, but beyond that, I had no idea of how we would pay any additional legal fees. I was gambling everything we had on the American judicial system. I did not even consider losing. I could not conceive of any judge or jury finding Kroc's actions legal. My friends called me naive.

December 31 came and went without any consequence. I did receive two communications from the McDonald's camp. The first was the visit of a gentleman who informed me he had just come to find out what my intentions were. Except for my vice president, John Zevchak, no one else in the company knew that I had hired a law firm. John had worked for me at General Motors and was an excellent worker but apparently not considered good management talent by G.M.'s standards. When I started American Pet Motels, I made John an offer to come to work for me and he accepted. I always paid him a salary, bonus, and benefits exactly equal to mine and considered it a quasi-partnership. When I told John what Kroc was doing, I was relieved that John agreed to quit if Kroc took over the pet motel. Without one of us to run the operation, it would have taken them months to learn the routines.

When this man from McDonald's asked me if I was thinking of hiring a law firm, I was a little surprised because John was the only other person who knew about it.

I told the visitor that I was seriously considering it, to which he replied, "Look. I just came from the Kroc's lawyers," he said sternly. "If you cause any trouble or hire an attorney they're going to look up every bar you got drunk in; every girl you ever slept with; they'll ruin you socially, politically, and economically, if it takes $685 million to do it!"

This was the one moment I cherished a comparatively virtuous existence. In response I asked him if they would like my war record also. I had done nothing that would add substance to their cause.

The visitor turned his back and then walked over to John and invited him to join him for lunch. To my surprise, John accepted. When John returned from lunch, he could barely restrain himself. With cold inconsideration he advised me that he had been offered the job of president of the new American Pet Motels. He went on and on telling me about all the things they were going to do for him. When he finished, I just stood there staring in disbelief. It must have suddenly dawned on my good friend and "partner" that I wasn't overwhelmed at his good fortune so he sought to comfort me with his logic: "Well, there's no sense in both of us starving to death."

There was one other communication from McDonald's. It arrived in a large envelope bearing a McDonald's return address but with no individual's name. Inside the envelope was a drawing of the earth with people standing on it shoulder to shoulder. From out of the clouds was coming a booming voice, *"Listen to Me Earthling, This is GOD! I am repossessing Earth and I want everyone off by the 31st!"*

Although many McDonald's executives regularly boarded with us, none ever mentioned the cartoon, let alone admitted to sending it.

Shortly before the end of the year, a special messenger carried a legal brief to the offices of Kroc's attorneys. It contained a copy of the documents in which I was charging the founder and chairman of the board of McDonald's Corporation with stock fraud. The suit was being filed in a federal court.

America's ground-beef baron would have to face a homesteader at the bar of justice.

Author's Notes:

Portions of this book were previously published by Dodd Mead publishing company just prior to the sale of the company and its subsequent bankruptcy.

After acquiring the rights to my book, their editors made a number of changes to the book which I felt seriously diminished its value. A major point of contention was the deletion of names and changing the title, but I was powerless to prevent it.

Shortly after publication, the new owners were unable to meet their financial commitments and filed for bankruptcy. The company was subsequently broken up and different divisions of the company were sold off to different publishing houses. This provided me with the opportunity to redress my concerns. Although some of the books reached the market, I re-purchased the rights to the book and also purchased the entire remaining stock of books. This entire edition I destroyed.

It was my wish to tell the entire story.

In re-writing the entire book, I have added sections deleted by editors of the first edition. I have also included the names of many of the people who figured prominently in these events.

It has not been my intention to be invidious, but to accurately convey the extent of our efforts and the depth of our despair and feelings caused by the perfidy of others.

There is another reason I re-wrote the book. I want to correct any impression that Ray or Joan Kroc was to blame for what happened.

Within a few days of the book's publication, I received a telephone call from Joan Kroc. It was a far different call than I expected at that time. She had just finished reading the book.

In a voice full of remorse and apologizing for everything that happened, Joan told me what she was sure actually occurred.

At the time Kroc's lawyers called me and told me they were taking over the pet motel, Ray Kroc's doctors had advised him he had only a short time to live. He was suffering from several health problems, including diabetes and cirrhosis of the liver, and was confined to a wheelchair. In order to protect him and make the last few months of his life as enjoyable as possible, Joan and the lawyers isolated Ray from all his obligations. For the last two years of his life, he and Joan traveled unencumbered by the demands and trials of business and public obligations. Joan described these two years as the happiest two years of their marriage.

The task of preparing his estate to deal with the death-tax obligation was left to his accountant and lawyers, Al Doty, Ed Lembitz, and Don Lubin. I heard later that a variety of ventures, from pie houses to our pet motel, were to be written off for tax purposes and then sold to their friends for a pittance of their true value. I do not know that this was correct. Although I can make an assumption, I have no knowledge that these men personally profited from these machinations.

According to Joan, neither she nor Ray ever knew one thing about what was happening to Peggy and me. The attorneys handled the entire matter.

Although my association with Ray and Joan was brief, I developed a strong respect for both of them. Ray Kroc was honest and extremly generous with those who were honest with him. With our exception, the people who stayed with him and believed in him, did become millionaires; wealthy beyond their wildest dreams. Joan was certainly no less honest but she also manifested a genuine air of concern not readily sensed in most people.

Based on the two people I knew, I prefer to believe they had no knowledge nor were they willing accomplices in what happened. For those who say that the blame stops at the top, I do concur. Contrition is not an easy thing for some people, but Joan handled it like the lady she is. I ask the reader to remember that the animosity and feelings I expressed in the preceding chapters were written prior to our conversation and the revelation of the true events.

When our telephone conversation was concluded, Joan suddenly said, "Robert, I want to make things right with you. How can I help you?"

I was caught off guard but my reply was instinctive. "Joan, there isn't anything you can or should do. It wasn't your fault and we don't hold you responsible."

It was impossible for me not to still harbor a degree of bitterness. What could anyone do to bring back all those wasted years of living on the brink of disaster? How do you erase a ten year nightmare and tear filled sessions? The begging and borrowing to meet a payroll or some other unforeseen contingency.

The economy had now improved. We were mortgaged to the hilt, but we were meeting our obligations and were solvent. There was really only one thing she could have done to help us. She could have re-invested the millions of dollars we paid them, but I would not ask that nor did I expect expect it. Outside of that, anything else would have been charity and I didn't want that.

"But, don't you still owe me some money?" she asked.

I hated that she brought it up at this time.

"Yes, I replied, "about fifty thousand dollars. But, we're current on our payments and we'll have no problems paying it off by the time it's due."

Then she asked me to hold for a few seconds.

A few moments later a stranger's voice came on the telephone. Apparently, Joan had a direct line to her attorney's office and had asked her to come on the line.

"Mr. Leeds," the attorney began, "my name is Elizabeth Ebey Benes. I am Mrs. Kroc's personal attorney. You have a note due to Mrs. Kroc for a little over $52,000. Mrs. Kroc has instructed me to cancel this note."

"That's not necessary," I replied. "I don't hold Joan responsible for what happened and I prefer to pay the balance of that note."

"You don't understand me," Benes replied in a firm voice. "I work for Mrs. Kroc and I do what *she* tells me to do! You will receive the cancelled note in a few weeks."

Despite my objections, Ms. Benes said she was canceling the note. In the end I just told her it was unnecessary and I asked her to thank Joan for me.

A few weeks later the cancelled note arrived in the mail.

When the end of the year rolled around I received some surprising news from my accountant. I owed the government an additional $18,000.in income tax. When I said that couldn't be, I learned that the cancellation of the note was the same as receiving $50,000 of cash income.

I couldn't believe my dubious good fortune. I was being taxed on money that I had never received and that was rightlfully mine in the first place. It didn't matter what I thought, it was back to the bank and another home equity loan to pay the additional income tax. In the long run, the cancellation of the note was a magnanimous gesture. It was appreciated more because we never believed she was a party to what had happened.

I know it is a terrible burden to carry the brier of betrayal into the twilight of life, but there are always some memories that continue to smolder in the embers of the mind. There are very few days when I do not look back without realizing that ten years of our lives were unnecessarily wasted. There are some things in life that can never be compensated for.

This occasion was the last time I ever spoke with Joan Kroc. I did receive one more communication from her a few months later. It was a letter written by her attorney.

" *Dear Mr. Leeds:*

I am writing this letter on behalf of Mrs. Joan Kroc. Mrs. Kroc has been extremely generous to you. Please do not ever contact her or ask her for anything again."

(Signed) Elizabeth Ebey Benes.

Prologue Chapter 22

LITTLE LOST PUP

Arthur Guiterman

He was lost! — Not a shade of a doubt of that;
For he never barked at a slinking cat,
But stood in the square where the wind blew raw,
With a drooping ear and a trembling paw,

And a mournful look in his pleading eye
And a plaintive sniff at the passer-by
That begged as plain as a tongue could sue,
"O Mister! Please may I follow you?"

A lorn wee waif of a tawny brown,
Adrift in the roar of a heedless town.
Oh, the saddest of sights in a world of sin,
Is a little lost pup with his tail tucked in!

Now he shares my board and he owns my bed,
And he fairly shouts when he hears my tread;
Then, if things go wrong, as they sometimes do,
And the world is cold and I'm feeling blue,

He asserts his right to assuage my woes
With a warm, red tongue and a nice, cold nose
And a silky head on my arm or knee
And a paw as soft as a paw can be.

When we rove the woods for a league about
    He's as full of pranks as a school let out;
For he romps and frisks like a three months colt,
    And he runs me down like a thunderbolt.

Oh, the blithest of sights in the world so fair
Is a gay little pup with his tail in the air!

22

RESOLUTION

The lawsuit was never filed.

It was a time when McDonald's was involved in numerous stock offerings and credit arrangements to finance their tremendous growth. Perhaps they didn't want their chairman to be publicly exposed in a federal court, or there may have been other reasons, but the next time I heard from Kroc's attorneys, their tone was tempered and conciliatory.

"Bob, what is going on here? What is it you want?" It was Don Lubin's voice. His voice sounded like I had done something that hurt his feelings. This time there was no chorus of Ed Lembitz's voice screaming across the line.

I told him what I had always told him. I wanted American Pet Motels!

Without a second's hesitation he asked me how I intended to pay for it. Kroc was quite willing to sell the business to me, but of course the price had to be $1.25 Million.

There wasn't any way we could beg, borrow or steal that kind of money, so I simply told him that it would have to be on terms manageable for us.

The sudden change in attitude convinced me that they wanted to reconcile this matter any way they could as long as the matter didn't go before a federal court and the public press. I didn't think it wrong to ask for reasonable terms.

The first terms Lubin offered would have been impossible for us to meet and after several exchanges I spelled out the terms I felt we could live with.

I agreed on the selling price of $1.25 million and to pay Kroc $5,000 a month plus 15 percent of all the profits for 10 years. They could keep all of the monies they had taken out of the company but in exchange, all of the notes for back-rent and interest would be cancelled.

I would have to pay a balance of $650,000 in 1986, and signed a balloon note to that effect with an interest rate of nine percent. I was confident that within that ten-year period I would be able to secure a private mortgage and pay off Kroc. It would be another parable to add to my long list: "No mistake is so great that it cannot be exceeded by irrational optimism and unreasoned confidence."

It was a horrendous price, but what price is too high to sustain a dream? The ten years I bought not only would give us time to get a mortgage, but it would give us the time to build the other two pet motels west and south of Chicago. I told Peggy a lot could happen in ten years. It certainly did.

The first warning was a request by our "personal banker" to come in and discuss new arrangements since Kroc was no longer involved with the company.

The next day I met with him in his office at the American National Bank & Trust Company of Chicago. I thought it was just to fill out new signature cards and other documents. Unforthantely, that wasn't why he had asked me to come in.

The bank officer began by reminding me that the bank handled millions of dollars for McDonald's, and then bluntly told me that under the circumstances the bank could no longer provide us with a line of credit. This was disturbing news since we made all our money during the summer months and sometimes borrowed money during the winter months. A line of credit is like a security blanket to a business. You may never use it, but if an emergency occurs, you can fall back on your line of credit.

What he told me next was even more disheartening. Under the circumstances, they would prefer that I moved my account to another bank!

Without realizing what was happening, I just picked up my papers and left. It wasn't until I visited several of the other large banks in Chicago that I understood what had happened. It appeared that Kroc's lawyers or McDonald's financial people had put out the word that if a bank wanted to do any banking business with McDonald's, they would not do any business with American Pet Motels.

With our options exhausted, we moved our account to a small neighborhood bank. Happy to have our business, they agreed to a modest, but important, line of credit.

Instead of finding refuge in the next 10 years, it seemed as if we were visited by a plague. The oil embargo of the late seventies and the consequent skyrocketing price of gasoline created havoc with the travel industry. People just stopped traveling. No longer did they board the family pet and take off on their extended vacations. Weekend trips to neighboring states became an unnecessary luxury, and our waiting list for rooms seemed to disappear overnight.

Yet, while airlines, hotels, and other leisure-time industries were losing money or going belly up in one of the worst recessions to ever hit the travel industry, American Pet Motels remained solvent, albeit with only modest profits.

With money getting scarce and interest rates higher than 20 percent, it became increasingly obvious we would not be able to pay our balloon payment of $650,000. Despite the fact that we could show an 11-year history of profitable operations, not one financial institution would give us a mortgage. It became apparent that the Krocs were going to win by default.

Our main problem was that our buildings were specially designed and if we defaulted, the bank would not be able to find a buyer for the buildings. In doing their appraisals of the value of all our $1.25 million in structures the banks appraised the value at only $100,000. That was the value of the land after paying to demolish all our buildings and clearing the land.

As 1986 approached, we realized the hopelessness of our situation, and we began to make plans for losing the pet motel.

My son, Marc, had returned from service in Korea and joined me in running the pet motel. During the height of the oil crisis, I had to even lay him off, and he subsisted on unemployment insurance until the crisis past and we were able to pay him a livable wage.

In reviewing our options, we decided to purchase a small 72-run kennel in Sarasota, Florida, and let Marc continue to operate the Chicago kennel. With the help of a Small Business Administration loan, we were able to purchase Sunshine Kennels and operate it as a branch of American Pet Motels. Accepting the fact that the Krocs would force us into bankruptcy in 1986, we structured the ownership of the Florida pet motel in such a way that Peggy's livelihood would be protected. Marc took over the operation of the Chicago Pet Motel and would run it until it was lost. It was a depressing period, but despite the gloomy outlook, we still refused to give up. Instead, we redoubled our efforts to obtain new financing to pay off the Kroc note.

Perseverance would finally be rewarded. But it was not until December 1986, only a few months before our note came due, that a savings and loan association in Lyons, Illinois, agreed to lend us a half million dollars providing we could raise the additional $150,000 from some other source.

The balance of the money we needed was to come from an unexpected source, Ray Kroc's wife, Joan. Although Ray Kroc had steadfastly refused to alter the terms of the note up until his death in 1984, his wife, Joan, did not remain indifferent to our problem. To save us from defaulting, Mrs. Kroc discounted the old note $50,000 and agreed to carry the $100,000 balance for five additional years at only 14 percent interest.

Final resolution of the note was like getting a new lease on life. Not a reprieve, but a vindication of all the past optimism, efforts and sacrifices.

When all the loan documents had been signed and the immediate future of American Pet Motels was reasonably secured, I remarked to Peggy that we had now reached a new financial milestone in our lives. We had achieved the dubious distinction of having a mortgage payment of more than $11,000 a month. Peggy's response amused me more than it reassured me. She reminded me of the time not too far past when a finance company turned us down for a loan to purchase a used Kaiser automobile because they didn't feel we could make the monthly payments of thirty-nine dollars. We had come a long way.

The realization of being able to continue in our quest again spawned the dream of building more pet motels throughout America, but we realized this could best be done if we lived in Chicago. With some reluctance, we sold the kennel in Florida and loaded our three dogs and our belongings into our van and headed back to Chicago.

Within a few years, we spent $635,000 to build a new "senior citizens" wing to the motel. This new kennel addition provided space for another hundred dogs and even included radiant heat in the floors so older dogs would always have a warm surface to lie on during the frigid Chicago winters. Unable to borrow the money, we found a leasing company that would lease us everything. We leased the concrete, the water lines, fencing, and just about every other thing that went into the construction. Our lease payments were substantial, but we paid everything off within five years.

Shortly afterward, we spent another million dollars to add a huge new lobby that included totally glassed-in areas for birds, rabbits, and small animals.

A modern state-of-the-art grooming parlor with fourteen workstations, a store area, and a large reception area were also included in this addition. We were now boarding more than 500 animals a day and still would have over 500 people on a waiting list for rooms.

Our new grooming parlor, O'Hair Port, looked like the

most modern ladies' beauty parlor, with individual hydraulic tables and a mirror for each station. In the center of the lobby was a huge new glassed-in aviary, and next to it, a bunny club and small animal room. As you entered the lobby, two human-sized interactive animal robots, Cecil, the dog, and Boo, the cat, automatically greeted you and you could answer by pressing a "yes" button or a "no" button. In the store was an area for children, where they could sit and watch cartoons shown on a nine-screen video wall.

With an investment of almost $5 million in buildings and equipment, we would reach a sales record of $2.5 million dollars in a single year. Continually building and remodeling to meet the increasing demand for more and better accommodations consumed a lot of our profits but it always resulted in improving our profit line. However, lending institutions still refused to finance an additional pet motel because of its unique design.

While we dreamed of building American Pet Motels all over the county, it would remain only a dream. On paper we were millionaires. In reality, we were like every other small business owner, working to exist. Our wealth was invested in bricks and mortar.

As 1999 rolled around, an unexpected solution to our dilemma suddenly appeared. We received an offer to buy the pet motel.

The offer came from an Eastern syndicate that had already purchased over 30 dog kennels all over the country. Marc and I listened, as a vice president explained their program to build first class pet boarding facilities throughout America. I listened, with a tinge of jealousy, as I heard how a Wall Street group, with no pet care experience, had put together an investment group with almost $50 million. Among their many investors was the Merrill Lynch brokerage firm and the family that published one of America's leading magazines. According to this gentleman, his company had millions and millions of dollars to spend and would have much more after a public stock offering. The company's objective was to bring good pet care to Main Street America.

The man readily admitted that he and the company's president, had visited our pet motels several times and, although they had optioned several prime sites in our market, they didn't want to build in the Chicago area unless they owned American Pet Motels. Several times he repeated the phrase, "We have no desire to go up against a bear." They felt they could learn a lot if they had us in their company. He came to Chicago to buy American Pet Motels and wouldn't go home without it.

There was a positive side to their offer, they wanted Marc and I to participate in the growth of the company.

While our attorneys confirmed the information we were given, Marc and I flew out to Hartford, New Jersey for a meeting with the president and his staff. In route, we stopped to inspect their newest prototype kennel in Norwalk. A brief inspection confirmed my worst fears. In addition to being a potential firetrap, their concept promised a number of serious operating problems. In addition, the company's plans seemed to include the violation of several serious federal laws.

Our meeting was extremely cordial. It turned out that the two men we were meeting with had been the ones who had taken Boston Chicken and TCBY companies public.

When I expressed my concerns with their prototype, they promptly acknowledged some of the problems with their first prototype and stressed that a large part of their current consideration was the acquisition of Marc and me to help guide their further development. We put on our rose colored glasses and returned to Chicago confident that we were doing the correct thing by joining them.

Believing what we heard, and assured that this company's policies for the care of animals were the same as ours, Peggy, Marc, and I sat down and weighed the alternatives.

In view of their financial strength, it didn't appear we had an option.

There was one other consideration, my health.

In 1984, I had undergone surgery for cancer. After surgery, I was given less than sixty days to live. Fortunately for me, their prognosis turned out to be incorrect. Two years later I was diagnosed with cancer of the mouth, the result of years of cigar smoking. This time I underwent surgery and a year of radiation treatment. Once again I beat the odds. I was seventy-one years old and selling now appeared to resolve several of our concerns.

The deal was clinched when we received their offer. The purchase price was much more than we had anticipated and included a considerable amount of stock in the company. In addition, Marc was given a two year employment contract, and I was given a consulting contract paying $1,000 a day plus expenses. The agreement included a minimum of ten days of consulting.

A few days before Christmas 1998, we affixed our signatures to the documents that made American Pet Motels a part of Best Friends Pet Resorts.

In the two years following the sale, things did not turn out as anticipated. The CEO and much of his staff were replaced and much of the investment capital appears to have been squandered on bad decisions. The rumor was that the new CEO was hired to find a buyer for the company. Things did not look promising for the new company.

Since my consulting contract required them to pay me, whether or not they used my services, I never understood their reluctance to do so. Despite their assurances, the term of our agreement expired without ever being called upon and they paid me thousand of dollars without one consultation. Apparently, running franchised fast food restaurants endowed them with all the knowledge necessary to run a chain of pet care facilities.

Our fear that it never was a concept for improving pet care in America, but strictly a concept for another lucrative Wall Street Initial Public Offering, has become a disappointing specter.

Only one consoling consideration remains. We retained first right to our pet motel. If they do not meet the terms of our agreement, we will recover ownership of American Pet Motels.

At my age it is not a goal I would seek but it is one I would certainly accept.

Prologue Chapter 23

THE VABABOND AND HIS DOG

Robert X. Leeds

A vagabond stood at St. Peter's gate
A mongrel cur at his feet,
And the line reached out to the dark of night,
As far as the eye could see.
And St. Peter looked at the disheveled two
And challenged the wretch to say,
What deeds he'd done, what praise he'd won
To walk in Heaven's way.

And the vagrant stood in his shabby robe
And not one word he spoke,
As though he heard not a single word
This man in the tattered cloak.
"What deeds have you done to think you've won
The grace of Heaven's line?
What honors earned? What evils spurned?
Pray help me be inclined."

But the wretched soul and his shepherd hound
Stayed on without a sound
As though no deed could come to mind,
As though no reason found.
"Can you not find one deed so fine,
To merit entrance here?
Can none attest some honored quest,
A challenge still unclear?"

And still he stood and but held the leash
That stayed the mongrel hound.
Until he knelt to feel the ground
And kiss the furry crown.
As love was cast in skin and bone,
He held the dog around,
And Heaven watched and Heaven judged
This vagabond and his hound.

"What seeds were sowed that a flower'd grow
When you'd depart the scene?
A single tree? One slave made free?
One clean and shining sea?
Was not one life made free of strife
Along the path you strolled?
Was not one child encouraged to smile?
No good that can be told?"

And all looked on at the vagabond
Who held the unkempt hound.
But not one voice to sway the choice,
No plaintiff voice was found.
And when at last, his patience past,
St. Peter bid unkind
And motioned on to the dark beyond,
"No reason you can find?"

"Not one but simple virtue be
That all of us may see?
Not one redeeming act of faith
Did bring you here to me?
In all your time can you not find
One voice for yours to plea?
In all your time can you not find
One voice to vouch for thee?"

And now at last his time though past,
The vagabond turned to speak;
And his eyes were filled with tears that spilled
And coursed the craggy cheeks.
And from his heart the speech did start
To argue not his sake,
But to plead the cause of the mongrel dog,
That lay in Heaven's wake.

"Perhaps it ain't for me to see
The paradise within.
I was a simple soul on earth
This hound my only kin.
But if the children's smiles count,
His cup's filled to the brim.
Oh, I can vouch for this hound, your grace.
I can vouch for him.

You should'a seen them laugh and run
When he was all their game.
You should'a seen the love he gave
And never once complain.
And when the tide of time arose
And naught was there to eat,
He shared the taste of an empty plate
And stayed at these failing feet.

It ain't for me," he whispered soft,
"It ain't for me I ask.
But don't deprive this poor old hound
For what his master lacks.
If caring and sharing and loyalty
Are virtues of your size,
Consider one who lacks of none,
Let Heaven be his prize.

It matters not what comes of me,
Or what may come about.
But it just ain't fair. It wouldn't be fair
To keep my poor hound out.

No friend has ever been so true.
No man has walked a line,
Who never strayed, but not this dog,
This hound that I call mine."

His fingers stroked the shaggy coat
And the dog licked back the hand;
And as much was said in the silence there,
Than since God's quest began.
And then abrupt, the hound looked up
And labored with its head
To lick this face of human grace,
This man of tattered thread.

And suddenly a calm would be
That tethered every sound.
And a warm breeze blew that embraced the two,
This vagabond and his hound.
And St. Peter turned to the mist beyond
And paused with uplifted head.
To heed the voice of Almighty **God**
And to do as **HE** has said.

"I've set the task and I have asked
For virtues held and shared.
To dwell in a world of every kind
And for every kind have cared.
And now I've seen dimensions dreamed
That seldom I've seen before,
A simple man and his faithful hound,
Denied at my own door?"

With pen in hand, St. Peter began
To enter on his list,
The names of those whom **God** had chose
To dwell in Heaven's bliss.
And one belonged to a vagabond
And the other he called his kin;
The man who vouched for an old hound dog
And the hound dog who vouched for him.

23

AGAIN . . . AGAIN. . . AND AGAIN

I was a vagabond standing before the virtual gates of what I perceived as a Heaven on earth. I stayed at the gates not to plead my own case, but the case of the millions of pets that add so much joy to our lives. It was never my desire to build the best pet care company in the world. My life was spent building the best pet care company for the world.

With the exhaustion of our youthful exuberance and the thinning line of sand in our hourglass, we are often challenged to ask ourselves just how far we really have come in life and what, if anything, have we achieved. These questions are painfully addressed each time someone asks us if we would do it all over again.

"Knowing what you were giving up and all the problems you would be encountering, would you do it all again? Was it worth it?"

We might pause, but the answer will always be the same. If there were twenty years filled with sleepless nights, there were twenty years of days filled with love and satisfaction beyond comprehension of those who have never worked with animals.

It is said that some people march to a different drummer. Ours was a beautiful symphony. A rhapsody of creature sounds filled with a quality of love and affection that is almost alien to the human society we live in today. There are some of us who will plead the cause of the mongrel hound.

The dream of improving the quality of pet care in America was not a fantasy. It was and remains a viable goal. From the time we purchased the Kroc's interest in American Pet Motels in order to preserve its integrity, until the day we signed the mortgage that lifted the uncertainty of our future, I never went to sleep without asking myself if it was worth it. Over and over during those first long nine years, I would awaken in the middle of the night and ask myself if it had all been a dream or some horrible nightmare. A quest of love or an obsession born of frustration? How cruel the prison of our aspirations can be. But what an education it was. An education for us, as well as for thousands and thousands of pet owners and people in our industry.

We learned that commercial boarding facilities *could* be designed, built, and managed to preclude the tragic consequences many pet owners experienced. Kennels *can* be clean and odorless. You *can* employ workers who are mature and caring and have a management that *is* concerned. Any pet *can* be boarded with the expectation that it will be alive and healthy when it goes home. Pet owners *do* have a choice!

Coming in contact with many thousands of pet owners awakened us to the very real bond that exists between people and their pets. Pets were no longer mere chattels of the law. We acknowledge them now as "companion animals," a term that implies a much deeper meaning. It is a term that explains the people who couldn't afford shoes but who went into debt to have their sick pet nursed back to health. We have grown up in a world where people have grown farther and farther apart from each other while growing closer and closer to their pets, and now we can understand why. Imagine what we would have missed if we had not dared to dream.

I often think of one of my favorite boarders, a little mongrel terrier named Trouble McLain. From the day he came to us,

Trouble always refused to eat his food from such a plebeian surface as the floor. When breakfast was served each morning, Trouble would pick his dish up with his teeth and set it at the end of his bed. Then he hopped up on the bed and dined in a reclining position. Breakfast in bed. That is how it had to be for Trouble. In France and other parts of the world, even formal dining with one's pet is an accepted custom. In Europe, I have seen well-dressed pet owners sit at tables with their pets and feed their canine companions tidbits from their own plates.

In exchange for their unique devotion, we have pampered our creature friends without the slightest tinge of guilt. There must be a million dogs that share their masters' toast each morning. There's nothing so unusual about dogs that get bacon and eggs at the pet motel. Or cats that drink chocolate milk. Or dachshunds that get a piece of beer salami at bedtime. Or horses that want to live a dog's life. If we hadn't followed our dream, we might have missed all of them. More than 250,000 dogs and cats, and thousands of other pets from a tiny mouse to some six-foot iguanas. They have added a wonderful dimension to what might otherwise have been a pedestrian existence.

We would have missed meeting the hundreds of veterinarians and kennel operators who have selflessly dedicated their entire lives to the healing and welfare of our creature friends. Those whose actions embarrass these honorable professions are insignificant compared to those whose daily endeavors distinguish them.

There are about 100 million households in America and three out of four include some kind of pet. More than 100 million cats and dogs and more than 17 million other assorted animals now share our daily living experience, and a recent survey confirmed what we have known all along: 80 percent of all pet owners consider their pet "a member of the family."

The mystique of pet ownership defies any simple logic. It is universal and all pervasive, but only lately have serious attempts been made to determine how significant a role pets play in our complex existence.

Certain benefits have already been established. At a recent conference on the human/companion animal bond, the chairman reported on the startling results of a documented study of two groups of patients who had been hospitalized for heart disease. Of the patients who owned pets, only 6 percent died within one year of their hospitalization. Of those who did not own pets, 44 percent died in the same period. Who is to say that the dramatic increase in our life expectancy has not in some measure been attributable to the accompanying increase in pet ownership?

A whole body of data is now developing to suggest that both our mental and physical well-being can be significantly enhanced through ownership of a pet. For those of us who have worked with animals, nothing that will be revealed in these studies will come as a surprise. Yet, despite all the benefits we derive from this association, our recognition of these benefits is often times woefully inadequate. Our concern for the proper care of boarded pets is but a small effort to redress this problem.

In our society, there is a tendency to equate wealth with success. If that were true, there would be many in this profession who would fail to meet the criteria. A part of our wealth is the satisfaction we get from providing the best environment a pet can have when away from its home. Sometimes this is acknowledged by the events we witness.

A few winters ago, a friend of mine approached her kennel one cold morning and was startled to see a large animal lying in front of the entrance, almost covered by the newly fallen snow. Its gray muzzle blended into the matted snow, and it sunken eyes peered up into my friend's.

As she got closer, the old dog struggled to its feet, and its tail began a back-and-forth motion. My friend studied the dog and then recognized it was one that had been boarded frequently in recent months by an elderly woman who required intermittent hospitalization.

Upon calling the owner's home, my friend learned that the lady had died the previous day. Neither of her two married sons wanted her old dog, so they had planned on having it euthanized after they finished loading their cars with their mother's "more valuable" possessions. Sometime during their goings in and out, the dog slipped out of the house and traveled more than seven miles to the only other place it felt it was wanted, the kennel where it had been boarded. The dog was right. My friend found him a nice home on her father's farm.

Would we do it again knowing all the confrontations, financial sacrifices, and heartaches that lay ahead?

No degree of achievement or failure is ever tarnished by the honest effort expended. It is not the quantity of life that matters, but the quality. I had once told my son the story of how my father used to conduct the details of his painting business at an ancient roll-top desk in the basement of our old frame house in Detroit.

It must have been around 1934 and I was only seven years old. I didn't understand the Depression years, but I loved to stand beside him and watch him do his paperwork. A single light bulb hung from a strand of wire and provided the only light by which he labored. This scenario of business held a compelling fascination for me. Shipped to this country by his parents in Ireland, he grew up in the back room of a Cleveland tavern owned by an uncle. Without any formal education he learned to read blue prints and to estimate costs, and when successful, he would get the job of painting a house or commercial building. He never owned an adding machine. A pencil and a yellow pad of paper were the tools of his trade. I would watch over his shoulder at the ponderous rolls of blue prints and study the long columns of figures he marked on those yellow pads. I was hypnotized and envious of his efforts.

This one evening, my father was just sitting at the desk, not measuring the details of any blueprints or scribbling a list of figures on one of his many pads of paper. He was studying something else. Even though he was owed more than enough money to pay our bills, he, like thousands of other Americans, could not collect enough to buy groceries, let alone meet our mortgage payments. Most of the papers that now cluttered his desk were past-due bills. One conspicuous document was a notification that the bank was repossessing our home. We were hopelessly in debt and his small company insolvent. Worst, there was not a glimmer of prospect for our future welfare. I shall always remember my father just staring and staring at his desktop until suddenly he seemed to become aware that I was standing beside him.

He gazed down into my unenlightened face and smiled. "Just think," he said, "someday all this will be yours."

With all the ignorance youth can muster, I relished the challenge and was enthralled at the prospect.

Only a few years before, when Marc and I left the offices of the Lyons Savings and Loan with the mortgage commitment that permitted us to escape from the clutches of Ray Kroc, Marc put his hand on my shoulder and broke into a big grin.

"Congratulations, Dad. You now owe almost a million dollars and your monthly payments are more than you make. Do me one favor, please. Don't promise me that one day it will all be mine."

I knew Marc was joking, just as his grandfather had been those many years ago. In the years since he joined us, Marc has shown all the signs of one hopelessly smitten by the concerns of this industry, and now works as hard for the new company as he did for us. He still relishes the idea of building our pet motels across the country.

Despite the uncertainties and financial impositions, his dedication and effort never wavered. Peggy and I were never alone in our travail and we think the world is much better off for the family pet than it was when we began this arduous quest.

Would we do it again?

The good Lord willing, again . . .and again . . .and again!

Recognition:

All of the poems included in this volume are reprinted from Robert X. Leeds anthology, *Doctor Leeds' Selection of Popular Epic Recitations for Minstrel & Stage Use* published by Epic Publishing Company. They were selected from among 195 old barroom ballads of the type recited by traveling minstrels on the kerosene lit, wood-planked stages in saloons of the old wild West.

We are especially indebted to Ms. Marcia Kramer, publications editor of the National Anti-Vivisection Society. Many of the poems about dogs included in the above anthology and in this volume originated in the NAVS publication, *The Dog's Scrapbook*. Contributions to further the efforts for a cruelty-free world for animals may be sent to:

NAVS
National Headquarters
53 West Jackson Blvd.
Chicago, Illinois 60604-3703

We wish also to acknowledge the assistance of Roseann and Bryce Lee in the preparation of this text. A special credit is due Gregory Erickson and T. Russell Wingate for their invaluable editorial assistance.

Correspondence to the author should be directed to:
Robert X. Leeds
C/O Epic Publishing Company
8814 Big Bluff Avenue
Las Vegas, Nevada 89148-1418